Robert Hayward

THE THIRTEENTH STEP

Ancient Solutions to Contemporary Problems of

Alcoholism and Addiction Using the Timeless Wisdom

of the Native American Church Ceremony

One Man's Odyssey of Recovery

The Thirteenth Step is a powerful and true recounting of the life of Robert Hayward. Hayward's life story weaves the real and the mysterious, the personal and the universal into a uniquely gripping story of self-discovery through his spiritual awakening within the Native American Church; an awakening that saved his life. The Thirteenth Step documents, for the first time ever, ancient ceremonies that have been conducted in the same manner for thousands of years, yet never shared with outsiders. Through Hayward's own journey of redemption, the reader will experience the words, wisdom, and teachings of The Native American Church, and encounter a spirituality that until now, has been accessible only to those born into the traditional Native American culture.

The Thirteenth Step is an introduction to an ancient way of thinking about our world. For more information about the ideas discussed here, to connect with Robert Hayward, learn of speaking appearances, and find out about future book releases, please contact us or visit one of our web pages!

We will periodically have giveaways and promotions…if you are interested, please visit our web page and sign the guestbook.

Native Son Publishers, Inc.
4051 Paramount St.
Las Vegas, NV 89115

http://nativesonpublishers.com

http://thethirteenthstep.com

Robert Hayward maintains a blog at:

http://roberthayward.nativesonpublishers.com

THE THIRTEENTH STEP

Ancient Solutions to Contemporary Problems of

Alcoholism and Addiction Using the Timeless Wisdom

of the Native American Church Ceremony

One Man's Odyssey of Recovery

Robert Hayward

Native Son Publishers

Published by:
Native Son Publishers, Inc.
4051 Paramount St.,Las Vegas, NV 89115
NativeSonPublishers.com

THE THIRTEENTH STEP
ANCIENT SOLUTIONS TO CONTEMPORARY PROBLEMS OF
ALCOHOLISM AND ADDICTION USING THE TIMELESS WISDOM
OF THE NATIVE AMERICAN CHURCH CEREMONY
ONE MAN'S ODYSSEY OF RECOVERY
BY ROBERT HAYWARD

EDITED BY Barbara Villasenor and Myra Wesphall

Native Son Publishers ISBN: 978-0-9836384-0-7
Library of Congress Control Number 2011923204

Front cover photograph by Mark Chambers.
Back cover photograph by Tim McGuire.

Body text rendered in Adobe Garamond Pro.

Book listing categories:
OCC031000- body, mind, spirit, ancient mysteries & controversial knowledge
OCC039000- body, mind, spirit, entheogens & visionary substances
SEL006000- self-help/substance abuse & addictions/alcoholism
REL029000- religion/ethnic & tribal
BIO028000- Biography and Autobiography/native Americans
SEL029000- self-help/substance abuse/twelve step programs

The experiences and events of this book are true. The people and events
described are real. The author has changed some names, but none of the
changes impacts the integrity of the story. The story and events described, and
the words chosen to communicate them, are the author's own.

This book is dedicated to my grandmother, Grace Glenway Hayward, for passing her deep roots and spiritual connection to this part of the world on to me, her youngest grandson, and to my parents, Tom and Louise Hayward, for their continuous and unrelenting prayers and encouragement that kept me alive and able to realize my dreams.

Table of Contents

PRELUDE

The drumming stopped after he sang his fourth song. Instead of passing the water-drum and staff to the next singer on his left, Red Hawk, the Kiowa Elder, began to tremble, tears seeped slowly down his face. Then he started to weep. He cleared his throat and prayed loudly in his native tongue, the few English words sprinkled into his discourse exposed enough of his intense sadness that the few of us who didn't understand his language still clearly interpreted the gravity of his plea to the Creator.

I tried to sit up, realizing I had slowly slouched to a very unacceptable position, appearing as if I was lying down. The medicine the Roadman, Sonny Hogan, had mixed for me hours earlier had me totally immobilized. Although I was keenly aware of everything around me, and in total control of all of my mental facilities, physically I felt paralyzed from the neck down. For all practical purposes, I was stuck in this embarrassing and, in fact, disrespectful position. Finally, accepting that I could not move a muscle, I gave up trying and mentally sat up at attention and listened.

When the Kiowa finished praying, everything went silent. Dead silent. The rain let up, the wind stopped howling, the fire burned soundlessly, even the river seemed to stop flowing. All I could hear was the subdued crying of many of the people in the tipi surrounding me.

Sonny Hogan, the Roadman, stood up to speak. I could hear his joints cracking as he straightened up, his body complaining about sitting still for hours being warmed in front by the fire and chilled behind by the frigid and uninvited air sneaking under the canvas. The night was slipping into early morning, "the bewitching hour," my dad used to say. The Roadman directed his words to nobody in particular, more to all of us spread out in that tipi on the mountaintop, and all of humanity crowded on the planet around us. The fire heated his words so they were seared into our hearts.

"We, as humans, have lost our way. We have gone off course, floating uselessly with the wind. We have no center, we have no balance. Our past, present, and future have become one straight line going nowhere. The circle is broken.

"Because we are no longer in touch with the Creation, we have lost contact with the Creator. Our souls cry out for peace, for harmony, for balance, for love, and we ignore the cry, getting farther and farther from the earth, the animals, this beautiful, wonderful world that God created for us, neglecting, rejecting, destroying, and we are paying for it in our own miserable existence. Using drugs, alcohol, sex, anything and everything to hide from ourselves, from God, from each other, trying to fill that hole in our hearts. We have forgotten the simple solution written in our souls that can restore us and our world to sanity.

"It is time to take our shoes off, run barefoot on the earth again, to feel the dirt and grass between our toes, the water from the creek cooling our throats and soothing our souls, the air from the wind in the trees refreshing our lungs, to get back to the basics, to what we really are about, to restore our connection to the Creator. To live every day like it matters, like we matter, that everyone matters. Helping everyone we can, giving back more than we take away, remembering our close ties to the earth, and how to live on it.

"This used to be normal. We didn't talk about it, it just happened. Now if I say these things, people think I am strange, crazy, someone out of touch with reality, when, in fact, that is the only true reality. All of this distraction and technology is pulling us away from that which is real, and confusing our spirit into thinking we don't need God or His Creation anymore.

"All of us—red, white, black, and yellow—we are all native to this earth, somewhere. We have forgotten that. Some of us by force, some by ignorance, others by convenience. But we are suffering from this forgotten fact now. All of us. We have to return to the basics now or we will drown in this rising sea of ignorance and isolation. We have become so smart we have lost all of our common sense and have forgotten how to survive in the real world, which is still here, just beyond the gated community and city limits.

"No other solution will work. Not another invention, not another law, not a better politician. We have to return to what has always worked for all of our ancestors, no matter where we come from. What we are doing now isn't just failing, it is destroying us. We are all dying from the inside out. The generations yet to come are relying on us to get back on that good path, that Red Road of Sobriety."

His eyes connected directly with mine when he said "sobriety". Suddenly, a profound feeling of shame overcame me when that word connected with my conscience. That conscience that until this moment had been drowned out with alcohol. Lots of alcohol. I looked away from him and around the tipi only to find all eyes on me. I closed my eyes, a big mistake, as that started the movie in my head with me as star villain. I watched a short clip of my wife and three children cowering from my

5

latest drunken rage in confusion and terror. Not a physical rage, but an equally devastating verbal assault against anything and everything my pickled brain could muster up. Ashamed and embarrassed, I opened my eyes, convinced everyone had just watched the same replay. Perhaps the Roadman did; when I looked up at him, he nodded as if in agreement with my self disgust.

The words he had spoken reached deep and grabbed me. Even though I had heard this type of talk many times before, it was always almost too simple, too cliché. But now I knew it was as basic as what he had said. It was all I needed.

The Roadman threw a big handful of cedar onto the hot coals and sat down in silence. The cedar crackled and burned, sending a swirling cloud of sweet smelling perfume in clockwise circles over the fire, spreading out among all of us and pouring out the open flap at the top of the tipi. But it wasn't the smoke in my eyes that made the tears run down my face. It had been decades since I had felt my heart break, and it actually felt good. At least I could feel something.

I thought this was the big event, the grand revelation I had so desperately wanted. What I didn't know, though, was this was only the bare beginnings of what was to become the longest, most intense, eye-opening night of my life. And before this night was over I would relearn everything I had ever thought to be true.

My life would never be the same.

THE SET UP

Under the radar, virtually unnoticed by contemporary society, every Saturday night, and often several nights a week, on Reservations, in national parks, campgrounds, wilderness areas, even suburban properties, all over this country, a traditional Northern Plains tipi is erected in the evening. And inside an ancient traditional ceremony is held all night. Before noon of the next day, it is down, the ground cleaned up and the area is as if nothing has happened.

This is the detailed account of one such Native American Church ceremony. Ceremonies are held for a variety of reasons, and this one was being held for the sole purpose of praying for my sobriety, a sobriety that was for all practical purposes unattainable, a lost cause, as was my career, my family, and my marriage. And those who came out of nowhere that night to pray only for me were until then total strangers. Today they are my relatives and closest friends.

In what is sometimes called the 12 hour version of the 12 Step Program, I walked out of that tipi at the Thirteenth Step; a person of total sobriety--the need and desire to drink permanently gone, even to this day, more than 12 years later. I went in there a hopeless drunk, and walked out completely healed. I was even spared the painful "detox" from alcohol dependence necessary after so many years that my body relied on alcohol to function. And I am not the first, nor will I be the last. In fact, I am merely only one of thousands, if not millions, of Native American people who have been blessed by one of the many miracles of sobriety and other supernatural healings that have come from this ceremony.

And there is more. Each ceremony imparts more knowledge, more insight, more solutions to everyday problems. While people think their problems will only get worse, there is a solution. It isn't New Age; just the opposite. It has been around since before the problem even began for the Native American people.

A chance encounter as a teenager with a reclusive medicine man set the wheels of fate into motion that ultimately brought me not only into this sacred ceremony, but also into the whole sub-culture of the Native American Church. I experienced a life-changing miracle that is recreating miracles in other peoples' lives and reconnecting them to their spiritual potential they didn't know existed.

It took many years of a personal relationship with the then current President of The Native American Church of The United States to gain not only his trust, but also his permission, to write this story. This is a secret and sacred ceremony that has been rightfully protected and guarded forever from outside influences and exposure. He only agreed to this story because he sees how it can help stop the downward spiral of alcoholism and addiction, not only among Natives, but also for all peoples affected by this nightmare. He also understands that as the world shrinks from the mass communication of the internet, it is best if the truth be told about this ceremony in a sacred way, to prevent the inevitable distortions created by half-truths, rumors, and outright lies. This is an opportunity to show that this is a very sacred and holy ritual that should not be abused, changed, or imitated, and one of the last elements of Native Spirituality that is to remain as it is, unspoiled, and respected from a distance, not a curiosity to be exploited. And those aspects of this ceremony that should never be revealed, remain that way in this story.

Never before has anyone taken a reader through this all night ceremony in such detailed specificity, explaining each aspect of this ancient ceremony that has retained every detail and ritual since its inception, relating it to its past origins, the present and its problems, and the hope for the future to those who would learn from it.

This ceremony, unbound by time and space, is a direct connection to the distant past, to a time when spirituality was an integral part of Native Peoples' lives, where circular thinking was the norm, when contact with the spirits and their Creator was as common as talking to one another. This was not the Hollywood or hippie romanticized version of the "spiritual Indian", but in fact, the day to day need to connect and converse with the Great Unknown for reasons of survival.

The connection to nature was necessary for daily living; therefore much energy was spent learning everything about the environment and what was good, bad, and ugly. Opposites were discovered, sicknesses pointed to cures, poisons found antidotes. Healings were part of everyday life. Faith was strong and left little room for doubt. God was not some secret mystery, He was part of life. Through this ceremony we are able to briefly return to that place of faith and spiritual innocence, where knowledge is freely shared, healings and cures are explained, when the Creator still interacts with Creation, where prayers are spoken to a personal God, and He answers them.

The time has come when these secrets and truths need to be reawakened and exposed, so our vague connection to the Creator can be re-ignited before we lose forever our ability to commune with Him, and in turn, lose our ability to live life. The general lack of ceremony and tradition in normal American life, coming from the fact that so many different heritages have been mixed together without any consideration given to the value of each person's customs and spiritual history, has inadvertently resulted in a confused desire for that ancient connection to our Creator. It seems unimportant, yet it is the cause of so much lack of direction and emptiness from which many of us are suffering.

It becomes painfully apparent when a community tragedy brings people together and the desire to show solidarity and support for the victim is manifest in a candlelight vigil. While the intention is commendable, the result is almost embarrassing to those who know ceremony and respect its value. There is virtually no beginning, no formula to follow, and no soul in the effort. It is not from lack of desire, only the simple fact that it has no basis in anything other than the flame on the candle, the ancient fire, and a distant connection to something in somebody's past customs, only nobody has any idea what it is. If only they had kept some thread of connection to their past, perhaps there would be some consistency and tangible spiritual value to the whole affair. It has become so difficult to organize a spiritual gathering, if only for the lack of centralized consensus on how to approach the ceremony.

God makes no mistakes. Everything and everyone He creates has a reason, a purpose, a duty, and a path to follow. And something happens in everyone's life, at some God-appointed time, that, if recognized, acknowledged, and accepted, can become the great turning point, sending us down that path of destiny.

That was the beauty of most native societies of long ago, through close direction of Elders and family, through teaching of the medicine man, vision quests, and just basic close contact and monitoring of children as they matured. That moment of cosmic insight and clarity was easily recognized and usually aided and directed by someone close by and experienced in spiritual education. In those days, the only excuse for not following your God-given path was rebellion, and--or lack of-- desire or commitment. Now, because of the weakened family structure and Elder teaching, along with the end of vision quests and traditional spiritual monitoring, it takes a very alert and informed individual just to even know there is such a transitional moment in one's life, much less recognizing and acting on it. How much easier our lives would be if we saw that special light turn on and followed it as our ancestors did.

I am aware of the theory that claims there is so much to be learned and gained by going through our trials, and I also understand the idea that where we have been is what makes us what we are and who we are. But who are we, and where have we been, that is so wonderful that we could not be that much greater and more beneficial to ourselves and to society had we not missed that open door so many years ago, stepped through it, and never fell off that good road? Sure, we have learned great things, things we can use to warn the next generation. And yes, we can personally empathize with those who are to fall into the traps we've crawled out of, and help them to navigate a better road. But how many generations have to fall away and fail in life before we have learned our lesson? It just seems too much of this short, precious life God gave us is spent trying to find our place.

Too much of this flash in time is wasted searching for that great meaning, the perfect answer, the correct process, the best 12 Steps, the illusive "higher consciousness", a new philosophy, the best way and the right place to live…talk, talk, and more meaningless talk.

The reality is, today most people have no idea what their true path is. Some get a glimpse of it. Many can feel that there is something more, much more, yet it is a fleeting feeling, and they have no way of pursuing it, because, as the medicine man running the ceremony said, the circle is broken. It's as simple as that.

It took this ceremony and a tipi full of complete strangers praying for my sobriety for me to relive that exact day when I was given the keys to open my mind to the solutions before I had the problem, 26 years earlier, exactly right where the ceremony was taking place. The events that unfolded in my life that brought me back to this place at this time are nothing short of miraculous and far beyond coincidental, an appointment with destiny that couldn't be stopped, even if I was aware of it all falling into place. Only the names have been changed out of respect for the privacy of everyone involved.

CHAPTER 1

MY STORY

Blessed Childhood, Troubled Teen

I was born to wonderful and devoted parents, number nine out of ten Catholic kids, six sisters and three brothers. Early on, my parents worked for and knew Walt Disney, so creativity runs deep in my family, which can be a blessing and also a curse. All of us are completely different, and at the same time very much the same. It seems I was the only one who ended up with a predominance of the Native genes of my Winnebago grandmother from Wisconsin, who had published a book about her state and poetry about Native life there, and that seems fitting as I was born on her birthday. There is a Native belief that the grandmother passes her spirit and power to her youngest grandson, and I am also lucky enough to be her youngest grandson, so much credit for what eventually happened to me in my life must go to her.

Because of my inquisitive nature, my father told me the following story of our ancestry, something completely hidden until, as an adult, I pushed the issue. Before he passed on he finally felt he could reveal his mother's true heritage, and he gave me his mother's moccasins and adoption papers from a Dutch reform school that stated her tribal affiliation.

Apparently, by the late 1800s, most of the Indian population of the United States had been reduced to a fraction of its original number, and the survivors had been relegated to multiple Indian Reservations across the country. The government was then faced with the daunting task of caring for a proud and yet broken people who were used to taking care of themselves. Numerous strategies were bandied about. The dirty little secret was they fully expected the Natives to die off from disease and starvation; they had no intention of taking care of them for any length of time. These Reservations were, in all reality, set up as large concentration camps with no options. Leaving the boundaries of these Reservations was completely forbidden, for fear of people actually finding a real food source. And to hasten extermination, there were some renegade government agencies that purposely introduced disease by giving certain tribes blankets infected with the smallpox for them to use on their sweat lodges, guaranteeing total infusion of this deadly and foreign disease. There was no way for the government to grasp that these were, indeed, a resilient people, and they were not ready to be exterminated completely. These were survivors, and are today.

One of the government's many ideas was an experiment tried in the Northeast and Midwest that was popular among the more conservative members of the Commission of Indian Affairs. It was the outrageous and misguided process called forced blood dilution, in other words, cross breeding. Cross-breeding was designed to assimilate the "primitive native blood and its associated heathen tendencies" with what was considered the "superior bloodline of certain European stock", thus eventually breeding the "weaker native blood" out, as the dominant white gene created a new generation without enough Indian blood quantum to qualify for government assistance. In effect, an entire race of people would disappear without any more government-provoked bloodshed.

The theory behind dilution was that within three generations, dark skin and brown eyes would be replaced with light skin and blue eyes, the "savages" would be civilized and could be accepted into the American mainstream. Among certain circles it was considered the most compassionate and caring help society could give these "poor, barbaric" people. They didn't realize that many of the schools created for this purpose would end up using these children as indentured servants, commonly known as child slaves, great for building missions and convents.

The Commission began by setting up orphanages, boarding schools and reform schools, forcing the Reservation Indians to enroll their children, often as young as three-years-old, or lose their food commodities. The children were taken from their parents, shaved, scrubbed, disinfected, and forbidden to speak their Native language or practice any traditional religion or way of life, or they'd suffer severe punishment and isolation. The Christian religion of the sponsoring school was forced on them. Parental contact was limited more and more until eventually the parents were prevented from seeing their children ever again. Then these children were advertised to newly-established European families of British, German, and Dutch descent as beautiful, lonely, abandoned orphan Natives. Adoptive parents were carefully screened for pure bloodlines, looking for assurances that the new children would eventually marry within the white community. The new parents would receive a legal certificate of adoption from the school. After six months, if there were no problems, they could trade in their adoption certificates for an official state birth certificate and register the child as their own natural born in the European and Mormon Ancestry.

The falsified birth certificates removed any legal paper trail as to the actual heritage of the Indian child, relieving the government of any monetary responsibility for the child, and preventing future generations of any possibility of tracing their true bloodline. It was a win-win for the government, and saved the European family any embarrassment over adopting a "savage from the wild".

An ethics commission caught wind of the program in the 1920s, shut down most of the schools that, in turn, promptly destroyed all records of the transactions. This left thousands of Indian families permanently torn apart, with virtually no connection to their past—mentally, physically, spiritually, or legally. A small percentage of unreturned certificates of adoption are all that is left of this tragic ethnic cleansing program sponsored by the US government on its original people.

Fortunately, my grandparents did save those adoption papers, and that enabled me to piece together my lineage somewhat, yet still deprived me of locating my great grandparents' names.

My grandmother eventually married a stoic Englishman, not consciously aware of the fact that she was continuing the dilution program long after it was over, as many Indian children did. Together, they had three boys. The eldest, Spencer, was diagnosed with diabetes in the 1920s. Since diabetes was common among Indians because of their new diet of commodity sugar and white flour, the government used half-breeds to experiment with insulin to find the proper dose to treat diabetes. As a policy, Indians and half-breeds were still not considered human, and did not get the right to vote until after the slaves and women were given their right to vote, so they were fair game for government experimentation. In one of the botched medical trials, Spencer was overdosed with insulin, and he died from complications.

My grandparents, as mad as they were scared, moved out of state and forbid their remaining two boys to ever admit they had any Indian blood. Being a good son, my father hid this old family secret so well, it really didn't exist anymore, until I came along.

And what became of the blood dilution program? It was so popular that it was copied by the Australian government and used on the indigenous people there, creating what is known as "the stolen generation," and to whom the Australian government recently made a formal apology. In our own country, after the government program to track blood dilution to measure diminishing "Indian-ness" was ended, ironically, each tribe started setting up blood percentages as a means of recognizing people with Indian ancestry so they could be affiliated as a tribal member and preserve the blood line, indirectly keeping a system in place for the government's use.

Back to my childhood. Although it has become all too common to blame one's parents or upbringing for the indulgent mistakes for which we are all solely responsible, I cannot even fake that claim in good faith. My childhood was nothing less than idyllic. I call it classic Norman Rockwellian: A large family, life on a small farm surrounded by wilderness, God fearing, church going, not dirt poor, but certainly not wealthy, yet rich in love. My hardworking father made time to interact with and teach the children, and my nonstop homemaking mother was always doing what it took to keep a big family functioning without most of today's modern conveniences, and without a single complaint that any of us can remember.

Our life was good in those days. I don't recall any major problems that weren't followed by simple solutions. The only scandal to this point was one older sister learning how to smoke cigarettes when she went to college in Wisconsin. I'm told I was the wild one early on, mostly just high energy, but lovingly labeled the black sheep, a name easily earned in a family of minor problems and well behaved children. Today I'd probably be labeled ADHD and, like many other overactive children, be forced to take medication that would stifle my creativity and sedate me enough to be easily controlled by my teachers and parents. I achieved the same result by self-medicating from a young age, which did not help my creativity, exactly the opposite. My joyful and searching mind was quickly shut down by my choice of drugs. I can only remember being minimally unmanageable as I reached my early teens, a challenge my aging parents of a different era did not deserve after successfully raising eight normal children.

More than anything, I believe it was just that weird time in history, the tail end of the 60's drug culture, when most all of us younger kids wanted to experiment, even though we could see the bad effects showing up in those older than us who had been using for a while. And that promised Age of Aquarius never really materialized. I think we still wanted it to, but the writing was on the wall. Excessive drug use was not bringing forth that bliss as promised, but we weren't ready to give up completely. Another problem was the decline of the purity and quality of drugs, and the subsequent introduction of overly powerful home lab drugs like crystal meth that was completely unforgiving to the mind and body. The psychedelic drugs of that time that opened many user's consciousness to a spirit world that we don't belong in and, for many, from which they could not return.

However, nothing in my memory of adolescence fits the standard excuse for blaming my experimentation and subsequent years of addictive behavior with drugs on anything unusual, irregular, or abusive during my upbringing. In fact, if childhood happiness were a predictor of future behavior, I would have led a wonderful, easy life to this point. But sadly, that was not the case.

When I think back to my childhood, I remember waking up with excitement and expectation, happy to be alive, exploring, learning, creating, living. A feeling that completely left me once I entered the world of drugs and alcohol.

I can remember one Christmas that exemplified the innocence of my early years on the farm. This year was special. The whole family was home for Christmas, even the older ones with their spouses and children, so we had many nieces and nephews to play with. We still had to go to bed on time, but there were so many of us in one bedroom that we were too excited to sleep. We talked, whispered, and giggled for hours, listening to the laughter, noise, and chatter coming from the kitchen. Twice I snuck up the hallway to peek into the living room to see if there were any new presents by the tree, nearly getting caught speeding back to the room to report any news.

As hard as we tried, we couldn't fight back the dreams pulling all of us to sleep. Suddenly, in deep sleep, I heard Mom at the bedroom door, waking us to dress up for church, Midnight Mass.

It only took a few seconds for me to remember what night it was. Then I was once again filled with that overwhelming excitement I had had a few hours before. I jumped up, yanking the blankets off anyone left in bed. The wait for one of the two bathrooms was painful and long, but soon everyone was in their Christmas best, running to the cars. I tried one last peek into the living room, but there were too many people guarding the door, and I was told, "Scram, Bobby, and get in the car!"

It was clear and cold outside, a slight, chilly east wind blowing, stars sparkling bright in the moonless sky, even a few Christmas lights still shimmering down the deserted street. We had to take the Rambler and the Pontiac to fit everyone. To my disbelief, there were a few in-laws who stayed behind, not convinced to go to church, even on Christmas Eve. In my limited experience and genuine naïveté, I really thought everyone had as much faith as I did in Christmas, and I couldn't comprehend not believing in the miracle of the Christ child. After that night I thought of them as outlaws, not in-laws.

Dad turned on the car radio so we could listen to Paul Harvey tracking Santa's sleigh across the country through the static AM signal. I stared out the window all the way to church hoping to catch a glimpse of the sleigh and reindeer.

As always, Midnight Mass was packed, overflowing the tiny small town church. We had arrived early because Dad directed the choir, so some of us went upstairs into the choir-loft with him, while the rest followed Mom to the front pews by the altar. With two brothers as altar boys that night, I felt we were all a part of the mass.

From high in the choir-loft I could see someone had put the baby Jesus into the previously empty manger crib, something I had looked forward to for weeks. I looked over the whole congregation, picking out the regulars and remembering the annual Christmas attendees scattered throughout the crowded pews.

I recognized the lingering smells of Christmas parties wafting up to us, cigarette smoke and specially made adult eggnog faintly passing by me and out the slightly opened windows. I couldn't wait to see who would faint this year during mass. I was told it was the lack of oxygen in the crowd that dropped a few every year. I learned years later it was usually the result of way too much consumption of Christmas 'cheer' earlier in the evening. Regardless, it was still fun to watch from above.

As always, Father Murphy said mass. The Christmas carols, Mom turning to smile up at us, Dad swinging his director's wand and singing loudly, happiness on everyone's faces; this was Christmas.

On the way home, we stopped at the furniture store in town with the window bedroom display that had Santa sleeping in bed for weeks before this night. As with every year before, and every year since until they closed forever, Santa was not in bed anymore, the blankets in a mess in his hurry to get to his sleigh. Paul Harvey crackled over the radio, announcing Santa had been spotted in the skies over the west coast. My heart raced and I could barely contain my excitement. I wanted to get home as soon as possible and into bed so Santa wouldn't pass us by for still being awake.

We didn't have a fireplace, so Mom and Dad promised to leave the living room door unlocked. Actually, I don't remember any doors being locked growing up. Falling asleep was easy this time; we were all too exhausted to talk.

I was the first to wake up, or so I'd like to think. I put on my robe for the first time since I got it last Christmas, and yanked the blankets off everyone in bed. At first, they were mad. Then they remembered what day it was. Suddenly, getting up was easy. We all crowded around Mom and Dad's bed, begging them to get up so we could go into the living room. We had to line up, youngest first, in the hallway, and wait for the door to be opened.

Because of the amount of family home for Christmas, the presents were everywhere. I will never forget pouring into that room that year and seeing mountains of gifts, piles of them, big and small, wall to wall. Our special Christmas tree, a silver-painted Manzanita tree, stripped of its leaves and covered with glass ornaments, lights and tinsel, was nearly buried in beautiful wrapped presents.

Behind the tree, by the window, unwrapped, was a giant wood handmade train set. Made by Dad and my oldest brother out of huge blocks of wood, with roller-skate wheels attached to the bottom, the individual cars were just big enough to sit on and roll around the cement slab in front of the house. My closest age brother got the engine, and I got the caboose. I don't remember any of my other presents, or what anyone else got. I loved that simple chunk of wood with steel, noisy wheels; I loved it for years, played with it forever. I don't remember any other presents over those childhood years that meant that much to me.

The rest of that Christmas is a blur, like many of those wonderful childhood years. Some memories are strong, others are gone. I will never forget that caboose, nor that Christmas, nor the love of family together at Christmas, in the innocence and awe of youth, when everything was right, growing up surrounded by love, laughter, and the Christmas child.

So my excuse for the later years is certainly not my family. Somewhere along the line, I made bad choices, real bad choices, and traded what could have been a beautiful life for self-made problems and abuse that brought me to the brink of insanity and death. It was a slow process that increased with intensity as the years went on. But God has a plan, even for those who try their best to screw it up.

Living fairly isolated from most of society, and going to a small Catholic school, I wasn't ready for reality when I was bussed 30 miles a day to the closest Catholic high school. This was during the end of the hippie movement, when drugs and getting high was still cool, before the "Just Say No" programs hit the schools. I was scared to death. Not so much because of drugs or getting high, more of not fitting in, not knowing what was going on. In my little school back home, I had more or less the same classmates for eight years. We had grown up together. And it was fun and secure. A couple of misfits kicked out of the local public school that joined our class during the last two years had educated us slightly on the goings on of the "real world", but really did not prepare me for high school, even a private one.

Of course, I learned real fast the private school was just as corrupt, if not more so, than the publics. The private schools had a lot more wealthy kids, meaning more and better drugs. It didn't take me long to realize, not out of any sort of street smarts, of which I had none, but just out of observable survival techniques, that drugs and alcohol, something completely foreign to me, were a fast tract to popularity with almost every group there. At least with the cool people. I didn't want to be the kid everyone picked on. I wanted not just acceptance, I wanted to be looked up to, and I found out fast the drug dealers were the way in, not the users. As well as status, they had lots of money as an added bonus, something almost more unknown to me than drugs.

The considerably older members of my brother's new rock and roll band proved to be the connection I needed to become the "dealer". Most of them were freshly moved from the big city, and easily set me up with all I needed to keep that high school fully saturated with the best marijuana of the day, along with the occasional harder drugs for a little excitement and infusion of big money.

Not satisfied with just selling, I began using, that way I could legitimately brag about quality. It was then I discovered my tendencies toward addiction of every kind. And it was also then that I lost all interest in family life, neglecting all of the farm animals and projects at the farm I had spent my life building up. My attitude went from positive, happy, and excited about life to negative, concerning everything I had always loved. My parents had no experience with this behavior, even with ten kids. I just happened to come into my own during a new generation of degeneration. Rather than reject and avoid the bad aspects of immoral behavior and abuse as my older siblings did and I was taught to do, I dove head first into the empty pool that the losers were swimming in, and became the swimming instructor to boot.

My folks were beside themselves, wondering where they went wrong. In fact, they never did go wrong. As I said, this mess was all of my own making. Yet they continued to pray for me, and I believe their prayers are what got me through it all alive. Many of my friends were not so lucky. I lost a lot of friends and acquaintances during that tragic time. And I definitely contributed in a big way to the downfall and undoubtedly the demise of many customers of mine, a fact that still haunts me to this day and is surely to blame for some of my problems over the years. Despite all of my fast living and total denial of responsibility and conscience, I have come to know that nobody lives in a vacuum, and all actions are accounted for, sooner or later, one way or another. I have reaped what I have sown, many times over, and none of it was undeserved.

It wasn't long before I was tired of taking a half hour bus ride to a private school, knowing the public school one mile from my house was the biggest party in town. I wanted to expand my customer base and expose myself to the locals. Business would be easier and closer. The problem was nobody in my family at this point had *not* gone to a parochial school. The trouble I had been getting into and the attitude I carried around at home was certainly not going to help me change a family tradition easily. Any mention of such a radical idea only brought on more strife and discontent at home.

Deep inside me, I was still that innocent, scared little country boy. But one of the benefits of drug and alcohol use, I thought, was how big, brave, and bad it made me. Not just with my friends and customers, but also with my family. I could stand up to them, argue with them and disagree with them, loudly, rudely, and especially nonsensically, without conscience or remorse. So I breached the subject of changing schools. That created a tension that would not go away. I was warned it was not an option, ever, period. That did not sit well with me and I pushed harder, louder, and longer. The higher I was, the more I pushed.

There was nothing to push. As a family, we had all we needed; there were no great unfulfilled desires. The argument for change really didn't hold water. So as I got more obnoxious, more of my siblings turned against me. As I carried on, I became more and more isolated at home. And that was big. We had all had our little squabbles over the years, but more on the lines of taking too long in the bathroom or eating one more scoop of ice cream than someone else. This was a major family blowup, and it was all about me, and all because I was putting personality destroyers into my system. Not only did I not know what the big deal was, I didn't care.

One evening I came home especially high, and began demanding that they take me out of my high school and transfer me. The argument fell apart fast. For the first time that I could remember, my gentle, quiet, reserved mother lost her temper. She had had enough. My siblings had had enough. I felt as if the whole world was against me. My pickled 14-year-old brain could not deal with anything rationally. I physically threatened everyone. When my dad turned his back to me in total disgust, I snapped. I jumped on his back, yelling and screaming, trying to tackle him to the ground. My mom, in shock, started to pull my hair. Two of my older brothers tore me off of my dad and threw me across the room. Life on the *Little House on the Prairie* was over. I had crossed a line none of us even knew existed. Darkness fell over me, and silence reverberated throughout the whole house. With tears in her eyes, my mom quietly, yet louder than I had ever heard, pointed to the back door, and said, "Get out of this house!"

I jumped up and ran out, slamming the door so hard the window on the top of the handmade Dutch door shattered with a crash. As I ran into the darkness, listening to glass hitting the patio, I was more frightened than I had ever been in my life. The glass breaking was the theme music to my final act. The window broke as my life shattered, and it all happened so fast I couldn't keep up with it. I heard someone come out the door and yell something, but I was running so fast I couldn't hear what they said. I ran to the street and down the block. I didn't stop until I could run no more.

I had aimed for a tree down the block that we had used as a fort as kids, then recently as a place to get high. It was more of a big bush, actually, right on the side of the road, totally able to hide everyone inside, yet gave a full view of all passing cars just outside.

I fell to the ground, confused, scared, and tired. I lay there for a long time, trying to make some sense of anything. I was high, drunk, and way too young and naïve to be experiencing this meltdown. It wasn't that long ago I was living a charmed life, without knowing it. I was just enough into denial to think my family caused this whole thing. What's the big deal with changing schools? Things have evolved since my last sibling had gone to high school. Plus, I could save them money going to a public school. It all made perfect sense to my newly twisted mind.

I lay down so I could watch the road, and nobody could see me unless they knew about this spot. I expected the cops to be searching any time. After a while, I dozed off. I would wake up briefly when a car drove by, which was rare. As the night wore on, I got colder, and began to slowly feel hung over. I had never been away from home after dark alone. As the high wore off, I fell into a well-deserved depression. So I was either asleep and cold, or awake, depressed, and cold.

Just as I started to actually analyze my whole situation, which would ultimately force me to face some real truth, I heard a familiar car in the distance. Both parents had 1965 Mercedes diesel cars. They bought them used, at an incredible price, and loved those cars. Not as a symbol of prestige, but because they were so pragmatic about fuel, just as gas rationing was kicking in, and diesel was about 39 cents a gallon. Gutless, nice looking cars, I had always felt like a special kid inside them. I only found out a long time later that they weren't limousines. And the diesel engine was noisy, like a truck.

So when I was drifting in and out of various forms of misery that night, I sat up fast when I recognized Dad's loud car turning onto this street. I got up and positioned myself so I could get a good look at whoever was in that car, and there was no way they could see me. I was sure the whole family was in there, searching for me. As it got closer, I became instantly wide awake and sober. I watched through the leaves as my dad slowly drove by, looking back and forth, all alone in the car. I could clearly see his face, and I could clearly see the pain on his face, searching for his youngest son, not understanding why I was gone, any more than I did.

As he drove by, I was overwhelmed with sadness and guilt. I had never stopped loving him. I didn't remember when or why I had become such a disappointment, it had happened so fast. I didn't want this. I wanted to go home. I wanted to back up time, forget the public school nonsense, and return to Eden. And, I had that opportunity now. I saw that in my dad's face as he drove by. Forgiveness was available; the ball was in my court.

I became very sad as I heard the car drive farther away. I wanted so badly to turn back time. This new life of popularity and drugs really wasn't me. It took the drugs to numb my conscience enough to make it all fly. Fun while high, fun with my newfound friends and customers, fun to have money, but at the cost of losing everything I had cherished since birth. Was I ready to exchange my true, happy self for the temporal rush of being not just accepted by the "cool" people, but even being—or so I thought—respected by them? As I sobered up, I fell deeper into remorse, farther into depression, regretting more and more. My life was changing so fast this was the first opportunity I had to really assess the damage.

If he came by again, I would give myself up and face the music. I dozed off, and sure enough, it wasn't long before the familiar, noisy car down the road woke me again. I got on my feet and edged toward the street, still hidden. I looked closely at the front of the car as he neared. The streetlight lit up his face only for a second. I could see the pain in his eyes. I can see that pain in his eyes to this day, if I allow myself to think about that night. It had changed from the look I saw earlier. The first time he passed by, there was a glimmer of hope in his sadness, like maybe he'd find me. This round, the hope had turned to failure. I saw something in his face in those few seconds that I never saw before. He had resigned himself to going home without me, and he was completely broken. Yes, I was number nine out of ten children, but he loved me as much as all the rest, and to lose me was to lose everything. He embodied the unconditional love God has for every individual person He has created, none more, none less. I was going to run out into the street, stop that car, and fall into his arms crying. It was not too late to fix this. And I couldn't handle that sadness in his eyes.

The car slowly rolled by. I froze. There was nothing in the whole world I wanted more than to go home with him. I started to cry. But I couldn't move. Something was whispering in my ear; "Let him suffer, let him pay, you deserve to go to whatever school you want. Besides, he has given up. He'll be okay. You have to stick to your guns. Don't be a wimp. He's the wimp. You've got plenty of people to see you through this. You're not a baby anymore. Who needs those squares? Life goes on. Grow up." I slipped back into the bush as his car turned the next corner toward home. I lay back down and fell asleep.

I wish I could say I went home the next day, apologized, and everything went back to normal. The reality was I barely slept that night. Between guilt, cold, and the effects of the drugs I took, it was fitful, at best. I don't remember much of the return home, other than it wasn't good. Life at home was forever changed. When I romance the idea that my drinking and drugging days were only bad in the later years, I conveniently forget the fact that from the very beginning it was bad. Not just bad. It took away my happy life. It ruined the happy life of my family, way back then. It stole my innocence, from the very start. Maybe I can remember good times—as long as I forget my family. I traded my family for popularity and ego, and it was not a fair trade. It was the beginning of an ugly pattern, where getting high meant more to me than anything: family, friends, work, career, then marriage, children, anything that competed with my current addiction.

Not long after that blowup at home, I was at school in my religion class. The teacher, a Catholic nun, was talking to us about rumors going around about certain students who really did not want to attend this school. She explained how unhappy students ruined it for everyone else. The faculty didn't want people here who weren't happy. She guaranteed she could convince even the most resistant parents to transfer their child elsewhere.

"It's really not a big deal," she said. "If you don't want to be here, come talk to me after class." Her next statement really got my attention. "Or you could just blow up the bathroom and for sure you'll be expelled." I had no idea she was dying to report some of us problem children to the hierarchy and to our parents. She had a definite agenda. But so did I.

The next day I brought a bag of quarter-sticks of dynamite we had snuck from Tijuana, Mexico the summer before; simple fireworks individually, fairly potent as a group. I borrowed a cigarette from a junior in the bathroom during first break, set it up as a slow fuse by the toilet, and went to class, the room next to the sports storage, adjacent to that bathroom. Less than two minutes into the class, the explosion surprised even me. I had no idea the power created when you put so many firecrackers together. One at a time was fun, this combination I put together that morning proved my religion teacher absolutely correct. The bathroom blew, and much of the sports room, even knocking shelves off the wall in the classroom I was in.

Too many people knew I was responsible. Within minutes after the blast, the principal, Pineapple Pete, was asking for me by name at my classroom door. He did not believe me when I said I was just doing what my religion teacher had told me to do only one day earlier. But he followed through with her promise. My dad had to pick me and all of my belongings up that day, never to return.

Dad didn't say much. I had won. And what an expensive victory that was. My family almost acted like I did not exist anymore, and that pushed me even further away.

Once I was established at the local high school two things happened. I fell right into the counter-culture, and I established an enormous customer base. At first, I had trouble keeping up with the demand for all kinds of drugs, even some totally new to me. By now I didn't care at all about my family. This was my new family. I went quickly from a member of a text book nuclear family, to the most dysfunctional group of misfits I could find.

Now, I appreciate the value of family and understand that, when all is said and done, family is truly the only thing that matters. I realize I threw away the most important part of my life, in the hope that this newfound high would replace my family and all of the beautiful experiences of my childhood. It did replace them, but not the way I had expected. Not in a good way.

CHAPTER 2

THE MOMENT

Somehow I Let It Slip By

Every summer, my family went camping somewhere special. I used to look forward to those trips. Early that particular summer, my parents announced that they had planned a short camping trip to a local campground at the nearby Indian Reservation. The idea was to get me, their 14-year-old rebel, away from town, and hopefully bond again with the family. I wanted nothing to do with the whole idea. However, in order to avoid another blowup, I agreed to go.

It was a beautiful place in the mountains. Our campsite was on a nice little river. It was hard for me not to like it. It definitely brought back great memories of fun times camping as a kid. I tried to keep up my macho wall, but without familiar friends around, it wasn't necessary. We were having a good time. I slept outside on a cot.

Late one night, I awoke to the distant, familiar sound of a party. I slipped out to watch a group of the local Indian teens partying around a big bonfire. Eventually, I got the courage to join them. After the initial tense meeting, soon a beer was in my hand and we were all one big group of lunatics. I stayed for hours, getting drunker, and got to know all of them. Early in the morning, close to sunrise, when most of my new friends were passed out or gone, the remaining few agreed to show me some local secrets.

We piled way too much wood on the campfire and snuck around the campground, as they took me to one rock shelf after another with ancient Indian drawings on them; nearly every one was directly over a campsite. It was then that I understood the saying "nobody looks up". For decades people had camped under these petroglyphs and I doubt that anyone had noticed them or reported them, or otherwise acknowledged their existence. It is so symbolic of life in general, rarely do we pay attention to what is going on right over our heads. It may also have something to do with the fact that most of the people who had camped under these ancient drawings were so drunk that they hadn't bothered to take in the beauty above them. Probably those few who had noticed the connection to the past, basically blanked out that insight and had forgotten about it by the next day.

After we finished that drunken, late night tour, we wandered back to our fire. When we got close, my new friends suddenly dropped to the ground and tried to hide. I realized they thought the camp security had seen our oversized fire and were waiting for us. Easy for me, I could just run back to my parent's campsite and fall asleep. As they crawled into the underbrush to hide, I began to slip off in the other direction. I always have had a strong sense of survival, and I kicked it into high gear.

But as I was sneaking away, they called me back. Even though I wasn't ready to be turned over to my parents in trouble again, they convinced me to follow them through the brush, slowly closing in on our oversized bonfire. As I peeked through the trees, I couldn't see the security truck or the Rez cops anywhere. My friends explained that anyone working at this camp was dead asleep by now, or so they hoped.

We had slowed down and crept closer. And there was a sight I had never seen or experienced before. As we drew nearer to the fire, and had a full view of it, I saw something that definitely made me think I was good and drunk. Our bonfire was still burning bright and strong. Only now, just before sunrise, very clearly and vividly, four men were dancing around that fire. And these were Indians in only breechcloth and war paint, a far cry from anyone I had ever seen, and as I found out later, like nobody any of my newfound friends had ever known. Though they didn't know them, they had seen these same four men dancing around a late night fire many times before.

I was secure in the thought that this was only drunkenness at its best. But I was feeling something that I never felt. This was not like any illusion I had ever experienced. I really struggled with the fact that we had all seen it, plus that they had expected it and were very familiar with it. On the other hand, I was definitely drunk. I was only awake at this odd hour because they had given me some street amphetamines earlier, little bennies so abundant at that time, commonly known as "cross tops". I was quite convinced that I was seeing the Ghost Dancers as a result of no sleep, all the alcohol, and drugs. Nothing new here. But as I looked over at my friends, I saw something that is just as vivid in my mind today as it was way back then.

I could actually see the reflection of the fire and the image of those Ghost Dancers in their eyes! And I realized that this wasn't just a game for them. They had come to watch these dancers many times before. At that moment, I had an overwhelming sense of compassionate sadness for them. It was their only door into the spiritual world, their only way to relate to their heritage and past was through alcohol and drugs. This was their religion. Not that I somehow knew a better way at the time.

But this alcoholic stupor definitely worked. It opened a cosmic door to the past, showing them something their alcoholic parents used to speak of with pride. Yet the abuse of this medicine--alcohol--was slowly killing them off. And this night, as we watched the Ghost Dancers, the cosmic door was suddenly slammed shut as the Tribal Police appeared out of nowhere and handcuffed my friends. They got sent to the Rez jail and I got lectured at length never to hang out with these losers again if I wanted to live long.

The Tribal Police walked me back to my campsite, just as the sun was peeking over the mountains. Luckily for me, everyone in camp was asleep. So I laid down on my cot, pulled the sleeping bag over my head, and passed out.

Several hours later, when it became unbearably hot and noisy, I got up. My folks joked about how late I had slept in. My head was pounding, my throat was dry, and I was in no mood for humor. They passed it off as teenage morning bad attitude.

I had breakfast and told them I was going to go for a hike. I wandered up the river, watching the young kids having so much fun, reminiscing about my innocent youth as I nursed a serious hangover. I went into my new friends' campsite, looking at the fire pit, now completely doused and dead. I shrugged off the memory of the night before, the dancing warriors, the petroglyphs, all of it was meaningless the way I felt right now. I knew nobody was here, so I opened their cooler, pulled out one of their last beers, and walked farther up the river.

I reached the end of the campground and kept going. I followed the river for a long time, until I ran into a broken down fence with a fairly serious No Trespassing sign, albeit very old and neglected. I crawled through the barbed wire and continued up the riverbed. After a while, I found what seemed to be another camp, but there were no people. It

had beautiful campsites and several waterfalls. It was a very special place. I couldn't understand why it was empty.

I found an incredibly comfortable boulder next to the water and settled down to drink my beer. We called it "the hair of the dog", nursing a hangover with more alcohol. This time the hair of a big, bad dog that had bitten me last night, my head was still pounding, and I knew the hair of that dog was my only hope for relief.

I was unaware that I had wandered out of the public campground and onto the local Indian tribe's private campground. Called Third Gate, or Indian Gate, it was only to be used by the members of the tribe, their family, and friends. Since I had come up the river, I hadn't seen the warning signs on the road at the gated entrance that made it abundantly clear how jealously private and exclusive this humble yet beautiful camp was. I was very much not invited, wanted, nor allowed here. I would find out at a later date just how fortunate I was that nobody saw me there that early Sunday morning. Normally there was always at least a handful of drunk or hung-over locals camping there, or just hanging out. For me to innocently meander into this guarded spot alone was more than a little dangerous. But for whatever reason, certainly not coincidence, on that fateful day, I was alone with my hangover. Hoping for relief. Wanting a nap and expecting nothing.

This was the beginning of a day that would determine which way my life would eventually evolve, far into my future, and I was not paying attention. It became that life altering moment, yet it took me decades to recognize, much less act on it. Looking back, I realize just how blind I was to miss something so obvious, so profound. But "if-onlys" and "woulda -couldas" didn't work then, and they don't work now.

As I settled into this big boulder with the awesome river view, something caught the corner of my eye. Descending the closest cascade, bouncing from rock to rock, was a tall Indian, looking out of place in this California Reservation. The vast majority of the local tribes were mixed with Mexican, German, Irish, and other nationalities, and did not look like this man--tall, dark, stout, with very angular and pronounced features. He had long black hair, more resembling one of the Northeast and Midwest tribes, and as he headed straight for me, I felt like a fool, slowly realizing I definitely did not belong here. I was just hoping he would pass me, but that did not work, so I began to get up and head back the way I had come. My beer was freshly opened, so I could use it as a gift to him so he would let me be on my way. Some of the stories of real crazy stuff happening on the Rez, told to me last night by my new friends now sitting in the Reservation drunk tank, started to come back to me. He was alone now, but who knows how many friends were behind him? Not that he needed any backup against me. I was still in major hangover mode, and in no condition to deal with confrontation.

Before I could move, he was sitting on the boulder next to me. Any illusion of him being close to my size was gone. This was a big man, well over six feet tall, and not lacking in muscular overkill. I was very intimidated, yet numb enough not to fully care what happened next. He began speaking to me as if continuing a long conversation we had started some time before. Totally non-confrontational, he spoke as if we knew each other, as if we were friends from way back. I thought maybe he had been sent by my friends from the night before, but he had a totally different feel about him, certainly not the personality of a man who drinks alcohol on a regular basis. Just the fact that he was so energized and awake this early on a Sunday set him apart from anyone I had ever known or had met up with here on this mountain.

He quickly shifted his conversation to focus on me. He told me I was definitely sick, and I definitely needed medicine to cure my sickness. As I lifted my beer to my lips, I said that I was anything but sick, just a little hung-over, and that was only because I had spent the night drinking with his relatives. He adamantly clarified the fact that the local Indians were not his relatives, possibly distantly related. And while he spent a lot of time in this area, just as his father and his father's father had done, these people were at best distant blood from his family. He was a modern day medicine man, son of a medicine man, and descendant of medicine men. He introduced himself as Chino, son of Padron Chino, a well known local Indian holy man. Perhaps well known to some, certainly not to me. He began to analyze me, as if we had an appointment.

He brought out a small leather pouch and dumped much of the contents into his palm. It looked like some kind of dirty, dried vegetables. He told me I needed to eat this medicine to get well. I protested that I wasn't sick, and probably would be if I ate these foul rotten-looking potatoes in his hand. Not meaning to be rude, I was quickly informed that I was disrespecting him, and worse yet, insulting the sacred medicine he was offering me.

He told me this medicine used to be found in many places, even in the local deserts near here. Now, it only grew in certain areas of Texas, and could only be found by those who respected it and used it in a sacred way. It was given to the Indian nations by the Creator to help them get through hard times, to keep them on a spiritual path, just as Jesus had given the Holy Spirit to anyone who would ask for it.

Chino said I needed to eat this medicine to open my eyes. Open them to the past before my lifestyle closed them forever. He spoke to me as if he knew me very well, and as if I needed his advice. I started to think he was just a little strange, a little off center. I had never seen him before, never talked to him before, and never heard about him before. Who was he to come along and tell me what I needed, and offer me what looked at best like some very old dried roots?

He then told me he was also watching the Ghost Dancers circling the bonfire last night. He said many people had stared right at those ancient dancers over the years, but very few, if any, had actually seen them. He could tell by watching me last night that I had definitely seen them. He said that because my grandmother had used this very same medicine long ago, and prayed that her youngest grandson would use it again in the sacred ways of her ancestors, it was for that reason I had seen the Ghost Dancers in the fire, and that he had come across me this morning at this location. He informed me this was an ancient ceremonial ground that even most of the local Indians didn't know about. Because of these things, I needed to eat the medicine, learn why I saw what I saw, and what I was to do with this knowledge.

Partly because Chino was a lot bigger than me, partly because I was afraid that he might get weird if I refused, partly because I was weak and hung-over, and partly because he saw those fire dancers and knew that I saw them, I decided to accept the strange-looking dried pieces of cactus. Not to mention the fact that there was the slim chance that he had a drug that I could make money on if it was good enough, so I needed to test the product. They couldn't be any worse than a lot of the garbage I had accepted, even paid for, from strangers, and ingested, looking for another high. I popped the whole handful into my mouth and started chewing.

Immediately I had a strong urge to gag and then an uncontrollable need to vomit. I was about to wash it down with my beer when Chino grabbed the bottle from me and threw it toward a beat up trashcan nearby. With a new tone of anger, he nearly yelled at me.

"These are polar opposites," he said, "and can never be mixed. To use this medicine in the way the Creator wants us to, alcohol has to be eliminated from one's life forever, so you can truly receive the blessings from this holy lifestyle." I agreed never to mix the two again. It was an easy decision, I enjoyed drinking beer and the effects it gave me. This so-called "sacred medicine" tasted worse than dirt, and was making me convulse uncontrollably. Beer won the competition hands down.

Yet, he wasn't finished. Chino dug back into his pouch and pulled out even more of his disgusting chunks of the "magic cactus".

"Chew. Chew every bit of them up. Waste none of it," he ordered. As if under a spell, I did as he instructed, chewing fast and swallowing hard, trying desperately not to gag as it got stuck in my throat on the way down. Tears came to my eyes. I shivered as if I was freezing, with a feeling of nausea building up from deep inside me like never before.

Suddenly I became very angry at this demanding stranger, and more so at myself for being so passive. Obviously, I had just been poisoned. Was this the infamous "loco weed"? The Jimson weed known to have killed scores of reckless fools who experimented with the dangerous native herb that only the local ancient medicine men knew how to prepare so it wasn't toxic? Had I just become the subject of another local practical joke, soon to be deathly ill out of total ignorance?

What had I done? Was I eating some foul poison from a complete stranger out of utter fear, misguided respect and stupidity, or was this the ultimate proof of a true addict, willing to consume anything that might get me high, looking for a new way to alter my conscience, without any normal caution, no basic survival instincts, no normal resistance to the possibility of being poisoned?

Fearfully, I asked him, "Why are you doing this to me?"

He replied, "You've been poisoning yourself for years. Now it is time to learn about the cure."

As my stomach started to settle somewhat, the medicine began to overtake my entire being. I started having questions, and more questions. I thought about what Chino, this out-of-place, mysterious medicine man who convinced me to eat this vile, nauseating cactus, had said about my grandmother, and about me seeing the fire dancers last night. How did he know my grandmother, since even I had never known her? Why did he happen upon me at this remote spot, and why did he give me this special medicine, even though he certainly didn't know me?

As I tried to sort out these questions, mountains of other thoughts poured through my mind to the point of overload, yet I seemed to be able to answer each thought in perfect order, moving immediately to the next question with total order and fluidity. My consciousness briefly returned me to my physical surroundings as Chino announced he was going on a hike down the river and told me to stay where I was until he returned.

This was not a problem, as I was completely immobilized, melted into this unusually comfortable boulder, my body molded into the water-worn curves of the rock, as if it were made just for my body, at this age and size and shape, holding me in a most natural position, able to see everything around me, above, below, behind, and in front of me. Slowly, I became the boulder and it became me. I lost the feeling of separation between me and all of my surroundings.

Soon I could feel it rhythmically breathing along with me, and along with the earth below us. The trees became acutely clear and vibrant, each corresponding leaf or pine needle reacting differently to the slightest change of air flow at each differing altitude. The sky beyond the trees was a beautiful dark blue, but I could see the color was actually a result of endless space, and I could see farther into that deep space, deeper into that blue color than I ever had before. I had a profound appreciation for even the most minute details around me, and for this brief interlude, I realized and understood how incredibly important and connected all of these simple, basic individual bits of creation were and how they all worked in unison, and how all of this was actually one organism, myself included, and needed all of it to function properly.

I lost all sense of separation from my environment, but it was unlike anything I had ever experienced. I had taken mega-doses of LSD before, and this was still near the era where Timothy Leary and the Rainbow Family were flooding the market with pure acid, unlike the garbage that passed as acid years later. I had also eaten psilocybin mushrooms, and in fact sold them to people on a regular basis.

But the experience I was having right now was not even remotely similar to any psychedelic experiments I had tried, mainly because those drugs had left me scared and confused, unable to direct any thoughts or cognitive brain activity. This was the opposite; right now I was completely conscious, totally relaxed, in absolute control of my mental state. This was more of a clear moment. Nothing was fuzzy, nothing was questionable. It was all as real as anything I had ever felt. I knew that what I was seeing was the truth, not a drugged-out illusion. I also knew that I would remember all of the details of today, unlike anytime I had taken drugs, when I forgot most everything that had happened. Something rang very true. And I wasn't exactly sure what it was, but I felt as if I was on the verge of finally finding out what this elusive "truth" was.

Unlike all drug experiences I had had until now, I was as clear headed as I could ever remember. My physical capacities, however, were less than useful; I felt nearly paralyzed, glued to the rock. But, rather than seeing things that weren't there, or distorting what was there, I was seeing my surroundings as they really were for the first time. The veil that I had always looked through to see life, was lifted. I saw the world as it truly was, without my or anyone else's interpretation. I could see the air and the molecules that made it up, I could feel the earth breathing. And I could hear all of the creatures, bugs, everything, making their individual sounds, and I could either separate them, or listen to the whole collection together, still able to discern one noise from another.

The loud hum in the air was nearly obnoxious, a collection of millions of insects communicating with their own kind, in their own language, directing their call only to each other, ignoring all other sounds. I zeroed in on one bug family, focusing on their special communication, blocking out all other sounds, until I was actually able to see what that particular creature looked like, and how it made its unique noise, where it was flying around, and how it narrowed its search to the exact member of its special family, so it could mate and reproduce, in complete order and simplicity, amid what seemed like total chaos and confusion.

I looked right through the broken beer bottles by the river bank, the aluminum cans floating by in the water, the piles of cigarette butts everywhere. I didn't notice the brown smog hanging in the air. I tuned out the loud roar of the long line of Harleys racing by on the main road above me. Instead I heard the ravens screaming at the red-tail hawks, the woodpeckers digging deep into the cottonwood trees, even the gopher pulling its favorite weed into its lair to feed its young, just below the surface. For some reason, I was able to filter out the day to day garbage I lived in and was able to pick up on the natural world, the world that really mattered. The world that has always been, and would always be, whether we acknowledged it or not.

Just as I was beginning to really enjoy this natural world, an uncanny silence fell around me, like someone had dropped the curtain to this act of the play. But it was an eerie silence that made no sense, as if I just hit the mute button on the movie I was watching. The roaring silence would have awakened me if I had been dreaming, but I was more awake than I had ever been before. All of the minute details of creation were still in full motion around me, I was still watching all movement, and also still able to focus in on any one aspect of life in detail if I chose to do so. Only now, the sound was completely off. So silent, all I could hear was my own heartbeat. Actually, I really only felt it, not heard it.

Quietly, I detected the faint sound of trickling water, like a leaking faucet. The only sound I heard was this slightly increasing movement of water, steadily getting louder, ever more intense, but only the sound of faster moving water, nothing else. As this particular sound increased, it reminded me of the beginning of a flash flood I had barely avoided when I was camping in the high desert years before. It was only because I had awakened early in the morning to a faint sound that somehow warned my subconscious mind that danger was imminent. This was a hauntingly similar sound, but I didn't feel the same fear of danger as I had then. I concentrated on the water, and as I did, my mind went to the source, way up the river, in the lake, where creeks and streams and springs kept it at a semi-constant level.

I followed the water, through the man-made weirs built decades ago in a futile attempt to control the water flow. The water poured out the chutes and churned its way down the boulder-strewn riverbed, roaring under poorly made bridges that broke apart every few years, as it cascaded down steep canyons. The water spread out on the level areas, backing up to waist high depths in the long stretches. It formed swimming holes that were used by the Natives for hundreds of years. They were, even now, some of their favorite wading pools. The river rushed past the narrow areas beyond the swimming holes, falling over rocks and tree stumps and branches, some stretches that had been widened by huge fallen trees, wedged across the river to form dams that rerouted the water into smaller tributaries that swirled around tiny islands, trapping and creating small ecosystems of life, altering that section of land forever with the simple shift of water.

I followed the water noise as it got closer, tumbling down the giant natural stack of granite boulders just to the left of me, slightly upstream. The water eddied in the small but deep natural pool at my feet, and suddenly changed its sound. It no longer was the rush of water, it eerily resembled human speech. I tried to sit up, startled to hear someone talking so loud right in front of me. Still unable to move, I tipped my head up just enough to look down into the water swirling around, just below my feet.

The words definitely came from the water. I looked around to see who might be talking to me, yet I was completely alone. It wasn't a vague, barely audible gurgling that I mistook for words. This was not some reaction to the medicine Chino had given me, because other than being paralyzed, I was totally mentally coherent, even though hearing water talk was hardly a sign of being in control of my mental facilities. Yet it was as clear as if someone was standing in front of me talking. I looked directly at the water churning at my feet, and as I heard the words spoken, I could actually see them form in the foam of the water. The words took on an indescribable physical form, so that as fast as they were being spoken, they formed a presence that was similar to steam above the water, and that steam seemed to surround me, entering through my ears as words, clear as any words I had heard Chino speak that day.

It took a few seconds to get past the absurdity of water talking, then I started to really listen. Not that I had a choice. The water began telling a story, the story of its existence. It spoke of ancient times, long ago, when there was so much water here, and everywhere. Before the aquifers were drained by thirsty ranchers, miners, oil men and new housing developments. Back when the springs and creeks were constantly flowing, pouring down this same river, only in much greater volume. It told me of pure, clean, pristine drinkable water, of the wild deer and bear that used to drink and bathe at this very same spot. It talked about the early people who first came to this river, who settled by it, who used the water but treated it with great respect, knowing how valuable it was. They caught fish, but only what they needed to eat. They taught their young to respect the water, and give thanks for its abundance.

Then the tone of the talking water changed. It sounded very sad as it described the river now, the way it was abused, the disrespect of the people who used it--the drinking, the drugs, the broken bottles, the urination from the banks, drains and septic pipes pouring into it, the dams, the diversions, the pollution dumping into it. It told me it was no longer a good part of peoples' lives; now it was just a means to move bad water to the ocean. The water, not all that long ago, was crystal clear. There were wild animals who drank from the lake, but not the hundreds and hundreds of range cattle now penned up at the source of this river, overloading the entire area with deadly bacteria that completely altered the chemistry of the water. No longer clear, the water is thick and heavy, and at every pooling section it has multi-colored foam, not natural bubbling effervescence.

Looking at these toxic suds reminded me of bath night at home as a child. Always doing what we could to conserve water and the gas to heat it, we would fill up the tub with hot, bubbly water. Starting with the oldest, each would soak in the bath, washing fast so the next sibling down the age scale would still get warm water. Being the second to the last to bathe, I always got stuck with lukewarm, dirty water, with only about a third of the bubbles left, usually mounded at one end, stained a brownish yellow tint, not really a very inviting sight. But I knew complaining would change nothing, and if I hesitated, the water only got colder. At least I wasn't the youngest.

This was the first time I actually saw just how much foam the river had, and how thick the water was. I had always thought how great this river was, it was all I knew. All of the creeks and streams around here looked just like it. The big rivers and lakes far north we had visited on vacation, were definitely much more pristine, but I thought it was due to water temperature and more flow, not the obvious varying levels of toxic pollutants pouring into each body of water all over the country. The water in this river represented more than I realized. I never really thought of the people who camped and partied by this river as bad, and, in all honesty, they probably weren't. At least not on purpose. But the reality was, they were the last ones to use it, not unlike me, when I was one of the last to bathe as a child, and the water was murky. Yet, they did not consider the river for what it truly was, a gift from the Creator, to be respected, protected, and enjoyed. Now, it was simply enjoyed for sport and *machismo*.

As the river explained its case to me, I began to feel weak. And then I realized it was crying. As impossible as was the talking, so much more was the crying, yet I could feel it, and I could actually see the individual tears mixing into the rushing water, with no possibility of discerning the source of these tears, only to know they were definitely coming from the talking river, as absurd as it sounded to what was left of my rational mind. And as I watched those tears multiply, soon the whole river was composed of tears. Gallons of tears, pent up for decades, pouring by my feet, mixing with the tears of all the rivers and creeks, rushing into the tears of the ocean, the ocean only a massive collection of all of the tears of the rivers, lakes and streams of the world, swirling around in sadness, the sum of all of the pollution. Of all the sewers, the toxic chemicals of all of the countries of the world; using the ocean as one big, infinite toilet, with no end in sight. As I listened sadly to the crying of the river, of all the rivers, of the ocean itself, I realized I was part of this river, part of all of the rivers, part of this dying ocean, and maybe that was why I was slowly dying, too. I realized that we were all part of this dying planet, all a part of its creation, and as much as we might think otherwise--that we were just another part of God's Creation--we were inseparable. Without this river, without these mountains, without these animals, trees, everything, we will also perish, no different than all of this beautiful experiment on God's Earth.

My mind started coming up with a host of revelations very foreign to me at that time in my life. Yet, they made sense to me. When we separated ourselves from the rest of Creation, we separated ourselves from our self, and we began a process of falling apart, individually, and collectively. Once we began to think and act as if we were not only separate from Creation, but also superior to it, we begin the process of destroying our environment, and in turn, destroying ourselves.

To honor the Creator, we have to respect his Creation as the ultimate manifestation of His creativity. Creation is God's greatest work, the outpouring of His spirit, His dream, His passion, a part of His soul, His idea of beauty, made for all to enjoy. To harm, to destroy the Creation is to blaspheme God Himself.

I understood that all of humanity has its roots in nature. All people came from some tribe, some group of natives that at one time in their history were fully connected to God and nature, if for no other reason than sheer survival. And deep down inside every one of us has that yearning to return to that natural, innocent state of mind, far from the chaos.

Revelation upon revelation, thought upon thought came to me. I lost track of time completely. Insights poured over me like a flood. I had never used my mind to this extent, at least not this fast. I was thinking and processing knowledge that I never possessed. My mind was filling up to overload, yet I was able to digest everything. I was learning about stuff that a 14 year old mind could not comprehend under normal circumstances. It was as if I was in a crash course on life, past, present, and future. And as strange as these images were being fed to me, I seemed to be absorbing it very well.

I mentally slowly backed away from the talking river, and tried to take stock in the whole experience. I felt sure that I had been there at least overnight. I started to get a feeling of panic as I realized that my parents were by now probably beside themselves with worry, and would have the Tribal Police searching for me. Once that thought entered my mind, all peacefulness and tranquility completely left me. I tried once again to sit up to look around but I found that I was still immobilized, after what seemed like hours. Now I started to get claustrophobic, thinking that maybe this "medicine" I had voluntarily eaten had permanently paralyzed my muscles. I had never heard of anything that kept a person in one spot, paralyzed for days.

As I sat there growing despondent, all of a sudden Chino was again sitting on the rock next to me. He began to explain the medicine. "It is like no other medicine. It has been known to heal every kind of disease, both internally when eaten, and externally when applied to wounds. This medicine has the discernment to find the ailment and attack only it, removing it from the body, sometimes subtly, sometimes violently, causing the sick person to vomit up what is hurting or killing them. And it goes beyond the physical, it works on the spiritual, cleansing a hurting person on a higher level." Chino called it an elevator. "It can take you up to the top floor, to our highest level of consciousness, where we can actually learn truth, feel truth, see truth, on a spiritual level, as God expects us to know truth. It has the ability to peel away the veil that covers our eyes now, a veil that wasn't there in our more natural days of existence, a veil we have voluntarily put over our spiritual eyes so we can focus on the carnal, the physical aspects of our nature, and do it without conscience or shame. With that veil lifted, we are able to see the spirit world, and all that comes with it. The medicine washes away our spiritual baggage, our pre-conceived notions of life, clears away the trivial day to day crisis and drama that we struggle with and get bogged down with, and opens our eyes to the big picture, to what really matters. It puts everything in perspective so we can break out of our self-defeating patterns and get beyond the superficial, meaningless, self-created obstacles that prevent us from maturing spiritually, from having a working, personal relationship with the living God."

As he continued educating me, I interrupted him as forcefully as I could, under the circumstances. "What about my family? My parents must have a search party out for me by now. I can't move, and you will probably be arrested for drugging me."

Chino smiled, trying hard not to laugh at me. "It has been about three and a half hours since I left you. I walked into the campground and, in fact, did run into your parents. I told them you were hiking up the river, and that they had nothing to worry about. They really didn't seem overly concerned about you, and were having a very relaxing time by the water with your little sister. So, I don't think there will be any search and rescue teams heading this way any time soon. You have a very important view of yourself, don't you? And you could move if you really wanted to, but I think you are more than comfortable right where you are, and don't want to move. Right?"

I felt much better when he said my parents weren't looking for me, but the three and a half hour part was impossible to fathom. Time had to have stopped, because there was no way everything that had happened to me, all that I had seen and learned, was possible to have happened in that short period of time. I knew that hours and hours had passed, if not a whole day. It was not conceivable that the whole river experience was that short. I just hoped that he wasn't lying about my parents. But one thing that was for sure, if I had been here as long as I thought, they would have come by now, and I would be in big trouble again.

Chino continued with his schooling. He told me that in the old days, this medicine was used more for its physical healing properties, because back then, before invasion, conquest, and removal, the great majority of tribes were living in guarded harmony, with minimal intertribal warfare involving not much more than shaming other tribes into allowing hunting on their traditional coveted hunting grounds. As with all humanity, there were exceptions to the rule--cruel tribes, mean individuals and bad seeds. But because they were spread out far enough apart and the wilderness was so vast and dense, most Indian Nations lived relatively peacefully with each other. There was plenty of resources to go around, land and game was everywhere, and the vast majority of people only used what they needed, and wasted very little. Over-consumption wasn't part of the culture, so the overall balance remained intact.

"So, in those old days, we as a people used this sacred medicine mostly for external wounds and some sicknesses. We didn't need an elevator to see spirituality, or catch a glimpse of higher consciousness, because we lived that way all of the time. God was not a distant notion, separated from us and living in some far away heaven. He was with us every day. The circle wasn't broken. Now, it is clearly broken. Broken into pieces. Life itself gets in the way of living. We don't know wrong from right, which way is up, what to do and what not to do. "Now we need this medicine as a spiritual tool. We need the elevator, so we can go back up to that top floor of life, get a glimpse of what was, of what matters, what is real, so hopefully enough of us will 'get it', so we can go back to that way of life, back to living the right way, back to the circle. With this medicine we have a chance to reclaim the spirituality that is still here, still deep in the roots of the trees, deep in the giant boulders, still in the tears that make up these streams, rivers and oceans, running like the blood of the Creator Himself, along with the blood of all of those massacred in the name of progress and civilization."

I closed my eyes and listened with ease. "Maybe we can get there with prayer, with meditation, with fasting and self discipline. But it hasn't happened yet, and we aren't getting any better, and we certainly aren't getting any younger. God gave this medicine to the Native People as a gift, as a tool. It only grows on this side of the world, and we have been taught how to use it properly. We don't know how to use alcohol, we were never taught that. It is not part of our history or culture, and because of that, every time we use it, we abuse it, because it is not ours to use. That is why it is such a problem for us. The same with marijuana and other natural drugs. God gave these to certain people who needed that medicine and taught them how to use it properly. Maybe those people are somewhere, using their medicines in the right way. Or maybe they've forgotten, we don't know, and it is not our business. All we can do is use what He gave us correctly, learn from it, and stay away from those things that we don't understand.

"We are fortunate to have this sacred gift, and even more fortunate that the secrets of how to learn from it have been handed down from generation to generation, with no changes or alterations. We can thank those who went before us, guarding this medicine and its ceremony from outsiders and those who did not understand. Thank those who gave up their freedom, even their lives, to protect and preserve these ways from extinction. We have been fighting and dying to retain this secret for hundreds of years, forbidden to participate in our own religious ceremony in our own land, by a new government that claims to have its roots in freedom of religion, as long as that religion isn't an Indian religion.

"The old ones say Jesus gave the white people the Holy Spirit in the form of tongues of fire, and gave the Red people the Holy Spirit through this Holy Medicine. This medicine helped the Native People survive the invasion. This medicine enabled them to retain a remnant of the old ways, to carry a piece of tradition and insight intact, through hundreds of years of every attempt possible to destroy all cultural and religious aspect of an entire race of people.

"One of the great mysteries and sources of power of this medicine and its ceremony, is the fact that the ceremony has stayed exactly the same as when it was first given to us by the Creator. Nothing has changed. It is our connection to our past, to our ancestors, our traditions, our ways of healing, our God. A direct link to days gone by, to a way of life nearly obliterated and forgotten. It has never been allowed to change, to adapt to the times or the surroundings. It is the one and only true constant in our turbulent lives to this day.

"The Anglo's say their Bible is that way, unchanged, a direct word from God, and it has remained the same over the centuries. I don't know if it is true, but those who study it tell me this, and I have no reason to doubt them. I know many people who try to follow this Bible, and they seem to be honest and sincere, so it must be good. The problem many of our people have with the Bible is from the first missionaries who did not understand that we had no knowledge or use of the written word, and they actually killed many Indian people for not accepting their foreign religion. In every organized religion there are people who go too far and ruin it for the rest. I know that doesn't mean the Bible is bad, it is just how it is read by intolerant fanatics that have no room in their heart for other cultures and other peoples' experience of God.

"This Native American Church, and this Holy Medicine, this is our Bible. It is the same as when the Creator first gave it to us. Many think ancient Native religion is long gone, because very few have kept it alive, but it is still here, as strong as it ever was, and we are still here, and always will be, as long as that Sacred Fire keeps burning in our hearts. If you could return to the past, hundreds of years ago, and walk into one of these ceremonies anywhere in these now United States, it would be exactly as it is now, on any given Friday or Saturday night, anywhere a tipi is set up for this sacred ceremony. You would know the songs, know what happens when, and what will happen, as far as the format goes. What is always new in each ceremony is the extent to how much God pours out His grace, His healing, and His instruction.

"This ceremony, with the use of this medicine as a Holy Sacrament, allows us to talk to the One God and hear His answer, to watch Him heal the sick, mentally, physically, and spiritually, to feel His presence, to know that He is still here to those who would call on His mercies, and to give us strength to carry on with our lives once we leave the ceremony.

"Only a small handful, a tiny minority, were able to keep these traditions alive through all of the troubles we've had. Now, seven generations have passed since conquest, and a revival is starting, ever so slowly. As this Seventh Generation is reborn, they will be able to help all people of all races return to that circular, intuitive way of life, living in harmony with Creation, with each other, and most important, with the One True God. Even though the time has passed where we can ever return to living on and with the land as our ancestors did, that way of life can still be achieved, only on a more spiritual level. A total societal attitude shift. But just as easily as this could actually happen, so too is the greater possibility that we remain only a small influence, and civilization will implode all around us. We already see it happening, on a grand scale. It will take an awakening of the spirit to stop the tidal wave. And within this ceremony, and through this medicine, and the direction of God Himself, we can all wake up, one by one. We just have to recognize that moment of awakening that comes upon every one of us, and act upon it as we learn the secret wisdom now available for anyone that desires to seek it out.

"Today, you were one of the fortunate ones who got to go on the elevator. One day, you will realize just how lucky you were, to go all the way to the top floor, and experience what you did. What you saw, felt, heard, and learned was all real, as real as it gets. More real than anything you have done up to this point in your life. How you react to today's lesson will either shape the rest of your life, or fade away until you no longer believe it happened. Now that you have taken that elevator, and seen reality, you must exit on the bottom floor, and start climbing the stairs of life, one step at a time. Tedious and tiring, the stairway is slow, yet necessary. Now you know what awaits you, the uncertainty is gone. But you must earn that top floor, it won't come easily. And on the way, you can tell others that there is more to life than the floor we happen to be on at any given day. The problem you will have is losing your faith, losing your direction, and falling back down the stairs now and again. You have to keep focused, keep climbing, keep believing, and get back up every time you fall.

"I wish I could tell you it will all fall into place soon, and your life will be easy, now that you have seen the top. But that is not your fate. You have an unusually long, curved staircase, and it is very slippery. Because of that, you must be wise, and be careful. You will learn many things in your climb, things most people won't learn and don't need to know. But these are all a part of your staircase, and from it you will be able to teach others to avoid many of the bad steps you have had to take to reach the end. There are no guarantees. Many have had a similar stairway, with great promise waiting at the top, but they got stuck on a bad floor, or fell all the way to the basement, never to get back up. You have to be steadfast and determined, and never allow a magnetic floor to trap you for very long. If you choose wisely, and allow those people put on your stairway to help you, all of the pain you will go through will be more than worth it. Remember this day, remember what you saw, and stay awake.

"That ceremony that I talked about will show you the way. Using this medicine in that ceremony will show you all you need to know. It is performed in a tipi, set up at sundown, and runs all night. One day, when you are much older, after you have been climbing your stairs for a long time, when you are about to give up, this ceremony will come to you to save your life, and finally make the climb easy.

"You will sit in your own tipi, right in this same spot we are now, right by this river, and learn how to use this medicine in a sacred way, exactly the way countless Indians have done before you. You will then remember this day, and once again hear the wisdom of the river, and understand how it can help you with the problems you will be immersed in at that troubled time of your life. In the meantime, I will take you through a more primitive ceremony using this medicine during the darker periods of your life, just to keep you on track. I can't prevent what has to happen to you, but I can make it a little easier from time to time. Don't worry, though. You don't have to decide to follow along with your life's plan. It has already been set in motion, and nobody can change it now. Like it or not, you have already begun the climb."

CHAPTER 3

THE SEEDS OF DOUBT ARE PLANTED

I completely missed the last part of what Chino said. When he began talking about "my tipi" at this spot on the river, I started laughing quietly. Up to then, it all sounded so "cosmic", so far out. I was enjoying the whole story, pretending I was being mentored by my own personal Indian Medicine Man hundreds of years ago. I actually was hoping it was real, except, of course, all of the talk about years of trouble and suffering before I finally found the light. I could do without all the doom and gloom. But, in my teenage mind, it really sounded like a great western novel. When he started talking "tipi", he took it a little too far, and brought me back to earth. I was laughing because I had been imagining it all as real, and also because we were sitting at Indian Gate, a private campground for the local tribe, just upriver from the public campground run by the tribe. While I had heard stories of this once being a "sacred ceremonial ground", that was all long ago. Now it was a party place for the least sober members of the tribe. It was amazing that none of the usual partying had been going on for the last few hours, probably because everyone was still sleeping off last night. Not only were the days of ceremony now replaced with sex, drugs, and alcohol, the idea of a Plains Indian tipi being set up here was totally out of place. These were Southern Californian Indians. Nowhere in their heritage was the use of a tipi a part of their culture, much less putting up a tipi at this crazy party spot and running some sort of religious ceremony in it. My attitude towards Chino, this unusual Indian, started to take a very negative spin. Maybe he wasn't even sane. A kook. I began to second guess everything he had said, and everything I had experienced. I started getting a sinking feeling that maybe this guy was just a nut, and I was just too drugged up to realize it. It all was going so good until he started mixing these Mission Indians up with Plains Indians, tipis and all.

This was that moment in time I spoke of earlier. That life-changing pivotal instant where, had I followed through, had I kept my eyes wide open and seen that spiritual path in front of me and walked down it, I probably would have avoided so many problems, so much grief and agony, and advanced spiritually so much earlier and gone so much farther. I would not have wasted decades of my life trying to wing it on my own, without the help and guidance of my Creator. Maybe. But I firmly believe I put myself through much more than was necessary, and could have avoided much of it had I acted on that moment when it was all laid out for me.

Instead, it was this little seed of doubt that grew into a forest that I couldn't see for the trees. Rather than asking questions and getting beyond the tipi dilemma, I threw it all away, everything I had just experienced and treated it as an illusion. Had I been born into a spiritual based culture that recognized my vision for the insight for what it was, things would have turned out differently. I would have been encouraged by family and friends to pursue my path laid out for me. Being raised in this time and space, with the years of problems associated with drug abuse, my mind was trained to go for the negative angle. While deep down inside my soul, I truly knew that what had just happened was much more than a psychological reaction to chemicals altering my neurons. I am blessed with an incredible imagination, inherited from both parents that worked for Walt Disney in the early years. But imagination has its limits, and if I really analyzed the last few hours, I would have to admit that even Disney himself would have had trouble dreaming up all that transpired.

My life could have definitely changed that day by the river. But, because of my sin of doubt, of disbelief, lack of faith, perhaps out of fear, maybe out of laziness, mostly out of ignorance, I didn't follow through. I used the statement about the tipi as an excuse to avoid the discipline necessary to do what I knew to be right. I decided I was having way too much fun drinking, drugging, and chasing girls to bother thinking about doing the right thing.

Still, a few times a year I would meet with Chino up in a secret cave for ceremony and spiritual guidance in an attempt to sober up. Then I'd dive back into the "good times" shortly after every retreat, each time getting deeper into abuse and needing relief even more. I thought I was fooling Chino, and fooling myself, too. But he knew what I was doing, and warned me several times that one day I might not be so lucky and lose it all, for nothing. The combination of being young and invincible, the lure of everything thrown at my feet, and the absence of any real consequences kept me coming back for more and more abuse. Chino told me time and time again, if I kept up my same direction, I would be lucky to last until the day I would sit up in the ceremony in the tipi, and, if I did, it would be a last minute gasp for air before I lost everything. I would need it just to save my life. Yet, every time he brought up the "tipi" thing, it was like a trigger for me to doubt everything he was teaching me. It became a very convenient excuse to go back to partying, so much so I hoped he would bring it up every time so I could justify ignoring all of the positive aspects of his lessons.

At home and at school, between parties, I began to read every book on Indians I could get my hands on. It was hard to find good material, most was from the perspective of Custer or someone related to him. The other extreme was the hippie angle, where the New Agers were taking what they liked from the Native American lifestyle and religious beliefs, infused it with some Eastern mysticism, Hinduism, and Buddhism, and made up their own version of Indian life. I had to look real hard to find anything halfway accurate about Indian history. When *Bury My Heart At Wounded Knee* came out, it was a real eye opener for me, and I'm sure for many others. The mid-Seventies were the beginning of the awakening of the American Indian Movement, but not only did the media cover a lot of it up, it sure wasn't allowed to be seen in my house. "Nothing but a bunch of trouble makers, best to leave it all alone," I was told. I didn't find out until much later why my family was in deep denial about all things traditional as far as Indians went.

Since the only classes I went to regularly were art, painting, and ceramics, I started making all kinds of Indian themed projects. I went to the Reservation to hang out with my friends I had met that fateful weekend. But hanging out with these Indians now was not teaching me anything about traditional Native life. While Chino was a wealth of knowledge on that subject, my new Rez friends schooled me about current life on the Reservation, where Native breakfast usually was a hot dog on a tortilla. We became connoisseurs of the campground store, or snack bar, to be accurate. And dinner was always beer, or wine if it was cold or rainy. On the crowded weekends, we hung out with the Indian war veterans in a site overlooking the whole camp, drinking dinner.

CHAPTER 4

TRAVELING FAST DOWN THE WRONG ROAD

I made enough money selling drugs all week at school to keep my whole group of Indians, young and old, good and drunk every weekend. I became very popular because I bought the beer. I got real involved with Reservation life at the campground, but not the traditional way Chino wanted me to do. Instead, I learned all about getting drunk and causing trouble from sunrise to sundown. The Vets always told me I needed to get involved in a good war to channel my energy in a positive way. They told war stories that gave me nightmares and gave them nightmares, too. Some nights I would hear them scream in their sleep, passed out under the trees. Still, most of them considered the war the best time of their life. To forget the bad stuff, they just passed the time telling stories and getting drunk.

At that time, being drunk was normal, accepted behavior for the majority of the Indians on most of the local Reservations, and many other Reservations across the country. Poverty was rampant, despair was the only constant. Many of the traditionalists and old timers had either died or were isolated in more remote areas, not wanting to participate in the spiraling depression and abuse that was overtaking Rez life. I watched families come together at the campground beginning their day happy, swimming, inner tubing down the river, picnicking, having a great time. And like clockwork, a little after lunch, when the beer and wine came out, the arguing began. By nightfall, every single weekend, the whole camp turned ugly. There were indescribable fights, beatings, knifings, domestic and child abuse. Men fighting men, women beating each other, drownings, and, of course, the occasional shooting. My friends and I would watch everything from the trees, out of sight. Sometimes, when we were drunk enough, we would beat up an isolated drunk that was getting sick in the bushes, just to be a part of the madness.

The Tribal Chairman at the time, Big Kamol, was a mountain of a man. He drove around on a backhoe. He was one of the very few sober men on the Rez. Whenever he got word of chaos at the camp, he would round up some of the oversized sober men from a neighboring Reservation and roll in on the backhoe, slap people around, tie them up, and lock them in the chain-link holding tanks for the night. He hated seeing his people drunk, and did what he could to discourage it. For as long as he lived, it was a losing battle. When Casino money entered the picture decades later, some of it went to help the people struggling with addiction, and Kamol would have loved that.

I watched as more and more of the older drinkers died from complications from liver failure, diabetes, and heart attack, often while they were partying with us. Kamol blamed many problems on me, saying not only were the old drunks a bad influence on me, but also my money buying them beer was killing them. He called me "Thunder" because I was always loud and carried a black cloud with me everywhere I went. He always told me to stay away. "Why do you want to become a loser like these guys? You have it made, and yet you come here to die."

Whenever there was a big problem, he came looking for us, so we could be blamed. I was the only one in the group that didn't black out, so everyone asked me for details about the night before. I used to sit around in a group in the morning and tell everyone what they had done the night before. No matter how evil, how disgusting, everyone wanted to hear what happened after they were so drunk they couldn't recall anything. And the hangover storytelling kept everyone laughing hard, so hard they'd be gasping for breath as tears rolled down their cheeks. It was all a big joke, the beatings, the fighting, the abuse. I was able to tell people where they got the big cut across their face, why they had a purple egg on the back of their head, why their truck was completely destroyed and in the river. It was a time of laughing and fun that was incomprehensible 12 hours earlier, during the war zone. I would pay close attention to the fighting, so I could tell a reliable story.

Slowly, as my disease progressed, my memory began to fail me. I started forgetting some of the night, then most of the night mayhem. Eventually, it really wasn't fun anymore as the effects of alcohol became fatal for too many people within my circle of influence. It got harder and harder to justify supplying the beer and wine to our close knit group. Funerals for friends who died from diabetes, heart attacks, and other diseases were a little easier to handle, even though we all knew the real cause was the alcohol. The frequency of deaths from drunk driving accidents, shootings, and suicide grew so fast that basic denial stopped working for most of us. The funerals for the older guys were bad enough; we justified it by pontificating how they had had a great, long, life. The truth was that they were dying at 45, 55, maybe 60, if they were lucky. We considered it old. But the increasingly commonplace death of friends and tribal members my age and younger became harder and harder to handle. More and more were giving in to their addictions, throwing away everything for nothing, giving in to their final escape routes, destroying their families, children, spouses, parents, friends, and ultimately, themselves.

The lies and deceptions thrown around by the priests, pastors, preachers, and other speakers at these depressing funerals should be illegal. So many times I wanted to jump up and shout the truth as they whitewashed the pitiful lives of the dead, glossing over the reality of what lead to their death. They emphasized the positive, usually stories of their childhood long before they became sick, and glorified their incredible ability to party harder than everyone else, as if this was a virtue. All were heroes, all the better for dying, victory was theirs. Never was it even hinted that the fact that all of these deaths were 100% avoidable, a direct result of foolish decisions and bad behavior, actions that most of us attending the funeral were still very much involved in. No lessons were learned at these funerals, because the truth was completely buried, as deeply as the latest body in the most recent coffin.

The drama at each funeral got more and more macabre. Whoever was the closest, by blood or relationship, had to out-do everybody else in sorrow and dramatic antics, throwing themselves on the body, slapping the dead or the nearest friend, running out of the church screaming, and then, of course, drinking or drugging themselves into oblivion (justifiably, you must understand). It got worse each time. The shock factor had to be greater than the last, the grief louder, more real, the self abuse more damaging. There were even a few who died from overdose or car accident in their desire to be the most distraught, the most grieving, the hardest hit. The double funeral had no rival in the antics of the bereaved. It would be comical, if it weren't true, or if it weren't so pathetic. Not to say I was immune. I did my share of dramatic grieving for some of my closer friends who killed themselves.

We came up with a "tradition" at funerals, where our group would wear a black bandanna rolled up and tied tightly around the left bicep. Soon, this caught on, and everyone started wearing black bandannas on their left arm at funerals. Then, you had to wear it as soon as you heard someone died. And it couldn't come off until seven days after the funeral. We constantly added new rules. If I were smart, I would have started selling black bandannas back then. There were so many funerals that we always had these smelly, unwashed bandannas on our arms. Lots of us. Tourists at the campground wanted to know the significance of the black bandannas on so many young people. Other tribes started asking about it. Thank God, there wasn't the internet back then, or You-Tube. People would be wearing rotting black bandannas on their left bicep to this day, in Siberia.

It got weirder. Someone said you couldn't wear the same bandanna for different dead friends. There were weeks where we would have three or four bandannas on our arms. We looked like fools, but we thought we were being respectful. Proud. Tough. Nobody remembered where or when the whole superstition started. Soon we thought this was some ancient traditional Indian custom, so it was sacred. If anybody questioned it, or much worse, made fun of it, that meant war. You were disrespecting an ancient tradition, and mocking our dead friend, someone who died a hero, for a cause. We became demented, fighting violently for something that didn't exist, over someone who was as pathetic as we had become.

I don't remember when the black bandanna thing faded away, but it did. However, to this day, occasionally I will see a couple of teenagers or adults wearing a black bandanna on their left arm at a funeral. All I can do is get on my knees and thank God I'm not still in the drama and insanity I was immersed in back then.

That wasn't "the" worst, there were many "worsts". When everyone you know is caught up in the drinking and drugging lifestyle, nobody is thinking rationally. Everything that happens is an emergency, all relationships are on the edge of breakup, nobody is faithful to anyone, and all emotion is exaggerated to the highest degree. Drama is the rule of the day, and the smallest incident becomes the greatest tragedy or problem, all molehills become insurmountable peaks. Especially when people are dropping like flies around you. Soon it becomes a badge of honor to *almost* die, to nearly commit suicide, to just about become the next funeral attraction. The attention is suffocating, and there is nothing an alcoholic or a drug addict craves more than undivided, suffocating attention. Soon the game turns into who can almost die, and how can the rest of us stop them from succeeding the next time. It is a sickness that feeds on itself, and has to have been dreamed up by the devil himself. It gets worse every day, until it's almost like we were all playing Russian roulette with a gun that had five bullets and only one empty chamber. The fun of the party is definitely gone.

We would always have a party over the grave of the latest victim of our insanity. And, of course, we would start out reverent, solemn, stoic, and strong. With four black bandannas covering everybody's left arm, usually a red bandanna headband, we would begin with funny stories of the deceased's crazy life, how they loved to party, how they were always happy, always the most popular, best looking, most friends, only the good die young, blah-blah-blah. Same stories, different corpse. Then, as we got drunker (especially once we somehow decided that a real wake required hard alcohol, that beer and wine wasn't good enough for the dead) the sadness began. The crying, wailing, screaming. Then, on cue, the anger. *Real* anger. Mad at the dead. Mad at whoever let them die. Mad at God. Mad at each other. Mad at ourselves. Always managing to pour shots of alcohol and pour it on the grave of the dead, so they, too, could keep enjoying alcohol even now, just as we were. We couldn't decide who was the luckiest; the ones who died, or those of us who managed to survive. To say the least, I became disillusioned with modern Reservation life, and wondered what had become of the proud, strong keepers of this great land, and why they had completely given up. Deep down inside I knew there were still some who hadn't given up, some who were still hanging on to that pride, that honor, and those traditions that kept tribes going even through the roughest of times. I knew there was another way, another path, a good road, one much nicer than this that many like me had not chosen to follow, but was still there for those who really wanted it. Somehow, I was so far away from that path I had lost track of how to find it again.

Occasionally, when it seemed I was at the end of my sanity, Chino would appear out of nowhere and drag me up to that cave above the desert. We would eat that bitter cactus and pray, and I would temporarily get back on track, swearing off all things negative, and sober up for a time. A very short time. And each time, the clean days got shorter and shorter, and the relapse was stronger and more devastating. I could return to drinking the same massive amounts to get less results in much faster time, and the guilt of knowing that what I was doing was totally opposite to what I knew I should be doing was debilitating. My resistance to bad habits was gone, but so was any resemblance of having fun when I did give in.

Somehow, I managed to get through high school. Sort of. I completely sat out tenth grade, partying every day in front of the school with a huge crowd of losers. I only showed up for art class, usually to make ceramic bongs to sell with the marijuana I was getting from high-end growers in Northern California. Lucky for me, the High School Proficiency Exam came along at that time, and if you could pass this test you received the equivalent of a high school diploma. I flew through the exam, acing it like no other test I had ever taken. I was amazed at how easy it was. I wasn't stupid. In fact, I did very well in elementary school, and in high school I was able to get pretty good grades in classes I actually attended. It was boredom, laziness, arrogance, and too much alcohol and drugs that prevented me from succeeding in high school. The equivalency exam was a Godsend. Soon after I passed, the rules changed and the test no longer replaced the high school diploma. The timing was perfect, like many other "coincidences" in my life. However, it didn't help me grow or mature; rather it tended to spoil me and absolve me of even more responsibility, winging through life waiting for the next lucky break.

I got the news that I had passed midway through my eleventh grade, while getting drunk in front of my school. Talk about a reason to celebrate. There was no way I would have graduated without adding a year or two of summer school. Now I was truly free. No real change in lifestyle, other than not having to pretend to show up for school. But the guilt and worry about how I would finish school was gone. I had learned to hate school, and now I never had to go again. This triggered a party that had no end.

After a while, my parents let me know that some sort of college was necessary. Art school sounded fun, so we searched until we found one that was minimally academic, heavy on actual art work. They would pay the way, but I had to really put out effort. First, I lived in a hotel near the college. Later, I moved into a nice house one block from the beach. Suddenly, I was completely on my own, in a distant community, knowing nobody.

Art school was a fantasy for me. The majority of students were female, and the few men there were predominantly gay, something I had never heard of and didn't understand. All I knew was it left more women for me to chase. So I was 18-years-old with no attachments, one of the few of straight guys among a harem of young, lonely women. To earn extra spending money, some were models for the Life Drawing class, a class that left nothing to the imagination. I started having after school parties at my house, and life was one big dream.

Soon I reconnected with my suppliers back home, and started up my lucrative drug trade in a whole new market. Through the endless stream of beautiful women hanging out at my house by the beach, I put together a new clientele that eventually even included some of the local police, corrupt and corruptible. This gave me a sense of security that led to a very blatant drug trade right in the middle of town. My lifestyle could never be repeated in the present political and social climate, and that is a good thing.

For all of the good intentions of my parents, college ended up becoming an exaggerated extension of high school, maybe just a little more sophisticated. My addictions only got stronger, my ego bigger, and my connection to anything spiritual dimmer every day. One of the better things that happened to me was meeting a street-wise artist a couple of decades older than me by the name of Bob Jones who taught me many life lessons, introduced me to the culture of the arts, and encouraged me to be very creative in new ways. His influence helped to round the sharp edges of my limited farm boy worldview, and we remain good friends even to this day.

Beyond improving my ability to paint, art school introduced me to a whole new medium, stone carving. Stone carving intimidated me at first, yet it wasn't long before I was hooked. I had a natural feel for this particular art. As a class we would go into the desert and pick out alabaster boulders at a quarry not far from the mountain where I spent nights praying with Chino. We carved these rocks into whatever we saw as we looked at the raw material. I got caught up into a sort of a cultish stone carving group along with my friend and mentor Bob Jones. We would begin every session smoking massive amounts of high grade marijuana, then staring at our selected alabaster stone until we saw the carving inside. We would actually see what we were about to carve, and eventually create what we had seen. I won awards for three of my best carvings: one of an Indian chief in full headdress, one a single feather on a warrior brave, and my hardest piece, a two-foot-long hand holding a peace pipe with a feather hanging off to the side. The undercutting and detail was very intricate, something my instructor assured me could not be done with the soft stone we worked with, and would surely break during the carving process. If it wasn't for the exhortations of my friend Bob, I would have never finished this remarkable carving.

I also stirred up some not so minor controversy with a project in one of my classes where we produced a short film documenting us methodically smoking our marijuana in a secret spot in the trees near the school, getting ready for carving class. It was real time, and accurate, and emphasized the repeated ritual we went through, hiding out, loading the sacred bong, passing the smoke to what were supposedly reputable members of the art school's teacher and student population. It won awards for production quality, and also separated some of the staff permanently. The art school had both ends of the spectrum, ultra-liberal, and very conservative. We managed to anger both sides with our project.

Another irritant I managed to arouse was with my final ceramic class project. I made intricately detailed individual victims of the Wounded Knee Massacre, with mutilated men, women, and children strewn across a snow covered landscape, with the Seventh Calvary laughing as they stood behind their cannons and Gatling guns, complete with the famous Native infant child trying to suckle her mother's breast in the freezing snow, with most of her body blown to pieces. My accurate clay figurine of Chief Bigfoot, frozen in a contorted angle in the snow, both arms blown off, was almost identical to the pictures of the actual event. The whole display was historically accurate to a fault. There was no disclaimer or excuse for the morbidness of the display. They couldn't accuse me of over dramatizing the scene because it was so close to the government's pictorial account of the incident, it had to be taken at face value. And it was anything but family-friendly art. When my parents saw the project, they were speechless, not in a good way, even though it received numerous awards for historical accuracy, emotional value, and going beyond the standards set by the committee. This was not their idea of money well spent. While they encouraged creativity, they shied away from dredging up old controversial issues. They did, however, enjoy my paintings and stone carvings.

Ultimately, I was given the opportunity to study stone carving with what was called "The Masters", in Carrera, Italy. I wasted this once-in-a-lifetime chance, which it truly was. But I was using marijuana and psilocybin mushrooms almost daily, and my mind was so messed up I had no idea what a great opportunity I was walking away from. I convinced myself, under the influence of the extremely mind altering effects of "magic mushrooms" and a group of very convincing New Age hippies, that I had all of the artistic education I needed, that my talent exceeded even the Masters in Italy, and I needed no more help to become a famous artist.

This was the beginning of a new phase of my addictive personality that I thought was leading me back in the spiritual direction I had fallen away from. I didn't realize how completely opposite the spirit involved in these mushrooms was, when compared to the true spirituality connected to the medicine of the Native American Church. I'm sure there are many who would say it is all the same, but reality says otherwise. If one analyzes the history of the cults associated with the use of the psychedelic mushroom, you can see a bizarre and confused society, connected with all sorts of demonic activity and sorcery leading to human sacrifice and torturous mutilations that never resemble anything positive and sacred, certainly not holy. And all of the people I associated with during my experimentation with this odd spirituality ended up being anything but holy, far from spiritual, and actually very scary in everything they did. While it had the feel of spirituality, it was very deceiving, made explicitly to lure Godly people away from the path, while acting like it was saving you from your current destructive behavior. Another perfect example of "the imitator".

All the while thinking I was somehow returning to my spiritual path, I was being lured farther away from truth. I stopped drinking, at least publicly. I embraced a cultish belief, very strong at the time, which told us we were the select few who were going to survive the end of the world. I dropped out of art school, sold or gave away way a lot of my possessions, and moved to a commune in southern Oregon. There I met the Rainbow Family, the last remaining remnants of the sixties hippie movement. They still held fast to the belief of the coming of the Age of Aquarius, were vegetarian to the point of extreme malnutrition, partook regularly of any and all psychedelic drugs, and still lived communally, sharing all, including mates or lovers.

They took me in happily, partially because I had such great stories about Indians, mostly because I still had "worldly possessions" and had to share with everyone. I only relented because some of the younger hippie women, or I should say teenagers, were not only beautiful without makeup, they had absolutely no hang-ups about sharing sex with strangers, and I was the new kid on the block, still a teenager myself, and way overloaded with hormones. From Oregon, I followed the Rainbow Family to Arizona, to a commune called Healing Waters. This was supposedly an ancient Indian gathering place, and everyone there pretended they were Indian. Only they were vegetarian, disregarding the fact that Indians were meat eaters, and most tribes would have starved had they been vegetarian. They had no clue about what Native life really was, and based their whole existence on drugs, group sex, and a made up spirituality combining Eastern mysticism, Buddhism, rebellion, drugged consciousness, and hopes of reviving the Summer of Love that had died out 15 years earlier. The carefree years got dangerous with the spread of venereal disease, a heightened sense of emptiness, realization that it was all leading nowhere, and increased suicides during extended periods of drug abuse and sex that often led the "free-loving" people into jealous episodes of rage and violence.

Eventually the advent of the AIDS virus shut it all down. When the Jesus movement hit the scene, the lines began to be drawn. Drugs were not the answer, in fact they caused the problem. Hippies embracing Jesus, after decades of hating all things remotely religious, symbolized a major shift of consciousness. All of the alternatives had failed. People were returning to what seemed to have worked long ago, albeit in a much more current approach. New warehouse contemporary churches sprang up with rock- and- roll bands that accepted the disillusioned hippies, and the new "yuppie" was born, again...literally. The backyard chemists brought crystal meth and crack cocaine, turning drugs from an experiment in fun into sickening, devastating, rapid addictions that destroyed personalities so fast it was no longer acceptable to associate with anyone in the counterculture anymore.

I returned to my hometown with my tail between my legs when the end of the world had not come as I had so strongly warned. I slowly returned to a semi-normal existence, moving into a small room I built in a greenhouse across the street from my childhood home. I tried to work for a while, soon to fall back into what I always did best. It wasn't long before I was fully immersed in the drug trade, now selling big quantities of methamphetamine made by a friend who was just released from prison, where he had perfected his drug manufacturing skills. Working my way up the ladder, eliminating any middleman in my way, eventually led to me dealing with the biggest and best known motorcycle gang. But I also worked with their enemies, doing whatever it took to make the most money, and also support my latest addiction: meth. Everything collapsed when a new partner who was constantly setting up too many contacts somehow got mixed up in a situation involving some stolen bars of gold, along with kilos of cocaine that I knew weren't his. He dropped them off with me late one night, against my loud protests.

They found what was left of his mutilated body way out in the desert, near the Mexican border, about a week later. Two other connections in my circle were tortured to death the next week. Needless to say, I was a nervous wreck. Innocent, but nervous. I gave the gold and what was left of the cocaine to a friend of a friend, and told him to return it to whom I assumed were the owners. I was wrong, and that brilliant move led to the assassination of him and three of his friends, which then set off a chain reaction that seemed to have no end. But, eventually, the right people ended up with most of what they were missing and it almost felt safe to breathe again.

One night, after getting good and drunk at my friend Franco's bachelor party, a big crew of us ended up at a local club, hoping to either get lucky, or just get a lot more inebriated. As we sat drinking and making fools of ourselves, a very pretty and petite young blondish woman approached our table from across the dance floor, obviously staring at me. She got about halfway to us, then burst out in hilarious laughter, turned, and ran back to her group of girlfriends. Every one of my buddies noticed, and started harassing me, daring me to chase her down. After a few more shots, I got up the courage and staggered to her table to ask her to dance.

I had definitely entered enemy territory. Her friends made every effort to make me fully aware of the fact. They protested my advances to her loudly, and strongly discouraged her from accepting my invitation to dance. Not easily dissuaded, and emboldened by the fact that she had made the first move, I sort of knelt down at her side, put my elbows on her knees, and rested my head in my hands, begging her to dance.

She laughed and laughed, then explained that she thought I was somebody else when she had approached me earlier. Realizing I wasn't him, she had returned to her seat, fully embarrassed. She was not trying to pick up on me and then got cold feet, a crushing blow to my drunk yet fragile ego. I insisted that she not be embarrassed, and her friends insisted louder that I *should* be embarrassed, leaning on the lap of a total stranger. I continued on with my pleading, while her girlfriends rolled their eyes and used every method of secret yet obvious hand and head motions to get her to send me away. Fortunately, my friends came over and started flirting with the other girls, and that took the attention off of me.

We talked. We talked, and yelled during the music sets, about a lot of nothing, typical drunken small talk, saying more than normal because of the alcohol, but still nervous enough to stay completely superficial in our conversation. She never gave in to my repeated requests to dance, but I did finally get her to write her name and phone number on a bar napkin, and I made sure she knew my name was Robert. To add insult to injury, not only did the cocktail waitress advise her against doing it, my friends even tried to prevent her from giving me her number.

When I woke the next morning with the usual pounding headache, she was a vague, blurry memory. Everybody and everything was scattered all over my house, yet in my drunken stupor I had managed to stick the bar napkin to the wall by my bed with a thumbtack. I struggled to remember what she looked like, but the memory was completely vague. She was small and cute, but her features eluded my tainted memory. My buddies swore she was a hot catch, way out of my league, but they had fooled me before, and put me in some very uncomfortable situations.

I did remember her laughter, and everyone agreed, she loved to laugh. So, by midday, my curiosity got the best of me, and I gave her a call. She laughed when she realized who I was, and I could sense she regretted giving me her phone number. Eventually, she reluctantly agreed to a sort of date the upcoming Friday.

When I picked her up at the end of the week in my freshly painted black 1959 Chevy pickup, I was undoubtedly happier than she was. Her name was Sandra, a tiny 5 foot 2 inches with a perfect figure. She had thick long hair, and a smile that turned into laughter at the drop of a hat. She was beautiful. Being four years older than me, and much more worldly than any of the girls I had ever dated, Sandra was definitely out of my league. Born and raised in upstate New York, she had moved with her family to the jungles of Costa Rica in her mid teens, where she became fluent in Spanish and got a job teaching in a local school. Hopelessly optimistic about everything, to her I must have seemed unbearably negative and jaded. At first, I thought her positive attitude was overdone, maybe phony, covering up something, but I was wrong. And she literally laughed at everything. Not just a subdued giggle, but a deep down belly laugh; loud and contagious. Being the annoying class clown my whole life, having someone continuously laugh at my corny humor was a real ego boost for me. But, not wanting a serious relationship at this point in my life, I tried long and hard to find fault with her, but I had no luck.

Once again, the timing was perfect. She was in the midst of trying to convince herself not to marry an odd fellow who had her hypnotized by his musical talent, but had some real serious personal issues that could definitely ruin any marriage. He was obsessed with his close friend who was to be the best man at their wedding. Sandra confided that she truly believed that deep down her fiancée wanted to marry his best man, and she should be a bridesmaid, not his bride. I could tell she was in love with this confused fool, but I also knew he would only end up hurting her in the long run, and did not mince words. I let her know how I felt.

She needed to get away for a breather to get a different perspective on what ultimately would be a colossal mistake, and I desperately needed to get out of the area to let the whole gold and drug deal disaster blow over, to clear the air, and probably save my life.

Sandra suggested we drive to Guatemala, and I thought getting out of the country sounded even better than getting out of town. Being a mostly localized traveler, I assumed Guatemala was a state or town in northern mainland Mexico, since I knew it wasn't anywhere in Baja California, which I knew pretty well. When she told me the map of

Mexico I brought out wouldn't have Guatemala on it, I was a little concerned. She pointed out the southern border of Mexico, showing the very beginning of the country of Guatemala, thousands of miles south of here, and I nearly backed out, thinking maybe she was a bit on the extreme side. I thought, "Why so far, when there was all of this beautiful Mexican countryside begging to be explored?" But I reasoned we could aim for Guatemala, and probably end up on some tropical beach in Mexico long before we got there. I didn't know at the time that when Sandra makes up her mind, the discussion is over.

So, for three hundred dollars I bought a 1973 Toyota Corolla with over 100,000 miles on it, and a huge dent on the entire passenger side with a sloppily spray painted "OUCH" on it. By not buying a nice vehicle, I was hoping to avoid attracting any attention. We appropriately name our car "OUCH", paid up rent for six months, cashed in all of my drug inventory, and headed south. Everyone we knew just kept shaking their heads, especially her ex-fiancée. Less than two weeks after meeting Sandra, we were on our way to the adventure of a lifetime that could fill several books with unbelievable stories.

We made it to Lago De Atitlan in Guatemala a month later, and stayed with a Native family for a dollar a day until the uprising of 1980 with the Nicaraguan Contras. When the local unrest spilled into our humble and peaceful pueblo and the violence and death became impossible to ignore, it became too dangerous to stay any longer. Ten thousand miles of driving all over Mexico and into Guatemala ended three and a half months later, after going through a few lifetimes worth of trials, errors, and fun, bonding us together like glue. Somewhere during that trip, against all odds, we fell in love. So when we returned, although emaciated, broke and worn out, we planned a wedding ceremony, fully aware that we had already started a family.

The wedding ceremony was a real outward manifestation of a spiritually confused couple. Both raised Catholic, both late-blooming hippies, and both currently devoid of any form of religious commitments, we were married by a guru at a Self-Realization Ashram by the beach. As if our Catholic parents hadn't been put through enough, this was almost too far out for them. But they attended, as did most of my family, making light of much of the ceremony, figuring it was just another one of my many bizarre, "soon this too will pass" phases. The reception was held in another section of the old greenhouses my home was hidden in, decorated like a tropical paradise, complete with a juggler and his act, and a well known Reggae band, long before Reggae became so popular. A real circus. My bright white tuxedo was finished off with a brand new pair of white Vans tennis shoes. The guest list was a Who's Who of some of the biggest drug dealers, suppliers, manufacturers, and, of course, users, for that part of the state. If the drug enforcement agencies had proper warning about the date and location, it would have netted them some real big fish, all in one spot, easy for the taking.

Bets were made all night at the open bar about how long the marriage would last, using my less than stellar reputation as a guide. Most bets were for weeks, some months, nobody gave us a full year before I would somehow screw it up. The big question was who was she, where did she come from, and why was she marrying me? It turned out to be probably the only smart decision I made in that whole period of my life, and the question still remained, why did she marry me? Though it has been no cakewalk for her, I am thankful for our relationship, which probably kept me alive all these years. As far as the bets, they all lost. One of the many valuable lessons I learned from my parents, and actually followed, was the meaning of commitment, and meaning what you say, especially before God and man. My parents were married for almost 70 years, and only my father returning to his Creator stopped that streak.

As a new husband, and soon-to-be-father, I attempted to turn over a new leaf. Once again I tried the legal job market, then the big recession of the early eighties hit hard. A friend set me up with the original spa entrepreneurs who used wine vats for hot tubs. We moved up to the northern part of the state to help run his business and start a family. Three years later we moved back, had a second son, and I opened my own pool and spa company. Twelve years later we had a beautiful surprise, a daughter.

All the while, I never abandoned my one true love, alcohol. I managed to somehow maintain a functional addict/alcoholic lifestyle. I strayed so far from my natural self, so distant from my connection to nature and to God, that it became only a faded memory, like a fairy tale. I did notice that with the more addicted and drunken friends I had, we all had a common thread of a distant spirituality that we once felt inside us and wished we could find again, but were resigned to accept it as a thing of our past, never to be reawakened. It was as if all the people I met that were mired in hopeless addiction were also very spiritual persons with great potential that had been drowned into submission with their drug of choice. Once in a while I realized it for what it was, we were all being taken out of the plan, one by one, so that eventually nobody would be left, and the circle would be irreparably broken. I would get so mad when I understood why we were all a bunch of bumbling drunks, when none of us should have been. Then I would numb myself back into submission, falling deeper into the abyss.

CHAPTER 5

THE BEGINNING OF THE END

The Final Fall From Grace

When Chino moved to Hopi Land, somewhere in Arizona, I was left without my periodic respite from insanity. He was the only connection I had to a distant dream that felt less and less like reality, and more and more like a fantasy, as if it was nothing more than a memory originating from my imagination.

I soon did my best to convince myself that what I remembered from that day long ago was nothing more than a collection of adolescent memories. I was young, hung over, and hungry for an experience that would justify the oddities of the hallucinations I witnessed at the fire that night, mixed in with my childhood desire to someday meet a real medicine man. All the rest was the culmination of a very active imagination. It may have worked then, when I was young and naïve, but now that I had a life of realities under my belt, I had to accept the fact that I wasn't living a well written novel about the wild west. I was just another drug addict and alcoholic with dreams of someday crawling out of this miserable curse and maybe returning to a semi-normal lifestyle. I was no different than all of the doped up losers who had dreamed of escape before me. The selfish hope that somehow I was some sort of a chosen one, that the secrets of a sober life were going to be revealed to me, was truly the delusion of a very sick individual, the type of ranting that landed so many other fools like me in institutions, perhaps where I belonged.

My disease progressed so that pretty soon everything I did was alcohol based. Specifically, tequila based. All camping trips, fishing trips, vacations, began to have tequila as the center of attraction. All travel was set up so I could stop at liquor stores at regular intervals. Restaurants that only served beer and wine were off limits. I worshipped tequila; I had a full blown affair with the golden liquid. I loved the energy it gave me, the ability to dance everybody else off the dance floor, to stand up to the meanest, biggest loudmouth at any party or bar, wanting to be the most obnoxious drunk there.

I threw giant parties in honor of my new love, tequila. I had live bands, open bars, and lots of drunk friends. Everybody brought me a fancy bottle of tequila. I got to know every brand, every distiller, the taste and proof of the best and the rarest, as if it were a fine wine. I used it to control me, and used it to control others. It became my black magic. I thought I was in control, but after a season, I was no longer drinking tequila, it was drinking me. I heard a Chinese Proverb at the time, thinking it to be very clever, and very funny. But it wasn't funny. "Man takes a drink, the drink takes a drink, then the drink takes the man." Tequila, like every obsession I drowned in before, was taking me.

Over the years as a husband and a father, in the midst of my disease, I tried as best as I could to maintain some odd form of normalcy, as functional as an addict as I could maintain. I built up a fairly decent business building pools, selling drugs on the side to keep one step ahead of the debt collector. I spent as much time as I possibly could trying to emulate my father, beside the fact that he never did anything to excess, not even ice cream. We did a lot of church shopping on Sundays searching for a religion that wouldn't hold me accountable. I was a 4-H leader for many years. We took countless vacations and fishing trips, and did what I thought was necessary to attempt to prevent my kids from turning out like me.

As a young family, we did manage to have a lot of good times, in between and around my drinking. My parents had instilled in me a deep love of vacations and travel to beautiful, natural, and rugged destinations.

In the summer of 1996, we were at a campground in the Sierra Nevada mountains, right on a lake among the most picturesque scenery God had to offer. My daughter, Jewel, was still just a two-year-old tow-head with an advanced vocabulary due to her older brothers' constant attention and teasing. To me, she was the cutest baby girl I had ever seen, full of love and wonder. Jacob, my handsome eleven-year-old son, was as obsessed with fishing as his brawny older brother, Storm. These two thick-haired, deeply tanned boys would rather spend all their waking hours competing for the biggest trout than anything else in the world. They had already perfected the fine art of fishing more than I realized was possible, having passed my skills long ago.

This particular area was known for its abundance of aggressive bears, and at that time, they easily ate from trash cans known for their consistent source of garbage, long before the bear-proof bins of today. About four days into this vacation, as Sandra, Jewel, and I were blissfully sleeping in late in our big military surplus green canvas tent, the boys popped in after fishing since dawn to "accidentally" wake us for breakfast. They made plenty of noise, pulling blankets and banging around the pots, pans, and ice chest. I was terribly hung over and couldn't open my eyes yet. Sandra had told the boys the night before she was going to sleep in this morning, something we tried to do every three or four days between getting up at the crack of dawn to fish with Jacob and Storm. She lay there wide awake and motionless, purposely not acknowledging them, more out of principle than actually being tired. They finally gave up and returned to the lake to fish some more.

When we emerged from the tent later for coffee, a neighboring camper told us about a giant three hundred and fifty pound black bear that had made the rounds earlier this morning, and he had film of him sticking most of his body inside our tent while we slept, rustling around for something to eat before pulling out and continuing on to the next camp. He wanted to know if we wanted copies of the pictures when he got them developed. As he was shocking us with his story, Storm and Jacob crawled out of the oversized tent.

As it turned out, they had slept in also, and it wasn't them making all of the ruckus early that morning. Papa bear was the early fisherman looking for breakfast in our tent.

That evening, the same bear was attracting a crowd as he rambled from trash can to trash can, knocking them over and getting wedged into them trying to get to the tasty stuff at the bottom. We walked over to watch. I brought my giant, outdated VHS video camera over and went right up to the stuck bear, waiting for a close-up of him as he popped out, sort of a payback for his trespassing at our tent that morning.

All of the sane tourists were keeping a safe distance, something I might have considered if I didn't have a few shots of tequila under my belt already. When that bear emerged, angry and disoriented, his snout bumped right into the camera lens, and bruised my face in the process.

While it made for great entertainment and rare video, it scared me to death. Fortunately, he was as scared as me at first, and took off running, turning once to return and sort of bark at me in between growls. I later found out it was a warning bark just before attack.

Even though my family considered it crazy, we had a great time reliving those moments that night around the campfire as we competed for the most bronzed, unburned marshmallow. Jewel kept repeating, "Daddy like bear. Bear no like Daddy," and "Yacub an Storn ketch feesh, Mommy?" until we could laugh no more. It was fun, and almost felt like we were just a normal family, having a great time. As drunk as I was, it seemed I could at least fool them, for now, and maybe even fool myself, too.

As I fell deeper and deeper in love with Jose Cuervo, my family had to sit farther and farther in the back of the bus. No longer a weekend thing, I had to drink every day. No longer in the afternoon, I had to start earlier each day. I would get all contact with customers, suppliers, clients, or anybody else in the public, out of the way as fast and as early as possible, so I could take my first shot of gold. I figured that if they didn't smell alcohol on my breath, they would never know I was drinking. The quality of my work deteriorated, as did my reputation. Word got out, slowly. Jobs were fewer and farther between. My office was a pig pen, my trucks filled with garbage, empty tequila bottles, and broken tools. My employees followed their leader, and without any chance for authoritative example, work turned into one big party. We took out-of-town jobs so we could go on five day drunken binges with a little work sprinkled in between hangovers and the next party. My employees' wives all hated me, but I kept giving raises when I was so drunk I couldn't think and my employees took full advantage of the situation, so their wives tolerated me.

But as time went on and my drinking accelerated, it became increasingly hard to hide my insanity. Storm, at 16, was now old enough to be disgusted with me. Jacob wasn't sure what made my moods change so fast. He loved to fish with me until the mean streak surfaced later in the day, and he probably got the worst of my temper, for no other reason than he was around when the negative aspects of tequila kicked in as the day wore on. Jewel, now four-years-old, was still young enough to think her daddy was a fun guy with lots of friends who threw wild parties where she could run around peoples' stumbling legs and have a great time. She was usually asleep by the time the yelling and insanity started, so she missed the worst of it. Sandra, apparently co-dependent since childhood, married me because I had the same problem as her father, and she was a born caregiver. Nothing else could explain why she stuck around, thick or thin, for better or worse, until overdose do us part.

In 1997, as a family, we took another vacation to that same lake with all of the trout and bears. By then, my alcoholism was no longer just a side note like it was the last time we were there. I had really looked forward to this trip for weeks, hoping to relive the past, and pretend all was well. My anticipation was contagious, and everybody wanted badly for things to somehow magically return to those early years of my disease. I was hoping that just getting away would do the trick. The problem was, I really never made it on that vacation. My body was there, but it was no longer me.

We had recently bought a little cab-over camper for my mini pickup, so we were done with camping on the ground level with the bears. We had barely finished setting up camp when I hit the bottle hard. For a brief moment, I caught that initial warm alcohol rush that pushed my Dopamine neurotransmitters right through the top of my brain, and felt on top of the world. It was that illusive feeling that had become so rare I had doubled my alcohol intake trying to get it back. Perhaps it was the new surroundings, the fresh mountain air, the breathtaking scenery, but most likely, it was the lack of oxygen at this altitude. Whatever it was, I wanted to share it with everyone. A big mistake.

I burst into the camper and gushed to my family how happy I was to be there, and what a great time we were going to have, reeking of tequila. Nobody shared in my exhilaration, and, in fact, they were terrified. Everybody but Sandra. She was at her wits end, and I just pushed the last button. "We're not here one hour and you are completely smashed, scaring the kids to death! I don't even know how anybody can get that drunk that fast. Why did you have to ruin this vacation, even before it started?"

I was furious with her. How dare she ruin my natural high because she thinks I'm drunk! I stormed out of the campsite and stumbled down to the lake to drink myself into oblivion. I would show her what smashed really was. I was drunk most of the time and everyone was on pins and needles. But on that vacation we still managed to fish, hike and roast marshmallows, but the magic was lost.

My wife finally could take no more humiliation. I really didn't care anymore, either. Our children would no longer ignore the fact that the bad heavily outweighed the good, and Daddy wasn't fun anymore, ever.

I had a new "wife and kids". I was drinking over a quart of Jose Cuervo a day. I was trying to book a permanent reservation in the gutter, only I had sunk too low even for that spot. Instead of attempting to turn around and start over, I just gave up trying. I had quit so many times only to find myself right back where I had started, it was time to admit that I was hopeless, a drunk destined to wind up dying from my disease, and accept it. The fight was gone, the tequila won, I lost.

To me, it made more sense to simply fade away, alone, leaving my family out of my final days, so they could move on, and not be forced to be a part of my slow suicide. The feeling was mutual; they stopped begging me to stay, to get help. They were done with the drama and realized it was time to cut the cord now, before it got really ugly. At least my youngest could easily erase me from her memory. My second son had built an emotional barrier and was probably already damaged. And my oldest, being the logical one, just wanted me to disappear. I barely dragged through each day, as my family looked for a way out. They didn't even want the house. They just wanted a fresh start.

CHAPTER 6

FALLING INTO PLACE

The Unrelenting Wheels of Fate

During that year of my rapid decline, something happened on the reservation. That same reservation where I had perfected my drinking and drug skills.

On one of the windiest days of the year, with a hot wind known by the ancients as the Santanna's, now called Santa-Ana's, gusting up to sixty miles an hour, a careless backyard trash fire on the Rez quickly turned into an out-of-control wild fire. For days, it consumed forest and rangeland, working its way to the main concentration of Reservation homes. Everyone was evacuated to the neighboring Reservations. Firefighters were flown in from all over the country. Some of the best of the best firefighters specializing in rough terrain in the country were Indians, and the elite were called the Hotshots, and still are. They would parachute in, drop in, drive in, and crawl into the center of the giant forest fires and are the integral front line of defense where nobody else dares to go.

Many times, when they heard of a fire on a Reservation, the Hotshots volunteered to go into the thick of it to help out. Some called themselves mountain goats, proud to show their expertise running up and down the mountainsides, controlling the flames and directing them to where they wanted them to go. A large contingent of Hotshots from the Pueblos of New Mexico was on this fire within a couple of days after hearing about it.

A small group of the Hotshots was deep into a canyon cutting a firebreak to divert the main blaze away from the housing area when a sudden gust of hot wind unexpectedly pushed the fire down into that canyon. With very little time to escape the flames, they had only one route out, straight up the side of a ravine. As fire-bombers dumped water on the erratic blaze and pumper trucks tried to re-position themselves to slow the flames, the Hotshots scrambled up the steep hillside as fast as they could. As they crawled over boulders through the dry brush, a big granite boulder broke loose above them, raining rocks down on them. It could have been a result of the high temperature, the wind, or maybe the moisture from the water-bombers, or a combination of all of those factors. Or, as stories are told about it now, it was fate, meant to happen, that big boulder that came loose at that exact moment, at that location, and did what it was meant to do. And the resulting repercussions were no accident either.

One of the younger Hotshots, from a small Pueblo tribe in New Mexico, was right in the path of that falling rock, and was killed instantly. According to the Elders at that Pueblo, because of the death of their Hotshot, known locally as Grayfox, two miracles happened at that moment. The fire, bearing down on the firefighters and heading uncontrollably towards the homes on the Reservation, inexplicably turned on itself at the instant the boulder hit. On the verge of causing massive disaster, the raging inferno reversed course against the wind, against itself, and turned back into the charred trees and brush, running out of fuel, and literally died of its own accord in front of hundreds of Hotshots, firefighters, Department of Forestry, and locals.

For a short time, chaos reigned, as the realization dawned that Grayfox was dead. Emergency crews scrambled to hoist his body up the ravine ahead of the impending fire, and everyone was caught between shock, grief, and panic over the fire about to overtake everything in its path. It took some time before it became apparent that there was no longer any danger from the fire, that it was not going to regain its strength and continue its destruction. Once everybody understood the fire was basically committing suicide, the reality of the death of one of their own sank in and hit hard. The brotherhood of the firefighting community is strong; even tighter is the bond between the tribal Hotshots. Everyone knew everyone, and this was almost more like losing a brother than losing an actual brother. The celebration of the end of the worst fire in this Reservation's history was muted, at best. Grayfox's death deflated the balloon of success before it ever got inflated.

However, what happened back home at his Pueblo, right when Grayfox died, eventually brought celebration, satisfaction, and honor to that day, to Grayfox, and to both his tribe and this local Reservation and its people.

The traditional tribal symbol of his particular Pueblo tribe is a ram's head, with a full set of curled horns. Periodically, they went on a sacred hunt and killed a large, mature ram for the head, used in ceremony and prayer, as they had done for thousands of years. In this new era of political correctness and well-meaning but misdirected over-reverence for animals, the resulting laws governing certain species often interfered with many Native customs and religious beliefs. New laws banned any hunting of the ram the local Native people not only used for religious purposes, but also for food, clothing, and a myriad of other uses.

It had taken months of legal petitioning by the Tribal Council to the Department of Fish and Game to finally secure approval of a temporary, limited hunt of one mature ram, for religious purposes only. Because of the typical bureaucratic red tape and delays, what should have been a spring hunt had dragged on so late in the season the chance of finding the right ram in the area designated and in the tiny window of time allowed was so remote they nearly canceled the hunt.

The Elders insisted the hunt go on as planned, as the need for a new ram's head had been put off for too many years already, and they were confident they would be successful, despite the extreme limitations put on them and the unlikely possibility of finding the exact specifications required by traditional protocol. But their faith in the Creator doing the impossible was unbendable.

The young hunters had been trained by the traditional Elders in what to wear, the prayers to say, how to make their own arrows and bow, just as their ancestors had done, centuries before there ever was a Department of Fish and Game dictating where, when, and how to practice their own religion. They did everything as it had always been done, with the exception of the new limitations on day and location.

After a very unsuccessful week, as their allotted time was running out, after they had covered nearly all of the approved territory without even a sighting of a ewe, much less a ram, they started getting discouraged. The Elders prayed harder and encouraged the hunters not to give up.

On the last afternoon, they spotted a huge ram on the hillside in the desert sagebrush, silhouetted by the setting sun. They crawled within range, and let two arrows fly. Both met their mark, deep into the chest

98

of the sacred ram. They recorded the time of the kill. It was discovered later the ram fell to the ground in that New Mexico desert sunset at the exact minute the boulder crashed into Grayfox's head, killing him instantly. When they went to retrieve the arrows from the ram, he was gone. They found the bloodied arrows at the kill sight. There were no tracks, and they never found the body.

Grayfox became a tribal hero, an icon. It is believed he became the sacrifice in place of the ram, that the ram became him, and because of that, the fire retreated on itself and ended its destructive rampage. He became a spiritual hero and saint to his Pueblo tribe, and some of the related tribes around that area. He became a cult hero to the Reservation here, the man who mysteriously gave his life so their houses and campground, their only source of income, did not burn.

One of my main drinking buddies from the Reservation called me unexpectedly shortly after Grayfox was killed during the fire. I had communicated with him periodically over the years, stopped in and drank with him once in a while, but hadn't heard from him for a very long time now. He had been sober for over eight years, turned his life around to the point that he was now the tribal chairman, the chief. Big Kamol, the tribal chairman back when we used to cause drunken mayhem together, now passed on, had to be rolling over in his grave. He had warned both of us back then that neither one of us would make it to adulthood the way we were headed. He was pretty close to accurate about me, so it was great to hear my old friend, Jump, was not only clean and sober, he was actually the leader of the tribe now.

Jump, or Chairman Jump, knew I had a pool construction company capable of many skills, and also was aware I had a creative streak in me.

He told me the story of the fire, something I was curious about, having followed the news reports that left the end of the fire a mystery, and the story of the firefighter killed in the line of duty only a small footnote. He gave me all of the details of the fire, and especially the story, now a legend on the Rez, of their new hero, Grayfox.

Jump wanted me to design a memorial monument for Grayfox, and if approved by the Tribal Council, build it. They were taking this project seriously, and had cleared a spot on the side of the public road above the campground, still on Indian land, at such a high elevation you could see the ocean to the west, islands to the north, and Mexico to the south. They had convinced the State Department of Transportation to pave the turnout for the memorial, and were in the process of making signs to officially name it the Grayfox Memorial Turnout, complete with parking and handicapped access. Once built, they were planning a dedication and memorial service at the monument inviting the whole Pueblo tribe, the firefighters, Jump's tribe, and various other officials.

Obviously not aware just how bad my life had turned out, Jump had complete confidence in my ability to pull off something great. It had to be, it would be on public display from the day it was dedicated until eternity. The only thing to destroy it would have to be a fire hotter and meaner than the one that killed Grayfox.

I needed all of the details of the Pueblo tribe. History, origins, tribal identity, traditional insignias, symbols, and everything related to the significance of the sacred ram's head. If I was going to accept this challenge, no matter how messed up my mind was at the time, I would give this my all, or not do it. Period. I was at the end of my sanity, but this opportunity out of nowhere felt like a life rope, tossed into my hands just as I was about to go under for the last time. I was aware that there was no way this would become a money-making venture; if I took on this project, it would be for spiritual reasons only. And there was a small, quiet voice telling me to go ahead with this opportunity. A voice I hadn't heard, or at least, paid attention to, for far too long. That phone call, from a friend shoved way back into my buried memories, revived a tiny flame so covered in darkness it was nothing less than miraculous, and it started to burn bright, ever so slowly.

Jump had called me to help out in honoring a hero. He could have called any number of people with the ability to construct this memorial. We hadn't communicated in years. But we established the bond long ago, watching the Ghost Dancers circle the bonfires we had brought to life, learning how to drink like the big boys, and carry their caskets when they went too far. I had completely forgotten a huge part of my growing up, but Jump had not. And deep down, I believed there was more to this than a random phone call from the past. Not ready to admit it to myself, I went about life as if it were the same. But I wanted to pursue this just in case it really was a light in my utter darkness.

This was in the late 1990's, at the dawn of the mass- computer age, before you could easily pull up any information about any subject with the simple click of a mouse, before most people even knew what a computer mouse was. Certainly long before I knew anything at all about those big fat white cabinets with the glowing blue screen. My investigations still relied on libraries, encyclopedias, and dictionaries. I had to dig deep to find any information about this tiny tribe in the New Mexico desert. Fortunately, Jump was able to get their tribal insignia and other pertinent information for me so I could design a respectable memorial. I drew it in detail, showing my idea of a permanent tribute to Grayfox, and an honorable display of his tribe's culture. When I presented it to the Tribal Council, they seemed to be reasonably impressed. Jump promoted me and my design vigorously, partly because we were longtime friends, and of course to cover his decision to choose me to create the design. The retired fire captain, an incredibly popular and well respected Elder called Chief, loved it and pushed it through. The job was mine.

The monument was to be over 14 feet across, 16 inches thick, and higher than 5 feet tall. Very Southwest in flavor, it was similar to the curved wall of a cliff dwelling, earth tone colors, flagstone accents on the face, desert stucco facade. I had a 24" round Pueblo tribal shield mounted in the center, with a solid brass plaque engraved with Grayfox's name, tribe, clan, birth date, date of his death, and a brief synopsis of how he gave his life so this local tribe could continue on. I mounted two small deer antlers at each bottom corner reaching to the ground. I built an altar in the front center of the memorial where we put a statue of Jesus in the middle.

The monument was built close to the cliff overlooking the broad valley below, with the view of the ocean in the distance. We built a railroad-tie retainer wall all around the memorial, with redwood chips inside, and a 10 foot tall cedar tree nearly touching it. Many of the forestry guys wanted to cut the tree down, to open up the memorial and not make it look crowded. A Marine base firefighter relocated to this area from a tribe up north claimed that to cut the tree was to completely negate the whole project. The cedar tree, he insisted, is the symbol of everlasting life, the evergreen that never went dormant. It was fortunate that it was here, and at the very least, extremely ignorant to suggest cutting it down.

Weekly, I would take a few crew members of my pool business and drive up the mountain to work on the monument. We would get a lot of work done for a while, then drink the rest of the afternoon away. Whenever there was anybody of importance on site, we acted sober and responsible. Once they left, we became the drunks we all were. Then there were the evenings where the crew left, and I was all alone, on top of the world, not one-half mile above where I had met Chino many years ago. If I walked down to a lookout point below the memorial turnout, I could see Indian Gate, and exactly where I sat on that boulder that changed my whole perception of life, in what seemed to be another lifetime.

That was long ago, and far away from reality. It was a dream, and I missed the ride. What a great fantasy it had been, young, innocent, and impressionable. Just when I started to get nostalgic, I would return to the present. Too bad life had kicked my tail. If only it had come about, as he said. If only I hadn't taken my love for altered consciousness too far. If only I was one of the normal people, those who could have a drink or two, and call it an evening. Maybe, just maybe, the stories Chino told me were real, but I would never find out. I had thrown it all away. For nothing. For the obsession of overdoing everything I put in my body. Nothing or nobody meant as much to me as getting high. And I hated that mindset. I tried to convince myself I was cursed. I did not wake up one day and say, "I'm going to throw away everything I know and love so I can stay high, so I can stay perpetually drunk." No, this landed on me like a lead ball, and I never asked for it, didn't expect it, and now, couldn't escape it. But that was all nonsense and denial of reality, the "why me" syndrome. I was denying the fact that I had a perfect childhood, knew exactly what I was headed for, I had asked for this misery, and deserved every bit of it. It wasn't just some mysterious curse; I brought on everything with my foolish choices. I had been warned over and over. I volunteered for this journey, and shouldn't be surprised as to where it took me. It just seemed now, I no longer could control anything anymore; it was now controlling me. I had given the steering wheel to someone or something else, and couldn't get it back. Self-pity and depression sank in, all alone and drunk on this secluded mountaintop. Anything could happen to me here and nobody would know how or why, and most people close to me would be that much happier if it did. The one and only reason I kept on was because my friend Jump had put his faith in me to finish this memorial as promised, and I at least owed him that.

One night, as I sat alone on that mountaintop, gulping down one tiny airplane bottle of Jose Cuervo Tequila after another, watching the sunset over the smog-lined ocean, I knew my life was setting with that sun. Everything that had happened to me up to that point was about to be washed away, forever. All of my thoughts, positive and negative, meant nothing. I had thrown it all away. My parents, sisters, brothers, nephews, nieces, wife, sons and daughter, my home, my career, I was about to become a bad memory for all of them. I was totally aware that my options were more or less gone. I couldn't stop drinking; now I actually needed the alcohol to function. I had a problem with my liver many years ago, back when I was a teenager, so I recognized the hardening and swelling of that area of my dying body now. Not turning yellow yet, I knew that was next. Almost 40 years old now, my body could no longer take this kind of abuse. And from what I had witnessed of many friends and acquaintances who died of yellow jaundice and liver failure, it was nothing to look forward to. Slow, painful, debilitating, and humiliating. All preventable. All because I was a weak person, not in control of my destiny. I had all of the information, all of the head knowledge required to prevent this tragedy, but I lacked the will power, the inner strength, something. It had been coming for a long time, now it seemed to be on fast-forward. My life was falling apart around me, all of it, and yet, I kept drinking, kept speeding toward that brick wall, and couldn't find the brakes.

I pulled out another tiny bottle and guzzled it down. The bite was long gone. It had taken years of practice to be able to down these bottles without even a slight grimace. I was proud of this achievement, loved to take shots in public at parties, bars, and other gatherings so people would gasp in awe of my ability to drink tequila like water. Or so I thought. What a macho man. I could generally drink almost anyone under the table and still drive home! I never got arrested for drunk driving, and also never drove sober after 10 a.m. In fact, I was usually the designated driver late at night to get more alcohol or snacks, just not in the current meaning of designated driver. I wasn't sober, or even close to it, I just had an untouched record of not being pulled over, so I drove. And without fear. I was brazen to the point of plain stupid, waving at cops, flashing my lights, all kinds of idiotic behavior testing fate.

All of that seemed fun then. Not anymore. I didn't enjoy drinking at all now, not the first drink, and never remembered the last drink. I sat there as the sun disappeared over the ocean, through the seasonably thick layer of brown and red smog. Self-pity surrounded me, ready to overtake my soul at the first sign of defeat. I heard my stereo in the truck making noise, music if I was closer. I dragged my defeated corpse back to the truck, leaned in, and cranked up the radio, attempting to get a second wind to drive down the mountain, back to what used to be my home. Knowing my family preferred I stay late, away from them as much as possible, while putting on a macabre act of normalcy until I stumbled in, everyone scared and not knowing what to expect, screaming and yelling, or just passing out.

I walked back to the edge of the cliff, overlooking the whole world. The radio was up way too loud, but there was only me to complain. The next song to come on was Elton John's "Indian Sunset".

A melancholy folksy type song, filled with stereotyping and misinformation, wrapped in romantic Indian lore, it never became a big hit, to my knowledge. But, years ago, just below where I was trying to stand right now, as a teenager and as a young adult, I had sat around many a campfire with my local Indian drinking buddies and sang this song as it came on some poor, innocent camper's radio that we had commandeered. We all knew the words by heart, no matter how late it was. And, for all of its inaccuracies and Hollywood tackiness, it brought up emotions in us we would be better off suppressing. The sadness, the hopelessness, and the finality of it made us fighting mad, and pathetically sad, all within a few minutes. If it was late at night and we had no chance of getting close to any members of the opposite sex, this song was our war cry and sent us on a rampage of destruction. But if we were in a group of females--Indian, white, black, brown, or even turning green--no matter how bad we looked, or how bad they looked, anything under 300 pounds was fair game.

But that song stirred up something strong in me this night, and it wasn't an act. I had nobody to impress, certainly not myself. The beat, the drums, the whole energy of the song cut deep into my psyche. Partly because it stirred up long ago memories of a better time, but mostly because of the sadness, the finality of the message. The song was about a last surviving warrior, finally giving in to his enemies' desire to wipe out him and all of his people. Tired of running and knowing his end was inevitable, he strung his bow to fight one last time, knowing he would be killed, but also knowing his misery would finally be over. As the song ended, I got overly emotional. I hadn't cried, really cried, for longer than I could recall. Even at the many funerals of friends, truly letting myself go was not an option. I had a reputation to uphold, a façade that couldn't come down every time somebody decided to die on me. I had been masking and burying my real emotions for so long, I forgot how it was done. Nonetheless, tears started pouring from my eyes and I began to cry uncontrollably, falling on my face to the ground, weeping. I let go. Completely. My fight was over. My time was up. I cried longer and harder than I think I ever had. Wailing in that lonely, dark emptiness, I was brought to an all new low.

Never an advocate of suicide, seeing too many in my lifetime, and watching that person drop to the level where he thinks he can not only end his suffering and run from reality, but also become some kind of a cultish hero when he pulls off his dramatic exit. True, a hero for a day, maybe a week, never more. Once the memorials fade away, the depression is diluted and people get back to dealing with their personal dramas, and even the promises of annual remembrances disappear. No matter how well liked, how well known, how tragic the suicide, the trauma fades fast, and people's memories are short. Very short. When I try to think of the many people I've known personally who took their own lives over the years, there are many. Too many. But for all of the energy put into each instance, they are just vague memories, some I can hardly remember what they looked like.

So, as hopeless and futile as my life had become, my inflated ego never really considered suicide as an out for me. But as I lay there, cold, drunk, running nose and eyes, a finer picture of pathetic hopelessness had never been painted. Finally giving in to my disease, and releasing all of those mixed emotions locked up deep inside me, I felt as if there was no reason to continue on. Nothing had mattered to me for a very long time. I was on autopilot; every day was the same routine, same pattern, same result: nothing. Building this memorial was the only activity I had undertaken that meant anything at all for years. I thought maybe doing this would somehow redeem me, but my drinking just found a new locale to reside. A prettier place to get ridiculously inebriated, go home, and get reassured of what a loser I was. Things were only going to get worse.

I turned off the radio, and sat back down on the ground, emotionally exhausted. Night had fallen, the damp mountain air sent shivers through me, or it could have been the tequila, no longer able to distinguish the cause or effect of anything anymore. Not a heavily traveled road back then, especially at night, silence took over this side of the mountain. The only break in the stillness was an occasional far away vehicle on a road way below and the yipping and sporadic howling of competing coyote packs in every direction.

I hadn't talked to God in what felt like forever. Actually, I had given up acknowledging His existence, because to do so would require at least some accountability on my part, and I was way past that. To say I felt unworthy of talking to God was an understatement. I was unworthy of accepting there could even be a God that would allow me to sink so low. As with all alcoholics and addicts, it was God's fault, not mine. Better yet, nobody's fault, because there is no God.

As I sat hunched over, shaking uncontrollably, out of my nothingness came a plea, the plea of every dying man. "God, if you are there, help me. I can't go on any longer. I can't do this alone anymore. I am finished with trying. I am a failure with this life. Take me out. Do something. Anything. End this misery. I hate you, I hate myself, I hate alcohol, I hate everything. Why are you doing this to me? Do you enjoy watching me suffer? Do you like watching all of us wither away and die, all for nothing?" I cried harder, screaming loudly. It didn't matter; nobody could hear me, not even God.

I sobbed, and cried out more hopeless drunken ramblings. As I wore myself out, I had one last heaven-bound request, the standard cliché of a desperate man. "Just give me a sign, anything. So at least I know there is something in that endless dark sky besides stars, some reason to hope, a spark from when I was young and full of hope and faith, before I threw away all of my innocence for nothing."

Now I was lying on my back, staring through blurred, tear drowned eyes at the clear, vast darkness sprinkled with stars and splotches of haze known as the Milky Way. My ranting had shut up all of the coyotes, crickets, and frogs. It was an eerie silence, the silence of wilderness without volume, the humbling silence of an unanswered prayer. I lay there waiting for the natural noise of the night to resume. I had no strength to get up and I was in no hurry to drive down the mountain.

It seemed to start far away, then rapidly closed in on me: a cracking, popping, then rumbling explosion so loud I jumped up, unconsciously leaping into the cab of my truck, slamming the door behind me. Even with the door closed, the crashing noise was deafening, louder, more popping and snapping, like giant firecrackers followed by smaller poppers. A huge crashing sound again, more snapping, the noise slowly getting less and less, then abrupt silence, only a rippling echo rolling into the distant hills.

I sat there, heart racing, completely at a loss for what had happened. I waited for more noise, digging into my memory trying to recognize that sound, only getting more confused the more I tried to figure it out. I opened the door and stepped outside, looking for any sign of trauma, a crash, smoke, cracks in the ground. Everything was normal, and the total silence persisted. I walked a little way toward the mountainside, nervously searching for anything that could make so much noise. Not feeling confident, in fact, feeling very insecure, I got back in and drove away. All the way home, I tried to understand what could have happened. I totally forgot that I had just finished demanding a sign from God, too shaken up to remember anything but the blast that left no evidence. The next morning I convinced myself it was my imagination, and that was that.

A few days later, while working on the memorial, one of the few local traditional Indian Elders stopped by to see what we were doing.

After a long conversation about the fire, he informed me he lived in a remote section of the Reservation near there, and was certain the death of the firefighter stopped the fire, and also saved his house in the woods. He said he was taking an evening walk in the forest just a few days ago, and an ancient, giant oak tree broke off at its base and crashed to the ground, breaking into millions of tiny pieces. He said it was completely unusual that this particular tree fell, as it was in excellent condition, but the wood from that tree would supply him and his neighbor with firewood for years to come. He said it was a good omen, a sign from heaven that good things were taking place nearby, so he wanted to meet us and see what we were doing. I asked him if a tree that size falling down could have been heard where we were working. "When that tree fell, we thought an airplane had crashed in the forest. It was the loudest explosion I have heard since the war. Scared us all to death. But you wouldn't have heard it, it was after dark, way after you guys quit working up here. If it fell any earlier, you would have jumped out of your skin. Definitely a sign from God."

Once we knew when the monument would be completed, the tribe scheduled a dedication and memorial service. They would fly the entire family of Grayfox, friends, and tribal Elders and leaders out for a ceremony on the mountaintop. I spent extra time on the fine details, wanting to impress the tribe, and all of the Pueblo Indians coming out.

About a month before the dedication, I forced myself to go up to the cave Chino had taken me to so many times before, and ate copious amounts of his medicine, hoping to sober up before I had to face the public in a big way, showing not only Chief, Jump, and all of the local people and fire departments, but, most importantly, Grayfox's tribe and

111

family, the monument I had created. Either I had to somehow miraculously sober up or I would stumble through the ceremony, embarrassing everyone and disgracing Jump and his people. Or I would do the honorable thing, and call in sick on the big day.

I sat on a big boulder on top of the cave we had prayed in so many times before. The sun had set, and I just stared down onto the desert floor below me, happy I made it up here without having a heart attack, having to stop and rest all the way up like an old man. It was as if something was trying to stop me from climbing back up here one more time. As the night wore on, the partial moon lit up much of the bigger outcroppings below, giving me glimpses of coyotes and other larger wild animals doing their nightly ritual of hunter and prey.

In the center of the clearing directly below me was a legendary ceremonial ground, pointed out to me by Chino so many years ago. We had seen faint whispers of Ghost Dancers circling a long ago ceremonial fire on many occasions, whether real or imagined, it was all the same back then, as my innocence, faith, and acceptance had opened up so many visions for me that there were some who disliked me for what I claimed to have seen. It was as real as Christmas morning to me back then; I expected it and it had happened. The unexplainable aspect was when we brought friends and new people to these impromptu ceremonies, and they all saw and experienced the same vision. What we saw out there was real, and we knew it at the time. Labeled as crazy wasn't odd for me, so I didn't care what other people thought.

Now, years later, jaded beyond hope, I questioned what I was seeing. I watched closely, moving my head back and forth, trying to erase what I saw, looking over the desert plateau for other odd hallucinations. Everywhere else I looked, it was normal, late night desert scenery. When I focused back to the ceremonial grounds, men were undeniably dancing around a faint, smokeless fire, and I could hear the drumbeat, if I really listened. I watched this group for a long time, hoping to see something different, something that was different from all of the times before.

Then I noticed something I hadn't seen in all of the years I'd been coming up here. As these warriors danced, there stood a lone man, off to the side, nearly hidden by the brush, looking on, as if he wanted to join them. He was moving in place, as if warming up to dance, unable to join in to the circle, and unable to leave the glimmering light of the fire. I watched his movements for a long time. He seemed stuck in time, or stuck in place, I couldn't tell which. I remembered each of the dancers in the circle, but this new outsider was one I hadn't seen before.

It suddenly hit me who this dancer was. It was Grayfox, the young firefighter who died in the firefight, unable to join in with the local dancers, and unable to go home. It made sense to me at that moment, as this revelation cut through all of the fog clouding my alcohol-deteriorating brain. I felt an urgency to tell his family that he was stuck here, and needed them to bring his spirit home to his people. I could relay this to the family at the dedication of the memorial, but had to be careful how I approached the issue. If I was drunk, or even had the smell of alcohol on my breath, as bad as I looked, they would rightfully call me a delusional drunk, and reject all I had to say. Not to mention the embarrassment I would foist on my friends Jump, and Chief, and the rest of the tribe. If I could maintain sobriety, behave appropriately, and because I was the one who had built the monument, they might listen. I regained a tiny sense of self respect that night, knowing the importance of the family freeing Grayfox's spirit, dancing alone and stuck in time, and helping his tribe at the same time.

A faint spark was kindled. I had a purpose and a mission. Once again I prayed, for the second time in many years, this time to fuel that spark inside me so I could help Grayfox's spirit return to his pueblo.

The day of the dedication, the memorial was hidden with a king-size Pendleton blanket. Local County Supervisors attended, eager for media recognition of their "monetary sacrifice", as if it came from their personal accounts. Police, local and distant firefighters, Department of Forestry, mountain residents, tribes, and friends, Hotshots from near and far, and tribal leaders and Elders of Grayfox's Pueblo attended. And, closest to the memorial sat Grayfox's parents, brothers and sisters, along with his widow and small child. Many more people came than I expected.

When Chairman Jump pulled the blanket off of the memorial, everyone was silent. I died for that brief second, not knowing what the response meant. Gasps were followed by loud cries, wailing and tears. Grayfox's parents collapsed in their seats, overwhelmed with emotion. His wife and siblings rushed to the memorial, crying loudly. They began touching every inch of it, praying aloud in their tongue, circling it, rubbing it, and eventually wrapping it with long strings of beads, like oversized rosaries. Their traditional religion had a combination of ancient ritual mixed with Catholicism from missionary influence in the Santa Fe, New Mexico, area over 600 years ago. The family spent a long time blessing the monument, smudging it off with burning sage, and mounting a gold crucifix to the face, just below the plaque. They even used sprigs of cedar taken from the tree crowding the memorial and used that for blessings also. They were in awe of the detail, and the attention I had placed on representing their tribal identity. They obviously had expected much less, as did pretty much everybody there, other than Jump, Chief, and on old man in the back, a new friend who lived nearby, who knew that when a tree falls in the forest, and there is nobody there to hear it, it still makes a noise, a loud noise, and very possibly, a big difference.

Several people spoke, but when I was asked to address the crowd, I only said a few meaningless words and sat back down. Struggling with my conscience, I felt a strong urge to talk directly to the family. After everyone spoke, I asked if I could speak again. Very nervous, and extremely self-conscious, I apologized and explained that what I had to say might sound very strange, but I didn't want to let this opportunity pass. I related the story of what I had seen a few weeks earlier up on the high desert, with the Ghost Dancers and the lonely man off to the side, unable to join in on the dance, yet also unable to move too far away from the fire. I told the startled family, speaking directly to them seated in the front row, that that lone dancer was Grayfox, and they needed to pray to bring his spirit home with them to his fire, back in New Mexico. Other than the handful of local Elders and traditionalists in the crowd, and the Pueblo Medicine Man that had accompanied the family from home, I was certain everybody in attendance thought I was crazy, a genuine lunatic. Had I not been the designer and builder of the beautiful memorial, I probably would have been led away in handcuffs or a strait-jacket by one of the many authority figures in the audience. If the family had taken offense to what I said, it might have turned ugly.

115

But they started crying again, and Grayfox's mother and father got up and hugged me, thanking me for the work I had done, and what I had said. Soon all of his relations joined them, surrounding me and crying. Then the thin, frail medicine man from Grayfox's pueblo inched forward and whispered in my ear that he was hoping somebody had seen "Gray's" spirit, because that was the Spirit of the Tribal Ram now, and he needed to return to the desert where he was from. While I had been addressing the family, I felt like I was making a fool of myself, but now I felt vindicated, and I knew all of this work wasn't in vain. And, if for only a brief second, I nearly felt normal, like maybe something in my life mattered again. I breathed deeply, inhaling years of long lost oxygen.

Even to this day, that turnout on the back-road up the mountain, now a very popular highway for weekenders, bikers, and bicycle riders, has a cult-like following where people regularly come to pray, to receive good luck and fortune, leaving mementos at the altar: crucifixes, bibles, money, even bottles of alcohol and memorial cards from funerals,

flowers, lottery tickets, casino tokens, and countless other offerings to the Patron Saint of Fire, Grayfox.

It had cost me several thousand dollars in labor and material to construct the monument. When my friend Jump, the tribal chairman, asked how much the tribe owed me for my work, I surprised myself with the answer. I told Jump all I wanted in return for building the memorial was a working key to Indian Gate, so I could go to the secret tribal campground on the river when I felt like it. I told him I was going to find a tipi, and one day set it up at the river at Indian Gate to camp in, and needed easy access to the area. I surprised Jump, along with myself, with the tipi announcement. It came out of my mouth, but I'm not sure where else it came from. In retrospect, undoubtedly I had a few shots of tequila under my belt when I said all of this, and was trying to sound really cool...or something. We had a good laugh about dancing around inside a tipi at Indian Gate.

We talked a little about what I had said at the memorial dedication. Jump teased me about still taking that crazy medicine that messes with your mind, and tried to encourage me about sobriety, bragging on his many years without drinking. I attempted to explain that the only time I got close to sobriety was when I ate that "crazy medicine", but he just laughed. Anything that makes you think you're going to camp in a tipi at Indian Gate has to be a little crazy. He was totally unaware how bad my alcoholism had progressed, and I wasn't about to tell him.

He gave me a copy of the key to Indian Gate, quite positive I probably would never use it, and definitely not put up any tipi there anytime soon. I wasn't any more confident, and was more worried about losing the key than anything else.

117

CHAPTER 7

TEQUILA PARTIES AND TIPIS

The Last Hurrah

Because Jump had teased me so much about the tipi idea, I felt like he had challenged me. My mind was always looking for problems, and I lived for alcohol induced trauma. Doubt me on anything, and I had to prove how right I always was. I could never accept defeat, no matter how wrong I usually was. That was the irony of my drinking problem. Years ago, if you called me an alcoholic, I would stop drinking for months to prove you wrong. Call me an addict, I would quit whatever I was abusing to show who was the boss. Always substituting one high for another, but I could control pretty much anything to a certain extent. Not anymore. Control was out of reach for me with my drinking now, and that frustrated and confused me to no end. A control freak from day one, this new total lack of control was almost harder to handle than the actual drinking itself. Then Jump made a few jokes about the tipi statement at the Tribal Council meeting, and word was out. If it was a joke when I had first mentioned it, now it was a challenge. If I never did put up a tipi at Indian Gate, I would never hear the end of it, especially after the teasing I was getting about my story about the "ghost dancers" at the dedication. They were calling me "Ghostbuster" and wanted to know if they could dance in my tipi. You don't build up a lot of credibility when everybody knows you are a drunk.

I started to ask around privately where I could order a tipi. I looked in magazines, checked phone books, but soon found I was in the wrong part of the country for this product. I found one aging hippie woman who made small tie-dyed rainbow colored tipis for kids' campouts, but that was about it. In town, a jewelry shop owner heard I was looking for a tipi. He had sat in on a Native American Church ceremony in a tipi. He connected me with an oil- rig roughneck in Long Beach, a Navajo whose mother actually sewed by hand tipis for people back home in New Mexico. She was married to a "Roadman", a medicine man who still ran ceremonies for the Native American Church in tipis all over the country. In fact, he was the current president of The Native American Church of The United States, whatever that meant.

I called Lilly-Ann Hogan in Aztec, New Mexico and discussed purchasing a small tipi from her. She wanted to know how big I needed it to be, did I need the poles, too, do I have the stakes and rope, what color did I want the stars over the door; all red, all blue, red and blue, or just white. Details that I knew nothing about, but wanted to sound like I did. She informed me that when she made someone a tipi, she prayed over every stitch, and when they delivered it, they performed a Tipi Dedication prayer service when it was set up. Usually her husband, Sonny Hogan, would run the Native American Church Ceremony, so she needed to know what the ceremony, or meeting, as she called it, was going to be for, and who was sponsoring the meeting, so she could focus her sewing prayers on that sponsor, or the reason for the meeting.

I didn't have the faintest idea what in the world she was talking about, and began having second thoughts. Surely I could find somebody who could just make me a tipi, without all of this nonsense. All I wanted was a simple tipi, some straight poles and a piece of canvas stretched over it, nothing fancy. I would probably camp in it one time at Indian

Gate to make a statement, not exactly sure what the statement was, and put it away, like most of the toys and junk I had to have over the years, only to lose interest in them once they were mine. This was way too complicated, too much mumbo jumbo. A simple price, and send it UPS or something, I'll figure out poles, maybe long trunks of the eucalyptus trees so plentiful around here. No dedication, no ceremony, just a tipi. Maybe another time we could follow up with all of the other stuff.

I called her son, Johnny Puebla, in Long Beach. An overly serious man, somewhat intimidating, he didn't understand. I wanted a tipi. She made tipis. The fact that his mom and step dad were willing to dedicate the tipi and run a meeting in it for me, a total stranger, was a big bonus. "He's not just any Roadman, you know. This is Sonny Hogan, a powerful and spiritually gifted medicine man, a healer from another time, another era, like that. He is the last of his kind. He still knows the secrets from the old days. Do you know how lucky you would be if they really did end up bringing you the tipi? Why would you pass up this opportunity? Like that. Don't you think it's strange that you called me, then talked with them, and now you want to back away? In that way, you do whatever you want, but don't call me after you buy some cheap junk tipi from some white guy in Northern California with thunderbirds painted on it, like that, in that way." He used the words; "like that" and "in that way" so much, and they didn't fit into the conversation. Later on I would learn these phrases were overly common with this tight-knit group, but for now, they were so out of place I had trouble taking him seriously. And what a great salesman this guy would make. Always degrade your customer. Such people skills. But a sales pitch like that worked best on me, because he was challenging me, daring me to do it.

Don't be a wimp. If you are going to order a tipi, get the best. Not just the best tipi, but the best Roadman and ceremony came with it. Who could top that? That would show Jump and everybody else what kind of tipi I could buy.

I called Lilly-Ann back, told her I would send her a deposit that week, and said I would get back to her on the sponsor and meeting thing. I asked her what a good size was. She said the smallest she liked to make was a 24, so I agreed. She explained we couldn't have a very big meeting in a 24, maybe 38 people at the most, unless we raised the bottom, then we would need a liner for that. I told her it would be impossible to fill the 24 around here so go ahead with that. Where would I get 38 people to sit inside a tipi? This was ridiculous, but I didn't want to sound like the ignorant fool that I was.

I went through all of my old Indian books, and then went to the library, trying to find out what I could about this Native American Church, and this ceremony. When I found out a "24" meant 24 feet across, 24 feet from wall to wall, I almost died. This was her smallest? This thing was an auditorium. It had to weigh a ton, as she told me she only used the heaviest gauge canvas so it would last. How tall was it? Was there even a cleared, flat area big enough at Indian Gate to set up this circus tent? I wasn't about to ask Jump if I could cut trees down to fit it in up there. She had given me a great deal on the tipi poles, so she said, so I had ordered them, also. How in the world was she going to transfer at least 23 fresh cut lodge pole pine tree trunks, over 26 feet long, and a huge tipi and door over a thousand miles from Aztec, New Mexico, to here?

These questions became insignificant once I started learning all of the intricacies of the ceremony they were planning. This was complex, to say the least. And talk about ritual and tradition. Growing up Catholic, I was accustomed to that concept. I thought the Mass was long and rigid. This was 12 hours, all night, with rules and details that made Mass seem like a holiday. Nothing had changed about this ceremony since its inception, no adjustments, no updates, no relaxation of protocol. If it had been in Latin like the Mass was when I was a child, it would still be in Latin. That was the easy part. There was no way what I read in the very few books I found touching on the subject was still true, at least I hoped not. The only comforting information I found was a few testimonials of supernatural healing and miracles from historians and anthropologists who had endured the unbelievably long night ritual, sitting and kneeling on a thin blanket on the hard ground, with no naps or breaks. Every ceremony had a sponsor, someone who had called for the meeting for one reason or another, and the whole ceremony revolved around praying for that sponsor and his particular request. Maybe I could sponsor a meeting for the family of Grayfox.

Life at home was as miserable as ever. When I was there, everybody was tense and tiptoed around me. Although my experience with the memorial had taken off some of my edge, I was still me. My quick trip to the cave and the vision I had with Chino's medicine that night definitely put a temporary hold on my drinking, but as always, it was very temporary. And as with every relapse in the past, when I went back to the inevitable full bottle, and fell inside, the walls of that bottle were slipperier than the last time, and it got deeper each time I fell in. Even the few days I stayed dry were no better, I was just a dry drunk. I didn't necessarily need alcohol to act like a jerk, it just made it easier. Everyone was completely sick of me, and my pretending to quit drinking only made things worse. The result was always the same.

My fortieth birthday was coming up, so as with every year a party was in the works. These parties gave an excuse for especially decadent and drunken fiascos. We always had fun preparing for these parties, but the last couple of years it had lost its allure. Jewel was now ten years old, and was excited, because this year the big party was a pirate theme, and as always, I went all out with the preparations. A beach, pirate ship, burning volcano, parrots and treasure, and, of course, the Copacabana Cantina, with every brand of tequila and rum ever dreamed up. We hired the start-up band for Jimmy Buffet, with impressive talent and ability to mimic all of Jimmy's wilder music. A day or two before the big bash I overheard my wife getting information on a rental apartment, so I pretty much knew this was going to be the final curtain for me, so I intended to make it memorable.

We never had any problem getting people to come to our parties. With fresh cooked Mahi-Mahi, live music, and an incredibly well stocked bar with professional bartenders, a hot summer night, hundreds showed up for the Big Forty, all with a bottle of tequila as a gift for me. Free food and drink buys lots of dear friends.

I managed to drink all day, and party all night. I ate, danced, and guzzled as if there was no tomorrow, and tried hard to assure tomorrow would never come for me. The center of attention, I was truly in my element. I made sure I kept my hero, tequila, at the center right next to me, toasting to the greatness of this wonderful cactus juice. Nothing mattered to me. This was my last dance, so I consumed far more than is physically possible without ending up in the ER or morgue. It helped that a few of the guests provided me with just enough artificial stimulant to keep me going.

Our property was large, over two acres, and neighbors were not close. Most of them were here at the party, but one with an unusually intolerant personality who I had run-ins with far too often, decided to shut us down; he called the police and signed a noise complaint. The over-zealous Sheriffs came to warn us about loud music, and I got excessively belligerent. I argued with the cops for way too long, and came very close to spending the night in their gray bar motel. A group of fellow drunks dragged me away from them, assuring the police the music would end. I knew who had called the authorities, and I was going to get even with him for raining on my parade. I stumbled down through the field and stood below the guilty neighbor's house, and started throwing rocks in that direction, screaming obscenities at him as he stood on his balcony, portable phone in hand.

One minute I'm ranting and raving at the top of my lungs, stumbling around searching for more rocks, the next minute I'm smashed into the dirt from a full speed tackle from my 18-year-old son, Storm. "Enough is enough!" he screamed at me, the words cutting all the way into my soul.

I broke down into drunken tears, crying like a baby. I attempted to apologize for 18 years of drunkenness that he had to endure. I promised him this was my last party, my drinking was over. Even in the darkness, as delirious as I was, I could still see his eyes roll. How many times had he heard those exact words come out of my lying mouth? How many times had I quit, this time for good? How many times had he, as a young boy, then teenager, up until now, tried so hard to believe me, always hoping it was true, always wishing that if he believed it hard enough, it was for real? Always let down, always disappointed, he had finally given up, just like me. His dad was a drunk, always was, and always would be. He was too old to believe in Santa anymore, and way too old to believe I would ever change.

I reassured him again, this was it. Tonight was my last bash. In a few weeks some Navajo Indians were bringing out a tipi made just for me, and they were going to run a sobriety ceremony for me. I was making up the sobriety ceremony part as I went on, or so I thought. I was trying a new lie, a fresh approach to an old and rotten promise. I was overcome with guilt and shame as I was laying in the dirt, mud on my face from tears and dust, my oldest son, now a man, looking down at me. I needed a story he had never heard, a totally different explanation of how this time things were going to be better, how this time, it was going to work. A sobriety ceremony in a tipi, he never heard that one before. Again he sighed and rolled his eyes. Tipi or no tipi, he knew me, and he knew my sobriety promises only lasted until my next drink, usually within the next six hours. It was a new line. These words meant less than nothing to him, but for some reason they suddenly meant something to me. I just wasn't sure what.

Two days later, still hung over and still dry, I called Lilly-Ann. "I have a sponsor for the meeting," I told her. "The sponsor is going to be me. And I have a reason for the meeting; for my sobriety." Lilly-Ann became giddy. She told me she was so happy I finally realized why she was making me a tipi. She had wondered how long it would take me to admit my problem, and finally ask for help. Now she could pray in earnest for me as she painstakingly sewed all the yards and yards of canvas together. She asked again if I was sure I only wanted a 24, worried it wasn't going to be big enough for everyone in the ceremony. I kept assuring her I was certain it was way too big; I would never fill it up with people. Especially in a prayer service for my sobriety. I knew nobody who would go to that. Ironically, I knew I could fill it up easily if I offered free beer to anyone who wanted to come in, but for sobriety? Who around here would come near that kind of gathering? I wondered if maybe she would bring her whole tribe out with her when they delivered a tipi. Nobody out this way ever heard of a tipi ceremony, as far as I knew.

Once again, I went back to my books to try to learn more about this ceremony I was dragging myself into. While there were some accurate facts about the ceremony, much of it was distorted and confusing. Nobody had ever been allowed to record or film a real ceremony, so anything that claimed to be real was usually a non-Indian charlatan exploiting the ceremony for his personal monetary gain or self-promotion. Chino had told me some small details, but assured me when the time came, it wouldn't matter what preparation I had, it would happen as planned no matter what. I still had it in my mind that he was a little crazy, so I mentally separated him from this whole episode I was going through, unconsciously disconnecting my past from my present and future. There was some written information that I later found out to be so far from the truth that it actually damaged, distorted, and insulted the real meaning of this ritual. Sometimes, *no* information becomes bad information, and wrong information can become damaging to those involved. No true Roadman was going to show much more than vague references to the actual event because anyone who wanted to record this sacred event up until now was only doing it to discredit native people and their traditions. It was only a matter of time before it was exposed in the wrong way, without the respect and honor it deserved, and those sacred parts kept hidden and secret. The few real accounts were mostly about the setting up of the tipi, the gathering of friends, some exposure of the instruments used, and the meal the next day, with some of the more common songs as background music.

I learned the ceremony was always held at sundown, usually in a tipi, no matter what the tribe. Sometimes it was held in a Hogan, sometimes even in a house, but regularly in a tipi, and the tipi was set up in a special way. Peyote, the small cactus that only grows in Texas and Mexico, was the holy sacrament of the ceremony, and was said to have been given to the Native People by God. The Native American Church was built on four pillars: faith, hope, love, and charity. And the symbol of the church was the water bird, a bird that spent most of its life flying, dove deep under water to spear fish and flew up to eat the catch. Inside the tipi, which faced east to greet the rising sun, there were some rules about how to move around. People were expected to always move clockwise, nobody ever walked in a complete circle in order to stay unwound, and nobody ever turned their back on the fire in the center. For whatever reason, everyone must always return to the same spot, and nobody can leave until the ceremony is over, other than a few short breaks, to keep continuity and consistence throughout.

I studied what I could about the mechanics of the ritual. The person who led the ceremony was a medicine man, called a Roadman. There were always other participants known as officers: the Drummer, the

Fireman, the Cedarman, and the Water Woman. It was clear to me that this was no sweat lodge, which I knew plenty about and was a regular participant until the alcohol made me sweat far too much, giving me away, or some other short ceremony that was sometimes done more for show than spiritual advancement.

So I was able to gather this much information about this "simple" ceremony I had signed up for. The deeper I dug, the more I didn't actually know. I finally realized I was going to have to go into it blind, and not try to pretend I had a clue about what it was. I had spent my whole life faking it one way or another. It appeared my phony days were coming to an end. My ancestors were calling me, and I couldn't quite hear them just yet. I didn't think I could fake this one, though. I got more nervous with colder and colder feet as each day brought it closer to reality.

I called Lilly-Ann several times, trying to postpone it, stop it, anything but commit to it. I told her we could do the dedication ceremony this trip, and maybe a ceremony later when I was ready. I had a lot to learn, and I didn't want to ruin the ceremony for them. She laughed each time I came up with an excuse, but she wasn't budging. She told me if I waited until I thought I was ready, it would never happen. She said I had been ready for a long time, they were just waiting around for me to call. That made no sense, because I didn't know them before the first call about buying a tipi.

Some days I would be so mad at myself for even starting this ridiculous process. Other days I was so scared of the whole situation I would almost cry. As my son already knew the night I quit drinking after the party, I still had to drink at least a few shots every day just to function. The emotional roller coaster I was on gave me yet another reason to drink. The only difference now was I tried my best to hide it from everyone. In fact, for the first time I could remember, I was ashamed of my drunkenness. I felt how you feel when you dream you are naked in school, or church, or some other public place, and everyone is staring at you, only they always stare downward at you in a state of shock, because you are always in the aroused state in these nightmares. Freud would have had a field day with them, but I always hated those dreams, and when I drank, I felt like I did in those dreams, unavoidable, shameful, self-conscious, out of place, alone, a big spectacle, standing out when you wanted to just disappear. I thought I was doing a good job fooling everyone; once again I was only fooling myself, and making a fool of myself. And the more I learned about this upcoming disaster I had set into motion, the more I realized I wasn't just a fool, I was really, truly crazy.

I didn't need a tipi, I needed a sanitarium.

CHAPTER 8

MY TIPI

Signed, Sealed, and Delivered

Almost exactly one month after my big party, the day was here. I waited nervously in the front driveway, hoping Lilly-Ann and my tipi would arrive soon, before Sandra and the kids returned from school. The last thing I needed right now was to explain the whole tipi story to my disgusted and fed up wife. I knew for certain she had no interest in socializing with these people. The only question on her mind would be how much my latest strange extravagance was going to cost, and who's going to clean up after these con-artists barging in on her life? An attitude completely justified, so my defense didn't exist.

Besides being anxious about a strange confrontation, I was almost 20 hours dry, attempting to sober up enough to give the whole experience a fair chance. An uncomfortable, mild case of the D.T.s was causing me to shake a little, and the realization that a couple of shots would instantly cure that made it worse, as I did not want to stink of alcohol on my first meeting of the mysterious tipi couple.

Around 11:00 a.m., a silver pickup truck with matching camper shell and a custom built rack carrying twenty-one 23-foot-long freshly cut lodgepole pine tipi poles, reaching too far in front and way too far in back came rolling down my driveway off the main road, accompanied by horns blasting from impatient commuters backed up behind them. A grand entrance. I could hear everyone inside the pickup howling with laughter. They honked their horn back in defiant response, laughing louder. "Thank God, I'm alone," I whispered to myself.

Driving the truck was Sonny Hogan, the "Roadman", who would run the ceremony; sitting next to him, his wife, Lilly-Ann, the woman I had been conversing with on the phone intermittently for the last six weeks, the tailor of my new tipi. In the cramped space behind them sat two elderly women introduced to me as Mom and Grandma. This crowded truckload of full-blood Navajos, or "Din'e", as they proudly call themselves, always naming their clan and location of birth on introduction, had just driven over 12 hours straight through from their home in Aztec, New Mexico, a tiny town near the Colorado border. They came to deliver my tipi, dedicate it, and run a ceremony in it, praying for me, a total stranger, the next night.

Sonny looked strong, healthy, much younger than his sixty-odd years. His dark, sun-weathered skin and braided long black hair gave him a classic "Indian" appearance, a multi-tribal look; he could have come from one of many North American tribes. When he was in his ceremonial prayer shawl and put on his eagle feathers given to him from a now deceased, famous Winnebago Roadman, when it was after midnight during a ceremony, he looked like one of the Plains Indian Chiefs of legend, born hundreds of years too late. I would later learn how that was no accident.

Lilly-Ann was robust, strong, extremely outgoing, very positive, reassuring in her demeanor, and laughing at every opportunity, a trait I would find abundant in everyone associated with the Church, happy about life. She was as anxious as me to get this show on the road, probably sensing my nervousness. She proudly described the new tipi in detail, grateful for another opportunity to show off what she loved to do. We talked briefly by the truck, then they invited themselves in for coffee, wanting to meet my family. I watched the time nervously, wanting badly to get on our way up to Indian Gate to set up the tipi, before there was any chance of an awkward meeting with my family.

Soon, Lilly-Ann's son, Johnny Puebla, arrived. He was from a previous marriage to a Pueblo Indian. Johnny was the oil-rig roughneck I had first contacted about the tipi, the great communicator and salesman. Unexpectedly, this turned into an emotional reunion for mother and son. Only communicating by phone for many years, this was their first personal contact in a long time. They hugged and cried, unashamed of their obvious love for each other. Lilly-Ann bragged how he was the spitting image of his father, a very tall, thin, and intense, long-haired man. I would learn later that his father had left Lilly-Ann when Johnny was very young because of her out of control drinking at the time. Up until a few years ago, Sonny, Lilly-Ann, and Johnny went from place to place running ceremonies for whoever needed help, barely surviving on Sonny's pension from the railroad and Social Security. Even though a mostly symbolic collection is taken up at the end of every ceremony, it never is enough to cover the fuel needed to get there, much less paying for all of the other expenses involved in putting on a Native American Church Ceremony. Most members of the N.A.C. live a very modest lifestyle, at best. Extra cash is not a common commodity, so the collection only serves as an outward show of gratitude. Nobody involved in putting on a N.A.C. prayer meeting does so with money in mind, other than trying to cover the costs. The returns are purely spiritual, yet they are more than worth the cost. That is why it continues on, the spiritual dividends are so great. Not geared to a monetary lifestyle, I would later discover they really charged far too little for the tipi and the poles. If you figured the time, energy, and material put into it, they got less than half of minimum wage for their efforts. So selling me a tipi wasn't much of a capitalist venture, done more to spread their love than anything else.

Johnny had moved out to California to work on the oil rigs, and Sonny and Lilly-Ann went back to running and attending church meetings closer to home. It had been a long time, and they were excited about running a service together again. Johnny was their Fireman, he kept the sacred fire burning perfectly all night long, something I would soon learn was far more than tossing logs on a fire to keep everyone warm. As I was about to learn, in a twenty four hour, impromptu crash course on the rudimentaries of the Native American Church Ceremony, not only is the fire of utmost importance, as the focal point and source of much of the revelation and magic that happens in the tipi, the firewood used in that fire is critical. No self-respecting Roadman or his Fireman would readily approve of running a ceremony using wood that wasn't prepared, that did not fit the standards of wood that had been used in this ceremony for eons. I came to find out that the fire was integral in every aspect of the ceremony. And the wood used in that fire showed preparation, always straight and clean, selected with intentions of a good fire, bright and warm.

I took Johnny out to show him the firewood I had gathered for this ceremony. Knowing what I had learned in the last few minutes about the importance of the quality of the firewood, I was ashamed to show him my pile of gnarled, short, bark-covered avocado branches, wood that I considered great for a sweat lodge fire. The problem, this wasn't a sweat lodge, or even close to one. Johnny didn't even pretend to cover up his reaction to my wood. At first he thought I was joking. Once he realized I was serious, he almost got mad. Didn't anybody tell me about the wood, the significance of it in relation to the success of the ceremony? I was intimidated, but I began to get defensive. No, nobody told me about your precious campfire wood. I had a hard time finding any information on this ceremony, and the only ceremonies anybody does around here consist of a stack of wood in a fire ring and a case of beer, maybe a pint of the hard stuff if someone just died. I thought, how am I supposed to know there were rules about something as mundane as the shape of the firewood; it all burns the same, and it all turns into ash, so who really cares? All I wanted was a tipi. Anyhow, you're the one who pushed this ceremony nonsense on me. Bring your own perfect firewood if you think I'm such an idiot.

Thank God he couldn't read my mind. It hadn't taken me long to go from nervous to neurotic. The lack of self-medication was starting to take its toll. I better get at least some alcohol in my blood before I blow this whole situation into a disaster. Maybe it would be wise to pay them off what I owed them for the tipi and poles, in case it gets real weird, real fast, and they just want to dump their load and head down the road. How many times had I turned a simple misunderstanding into a major crisis, making a complete fool of myself, ranting and raving about absolutely nothing, then regretting it the next day, unable to undo the tangled knot I had just tied? The beauty of my disease was that I developed the talent to totally destroy a beautiful situation without any effort at all; it just fell into place without me even trying. Why would this be any different? I could see the potential for meltdown any second, if we were already clashing on something as irrelevant as the wood that was going to get burned up.

Mentally I started the process of setting up my backup plan. I always had a backup plan in everything I did back then, knowing my original plan could implode at any given time. My backup planning caused many of my problems, as often times I could have easily diffused a situation, but in the back of my mind, I knew there was another way out if I did explode, so nothing prevented me from crossing the line, a line I would never have considered approaching if I were sober. Many times I seemed to force problems, creating the need to fall on my backup, which was always the unhealthier avenue of retreat, always using excessive alcohol to complete the process. So as Johnny talked, I worked out a plan that would assure I ended up with the tipi, whether these guys stuck around or not.

CHAPTER 9

PREPARING FOR THE NIGHT

More Than I Ever Expected

Johnny decided it was time to educate me about the importance of the fire, relative to the whole ceremony. He used certain phrases and words repeatedly that I later learned were common to this group associated with the Native American Church.

"Grandpa fire," Johnny explained, "is the center of this ceremony, like that. Our ancestors are in that fire. Most people connect fire with hell, evil, bad things, in that way, like that. They forget, or don't know, Moses received the Ten Commandments from fire, like that. They also don't connect the fire with the tongues of fire on the head of the disciples when they received the Holy Spirit, in that way. There is the heavenly fire, like that, the ceremonial fire that reveals all truth, and in that way, there is hell fire, where demons end up, where God has sent those who have rejected Him completely, like that. Yes, it is real, they are both real. As with everything spiritual, there is the truth, and a direct impostor, a deceiver, the lie, in that way, like that. They are identical in appearance, to fool the casual observer. Discernment is king, like that. Without it, everyone is fooled, misled. In that way, you have to know what is true, and what is there to lead you astray. We have always said, there are two Jesuses, like that. One, a blue-eyed, blond-haired man, here for the white people, but not really, he is the impostor. He is the Jesus of the missionaries, who misled thousands of well meaning "Christians" into hating the Native People, like that, to the point where he commanded them to kill these heathens, to cut their children from their wombs to be killed, so they could be baptized and their damned souls could be saved. In that way, then there is the real Jesus, the dark-skinned, long haired Native man, who, like that, lived off the land, walked barefoot through the countryside, preaching peace and love, fasting and spending His nights praying, from the tribe of Judah, who came to save all tribes, like that, all nations, that all would know the truth. We knew about Jesus before any missionaries came. He said He came for humanity, not a tiny part of the Middle East. There are many years of his life where He seemingly disappeared. He came here. All tribes have in their history the stories of a bearded "peacemaker" who came from the east, in that way, and gave us a peaceful way of living.

"The problems arose from the missionaries insisting we learn about a man we already knew, but we had to learn from the Bible, like that, and the written word was completely foreign to us. Forcing us to accept the Bible's Jesus, all or nothing, only caused confusion, as the men who insisted on this showed none of the characteristics of the Jesus we were accustomed to, like that. We did not understand why we had to abandon our culture and cut our hair to follow this new Jesus, risking death if we refused. We believed then as we do now, in that way, Jesus gave us this sacred medicine, Peyote, to help us on our path, just as He gave the tongues of fire to the disciples when He left them. Many of the aspects of this ceremony came from Jesus, like that. The 12 eagle feathers in my dad's fan represent the 12 tribes of Judah, like that, and the 12 disciples. The staff, called the Staff of Life, is modeled after Moses' staff in the wilderness. The medicine itself is called the Teardrops of God, in that way. And the fire, it represents God, and looking deep into that fire will reveal secrets about yourself, about life, like that, in that way.

"The fire in this ceremony will determine your fate, like that, whether you succeed or fail is dependent on the fire, on you, and on your faith. You will be looking into this fire all night, interacting with it, experiencing it, learning from it, in that way. I have nothing but utmost respect for the fire, or fireplace, as we call it. "Every Roadman has a different fireplace, or type of fire. It has been given to them by a Roadman who they learned from, one who has gone on before them, like that, and in turn, every Roadman gives a deserving man his fireplace, to carry on the fire in that way. Sonny's fireplace was given to him by a powerful, well known Ho-chunk Winnebago medicine man and Roadman, along with his staff and many of his eagle feathers, like that. He also gave him his Peyote Chief, an ancient, dried, sacred peyote cactus button that sits on four tiny sage leaves on the moon altar in front of him, a symbolic focal point of the ceremony, bringing the past into the present. In that way, I will tell you about the Chief later. Looking at your firewood, you have a lot to learn, and not much time to learn it, like that.

"I am very particular about the wood I use in a ceremony. Some Firemen will use poorly prepared wood, but I don't. Normally a sponsor starts preparing his wood months, like that, or at least weeks before the ceremony. The ideal wood is fully cured, but not rotten or termite infested, burns bright and hot, never smoky, and burns slowly, in that way. It is 4 to 5 feet long, 2 to 4 inches thick, perfectly straight, like that, no branches, and all of the bark taken off, clean. And as the sponsor cleans each piece, he prays over it, for himself, for the success of the meeting, so that as the wood is put into the fire throughout the night, the sponsor recognizes each piece, and remembers those prayers in that way. That wood represents your life from now on, like that, straight, clean, and holy, in that way, like that.

"You want that wood to represent your new life. What you put into that wood, what you put into that fire, is what you will get out of it. You don't want short, gnarled, crooked and branched old wood, like that, covered in bug-infested bark in your fire, or it will affect your prayers and life in that way, like that. This wood you have here represents your life now, a mess. You want to leave that mess behind you, not bring it into the fire with you. In that way, your firewood is part of your prayer, and the quality of the fire is important and necessary to bring about the new qualities you want in your life.

"And not only the wood, everything that goes into this ceremony, every instrument, every object, every act, thought, and prayer, like that, all that is part of this ceremony is of equal importance, in that way, every detail, every nuance is done with purpose and good intentions, like that, it will all effect the outcome of your prayers. This is why nobody can change or alter any aspect of this ceremony, in that way, because everything has a reason, a purpose, a cause and an effect, like that, and one simple, seemingly innocent change can completely retard the outcome in many ways.

"Nothing is taken lightly, like that, nothing is ignored or omitted, in that way, nothing added or subtracted. From the preparation of the wood, in that way, to the careful, deliberate setting up of the tipi, in that way, poles laid in traditional order, canvas pulled tightly, no wrinkles, door facing direct east, not just "somewhere towards east", like that, to the direction you must walk, like that, and all things passed inside, how you sit, what you say, nothing is accidental, in that way, everything has a reason.

"The power of this ceremony is a direct result of the painstaking energy put into every detail, like that, and the fact that it is exactly the same as it always was, it is the one true constant, the one thing we can always count on as being as it always was, in that way, and always will be, God willing. The moment that Chief is put upon the altar, like that, it is no longer a canvas tarp over some poles. The laws of cause and effect become absolute reality, in that way. It is a sacred place, the womb of Mother Earth, where we can experience total rebirth and rejuvenation, like that."

"Oh, is that all?" I thought, nearly out loud. We had started talking about firewood, and now we were talking about the cosmic order of the universe, and how it is affected. And all of this "in that way" and "like that", what was that all about? Please tell me I'm dreaming. This isn't anything like what I read about in the storybooks. And now I know why. Nobody would believe it. And, if I had any idea it was this involved, this serious, I would have never agreed to it. If they had told me about the firewood, even just a little of what I just heard in the last few minutes, I would be buying a tie-died camping tipi from the hippie girl in town. We were going to camp and dance around this tipi at Indian Gate to prove a point, not try to direct the order of the universe using an ancient formula only used by the great Medicine Men of the old days. I really needed a drink.

Johnny asked if there was a place nearby where we could cut some acceptable wood for tomorrow night's ceremony.

We hopped into my truck and drove to a few locations that had what I thought was decent wood. After several reprimands, I started to doubt we would find enough of the right wood in time for the ceremony. This might be a blessing in disguise, the ideal excuse to postpone what I saw as a long night of punishment for the years of drinking I had done. While I could appreciate the reasoning behind this extreme selective traditional dogma, I was anxious to get away from my house, and even more anxious about denying my intensifying need to self-medicate. More than anything else, I needed a shot of tequila. I told Johnny we could definitely find the perfect wood on the Reservation near the site where we were going to set up the tipi.

I had stocked up my small motor home with canned goods, meat, and other food and drink, hoping at least this would be acceptable. I even put some thawed out buffalo meat in the fridge, hoping that could be utilized, remembering a vague reference in a book about a meal related to the ceremony. I braced myself mentally for the inevitable onslaught of criticisms about the wrong food, the incorrect labels on the drinks, the non-traditional breads, on and on. If the firewood was so all important, God knows what else I had done wrong.

Johnny drove the motor home, Sonny drove his truckload of women and the insta-tipi kit (something I thought up, but didn't dare to vocalize), and I led the way in my truck. After a little over an hour's drive up through several different small Reservations, we arrived at Indian Gate. As had become typical, the gate was locked. I pulled out the key. For a brief second, I got this sudden fear the key wouldn't fit. It slid in, the padlock popped open, I swung the gate forward, and drove down the rutted, washed out dirt road, winding through overgrown trees and brush, over fallen branches and rocks, watching closely in my rearview mirror to make sure the tipi poles on Sonny's truck were going to make the sharp turns on the road without getting hung up in the jungle-like trees crowding the path. This was the first time I had been at this neglected camp since my teenage drinking days, more than 26 years ago. What used to be a nicely maintained private Indian camp, used primarily for excessive drinking and drug use, had obviously fallen out of favor with the current generation. Video games, computers, wide screen TVs and casinos had replaced outdoor parties by the river, actually, a good thing for the river, trees, plants, and animals. But the area was in pretty bad shape. It was going to take some energy to clear it up enough to set up the tipi and have room for the motor home and other cars. Had I known, or at least thought about it, I might have come up here last week and cleaned up some. Thinking and planning ahead weren't part of my routine lately.

The Navajos were going to spend the night here in the motor home by the river, and I would return tomorrow morning so we could search for the elusive perfect firewood, then set up the tipi for a dedication, and after that, prepare for the big night.

On my way home, I detoured to pick up a close childhood friend I hadn't seen in years, who had flown in from Phoenix after hearing about this ceremony. Franco was my old friend whose bachelor party ended up with me meeting Sandra at the bar. Over the years, we only talked periodically on the phone, but he was from my close circle of party friends from way back, one of the inventors of the arm bandanna for funerals, and he really wanted to see this ceremony I had told him about on a recent call. It also gave him a great excuse to visit his father with whom he had an unusually close relationship. He didn't believe me about my excessive drinking, thinking it was just another one of my many phases. He started to catch on when he couldn't help but notice my shaking and sweating.

We stopped at a K-Mart for supplies. Johnny had given me a list, the most important was lots of rope, had to be real fiber, not polyvinyl, and 26 metal stakes to anchor the tipi to the ground. I finally ended up buying giant nails, spikes to be exact, with huge metal washers on each, just hoping they would be allowed. Franco, whose nickname was Pancho Villa, was as loud and overbearing as ever. When I told him about the firewood controversy, he broke out laughing, more like bellowing, loud and obnoxious, in the store. "The right kind of wood for a campfire," he screamed embarrassingly, "what kind of crapola is that? You're kidding me, right? Hell, I'll straighten this crazy Navajo out about firewood. We know how to build a fire that brings ghosts to dance around it!"

People were starting to stare at us. I had somehow forgotten how loud Franco was, or maybe I had hoped he had outgrown it. Why, I don't know. I hadn't outgrown any of my bad behavior, why should he? All I knew, at that moment, was this was probably a huge mistake, inviting this loudmouth to a sacred ceremony, old friend or not.

After checking out of K-Mart, I walked over to Lucky Jug Liquor and bought two pints of tequila, hoping Franco didn't want much of it. I didn't even make it to the truck, literally yanking the top off, and guzzling half of the first bottle in a matter of seconds in the parking lot. Nearly strangling myself, it took a few moments of gasping for air before I could get a full lungful of oxygen. Soon that warm feeling filled my insides, my neurons receiving the signal to release dopamine, calmness returned to my psyche, and the whole world was once again at peace. The uncontrolled shaking left, and the edge was taken off, all of the corners rounded again for a short while, until the depression and anger set in. I finally relaxed enough to offer Franco a drink. When I looked at him he was just standing there, looking at me in shock, mouth and eyes wide open.

"Man, you really are sick, dude. That was the grossest thing I've ever seen, man," he yelled, for some reason unable to just *say* things. Everything out of his mouth had to be amplified, so the whole immediate world around us could share in his thoughts. "Dude, you better hope this ceremony helps you, you're like a goddamn drunk in the gutter!" He turned down my drink offer, said he had lost his appetite to drink after watching my act. I was relieved, since the bottle was nearly gone, and there really was not enough to share.

Back at home that night, with me in a calm stupor, Franco reminisced about the good old days with Sandra, who was in no mood for his boisterous, extroverted chatter about past excesses and conquests. She retired to the bedroom early to escape, while the kids stayed up late loving his entertainment, laughing half the time with him, the other half at him. Here was a guy louder than Dad, and he wasn't even drunk. I had to stay just coherent enough to censor him when he crossed the line about our sordid past.

We were up with the sun on Saturday, Franco wired and loud at first light, me trying to crash through yet another outrageous hangover. We loaded up a couple of chainsaws and last minute supplies and headed back up the mountain. The tipi site was bustling with activity when we arrived. The two elderly women were cooking corn and stew on a small fire in the rocks, Lilly-Ann was cleaning out what I mistakenly thought was a fairly organized motor home. Sonny and Johnny were clearing out an area to set up the tipi. Franco introduced himself in his usual thunderous voice, and we started to prepare the tipi for set up.

We lined up the tipi poles on the ground nearby according to length. Sonny culled out the two longest poles with strong tips for the "ears" to be put up last to control the smoke flaps at the top of the completed tipi later. He chose the strongest pole to be the "main pole", to be used to rope the canvas to that created the tipi covering. Then he picked out three varied sized poles for the tripod that starts the tipi process.

We measured out a 24 foot circle in the dirt, making sure the treetops didn't interfere with the top of the tipi. With a rope and string,

attached to a stake in the center of the circle, I etched a perfect circle in the ground, dragging the stick tight against the rope as I rounded the 24 feet. Sonny had watched the sunrise and marked exact east. Using that as a reference point, he marked out the four directions on the circle; due east would be the doorway. The three poles were stacked together on the ground across the circle, tied together with a long rope about two and one half feet from their tips. We fanned the stack out, putting one base at the east side of the door, stretched the other two to the west side of the circle, one man put his feet on the base of one pole, the process repeated with the other two. Sonny pulled the rope and the tripod rose up into the air, and was eventually able to stand on its own.

Starting with the shortest pole in the pile, we began to lay them up against the tripod, beginning with the northeast wall and spacing the bases about 6 feet apart on the etched circle, while Sonny ran in a wider circle around us, pulling the long rope tied to the top of the tripod around the pole as they set against the top of the growing tipi. He would whip the rope up and down as he went, forcing it tight against the top of the poles, cinching the tips together. Almost every pole I put up was in the wrong slot. I just couldn't get the pattern down in my mind. As with everything else, each placement was critical. They had to be in the exact position, in order, and set right.

Once the north wall was laid up, we repeated the process on the south side, starting with the shortest pole left on the ground, setting it on the south side of the door, putting the next size up in order, working to the west pole, eventually meeting up with the last north wall pole. Sonny cinched the frame all the way around. Completed, it was impressive, with the tips of the poles suggesting the shape of two hands clasped together with fingers outstretched toward the sky.

Sonny pushed the two poles framing the door together at the base, thereby separating their tips at the top, creating an open slot for the main pole to wedge into when leaned against the opposite side of the tipi frame. We pulled the pristine canvas tipi out of the custom sewed tipi bag and unrolled it onto a plastic tarp laid on the ground at the west side of the frame. Johnny brought the heavy main pole and laid it on top of the unrolled tipi canvas. He tied the canvas to the pole about two feet from the tip, wrapping a short piece of rope around the special flap at the top of the canvas several times, folded the flap over the rope, and wrapped it again, pouring a little water on it from his drinking bottle as he wound and tightened, so as the rope dried, it would shrink even closer to the pole. He lifted the end of the pole off the ground, and Sonny brought over an eagle feather and tied it to the tip, wrapping it securely with a long, thin piece of leather, everyone being careful not to let the feather touch the ground.

Another detail, not just for this ceremony but universal among the North American Tribes, the revered eagle feather is a sacred symbol, the flag of every nation. It is never allowed to come in contact with the ground. This is a sign of disrespect and bad luck, and if it happens, there is a certain protocol on how to retrieve it and bless it *and* the person associated with the accident, usually involving sage and cedar, and plenty of prayer. Letting the eagle feather touch the ground even before the tipi is set up for a meeting is at the very least not a good sign, definitely an indication of a very intense, hard ceremony coming up. Once I learned that, I made extra certain that feather, or any other eagle feathers I came in contact with, were given extra protection. Call it superstition, call it what you want, I called it keeping the scales tipped in my direction as far as humanly possible. I had been tempting fate for so long now, I needed all the leaning in my direction I could muster up, real or imagined. As the day progressed, and as my crash course evolved, all reality became very subjective. I was now along for the ride.

With the canvas secured tightly to the main pole, two of the women stood with their feet pushed tightly to the base of it while Franco, Johnny, Sonny, and me lifted the now very heavy pole and canvas, starting at the tip and working our way down the pole, pushing it up until it was vertical. Straight up, it was unstable, balanced precariously midair, now we had to lower it down into the gap made by spreading the two door poles, wedging the tip of the main pole in between the two tips now open. The women worked their way around us, keeping their feet wedged against the base of the pole so it wouldn't slip out and drop to the ground. As we slowly tilted it toward the frame, the weight made itself known. Top heavy and unbalanced, we all strained to keep it in control as we aimed it into the open gap, avoiding the thin tips of all of the other poles. If we missed the spot, we had to lift it back out and try again. If we dropped it too fast, we could break its tip, or tips of the other poles, or if the base slid out, it could crash to the ground. None of these options were good, not just in regards to the effort involved, but also in the spiritual realm. Just as a dropped feather has repercussions, any aspect of the set up that has unexpected problems is always interpreted as a negative, requiring prayer and meditation to understand the meaning and clear the air. From here on out, the outcome of this ceremony can be altered in a good way or a bad way, depending on how well it goes, and how much attention we pay to detail.

The main pole slipped right into place. Everyone sighed in relief, then cheered. I had assumed setting up a tipi had to be a chore. I never considered how the canvas actually got put over the top. It was hard installing the main pole, but that was really the worst of it.

Sonny once again circled the tipi with what was left of the long pole rope, whipping it tight against the last pole four times guaranteeing its security. Then we pulled the folded canvas bunched against the pole. Sonny grabbed one side, Johnny the other, and they ran fast around the tipi frame toward each other, pulling the giant canvas wings behind them, the material bellowing up and settling down on the skeleton, covering it with pure white canvas, turning it instantly into a beautiful tipi, only in need of tightening and securing. They kept pulling on it, flapping the material against the poles, stretching hard as they went, flipping out the wrinkles and closing the gap between the two sides. Once it was as far as it could go, they laid one side over the other, leaving only an opening for the door. The overlapping canvas was then laced together with 16 inch long, smooth pins, specially carved for this tipi. The pins were threaded into a hole from one side, down into a hole from the other side flap, across the front, then down into the holes on the other half of the flap. Starting at the bottom set of holes, and working up, soon it was too high to reach. We rolled over a barrel trash can, stood on that, and finished weaving the pins through the flaps, pulling and tightening as we went, each pin harder and more difficult as the tipi strained against the poles.

Lilly-Ann was giddy as she walked around the tipi, and not the least bit shy about how proud she was of her latest accomplishment. And proud she should have been, since the canvas fit the size layout of the poles like a glove, not a crease anywhere, truly a work of art. I was so busy thinking how nice it was, I completely forgot it was *my* tipi we were complimenting. What a revelation. Never in my craziest drunken stupors had I ever thought I would really have a tipi, and I certainly never envisioned anything as beautiful as this. In fact, this was the first tipi I had ever really been close enough, or interested enough, to really appreciate. I stuck my head inside, and was in awe of the size of the space, and the artistic beauty of the poles meeting in perfect order at the top, directing our sight right through the opening and into the blue sky above. My appreciation grew tenfold for her talent, the process of set up, and the myriad of characteristics represented by this structure that for eons kept uncounted tribes alive and protected.

Sonny took my newly purchased spikes and went around the base of the tipi, pounding one through each cleat, alternating from side to side, pulling it tight to the ground, making it even more taut, eliminating the last stubborn wrinkles, so tight you could play it like a drum. He strapped the canvas roll-up door with a small rope over the opening, closing the final gap. He slid the last remaining poles, one at a time, up the side and into the pocket in each smoke flap, using up the original poles he had set aside for the "ears" of the tipi to be adjusted by the Fireman throughout the night according to air flow, smoke content, and rainfall or wind gusts. In a little over one and a half hours, the tipi was up, perfectly fitted into place. And anything less than perfect will not do for this ceremony, especially a sobriety ceremony, something that requires no flaws to assure success. For this tipi to go up so smoothly, without any "do-overs", was a tiny miracle, one that was not lost on Sonny, and definitely not missed by the two Elders, who made very certain I was made aware how blessed I was for this to happen, and how great this ceremony was going to be. I was just happy it went well, and that they were happy. I didn't need to get blamed for more mishaps and bad omens, not since we still didn't have one single stick of firewood for what was looking to be a cold night. The fog wasn't lifting and it felt more like rain each passing hour.

As soon as everyone was satisfied that the tipi was perfect, they all got busy cleaning themselves up, and dressing up for the dedication. It was tipi dedication time, time to present me with a ceremonial tipi, a church, not just poles and canvas. Sonny built a small fire and got it going in the center of the tipi with the few pieces of semi-straight wood he had gathered earlier in the morning. With no fancy clothes to change into, I followed everyone inside. As he entered the tipi behind me, Franco bellowed out in his boisterous way, "Holy crap! This place is cool!"

Sonny sat in the Roadman's spot, due west, facing the door on the east side. Lilly-Ann sat to his right, me to his left. Franco sat to my left. Just as we sat down, Steven, a friend from the early days, popped in, more out of curiosity than anything else. He saw Franco and sat next to him, as they exchanged loud, crude greetings. The old Navajo women sat to Lilly-Ann's right, commenting in their native tongue in obvious frustration over Steven and Franco's loud carrying-on. Johnny sat by the door, stoking the little fire in front of him.

Sonny rolled a traditional tobacco smoke, using a dried corn husk to wrap his sweet mix of tobacco and mountain herbs. As he rolled, he spoke. This finally caused Franco and Steven to shut up. He thanked everyone for being there, and thanked me for asking for the tipi and for the meeting to follow tonight. He thanked his wife for making the tipi and helping him dedicate it, and thanked the elderly women for making the trip out so enjoyable, Johnny for taking time off work to help set up and help tonight with the fire, just like old times. He thanked Steven and Franco for coming in, and when they began to respond, he stopped them with a piercing look, so he could continue uninterrupted. Johnny handed Sonny a burning piece of firewood, and he lit his smoke.

He started praying in Navajo, with a few English words inserted occasionally. His prayer was sincere and intense. Nothing like the Catholic prayers of memorized repetition, he was actually talking from his heart to God. He got emotional, starting to cry. He was asking the Creator to have pity on us all, to forgive us, and to help us. He prayed for me in Navajo, saying my name in English, asking for the Heavenly Father to stop my need for alcohol. Sobbing now, he prayed in English only, so we could appreciate his plea. He asked God to heal me tonight of this terrible disease, to end all desire to drink. He wailed when he talked about how many people, friends, relatives, even sons and daughters who were suffering from this evil alcohol, people who he wished would also ask for help, just as I was doing, so they could get better and return to life. He thanked God for all of the times He had answered his prayers, and begged Him to answer one more time. He asked again for forgiveness, for understanding, and for direction. Tears falling down his face, he looked at me and said, "Thank you for asking for help. I wish more would ask, because the help only comes to those who ask for it. Thank you." I nodded, tears filling my eyes, more out of guilt than anything else. I looked down in shame, unable to face him again.

I started to realize the importance of everything that was happening, and what was about to happen. I stepped out of my overgrown, selfish ego just long enough to appreciate what was going on. These people took this very seriously. Nobody asks for a tipi, for a sobriety meeting on a whim, much less a dare, or a challenge, even though that's exactly what

I had done. Even if I tried to explain that to them, they wouldn't have understood or believed me. I was the odd one out here, once again. Somehow, I had landed in a lake of compassion, while drowning in a river of self-pity and defeat.

Sure, I had wanted a tipi, maybe even a ceremony. But the wheels of fate I had set into motion were not what I had expected. To these people, this was all-important. Lilly-Ann had just spent weeks sewing this tipi, praying for me with every stitch. Sonny had gone with a friend and hand selected these lodge-pole pines, with this ceremony in mind. The elder women never traveled anymore, but heard someone had actually asked for sobriety, and they came along, crowded in the back of the truck just to help out, if only with the food and the prayers. Johnny hadn't been to a ceremony in years, but took off time from work to be here, for me, a total stranger, someone who was tired of the curse.

This wasn't a whim to them, not a bet, not a challenge. This was what they lived for. Someone needed help. Someone actually asked for sobriety. That was significant. Rare. Special. Many people they knew, many of their relatives, they needed sobriety. They needed help. But it was very rare that anyone let their guard down long enough to ask for it. When someone calls for a sobriety meeting, many people want to be there, to help, and to be helped. In helping yourself, you helped others. Me, I had just wanted a tipi, or so I thought.

When Sonny finished praying, he passed the smoke around. One of the Elder women spoke up. She explained the importance of the tipi. It was now my home. I was to respect it, to guard it, and to take special care of it. It was to be used for me, for my family, for my relatives, and for my friends. It must be protected from people with bad intentions, and only used for important reasons. This was my home, and my church. Tonight, it would become my sanctuary. It would become the place where my life would change forever.

Her name was Eloise. She grew up in the Native American Church. She said it used to be harder to get into a ceremony. The ceremony hadn't changed, but people sure had. Many don't take it seriously anymore. They don't respect it the way they did decades ago. They take it for granted, and don't receive the blessings available from it. The church has gone in two directions, now. There is a new awakening for the young people coming about, and the Elders are happy to show them the way. At the same time, there are some who do not respect these ways, do not understand them, and are getting into trouble because of it. She warned me to be very careful and watch what I say and do, because now that I owned a tipi, I would be approached by people on both ends of the spectrum. I must become very discerning, something that is impossible if I am to remain a drunk.

She said if I never forsake my tipi, it would never forsake me. She asked where my wife and family were, and if they were coming in to the ceremony tonight. She said I could not go forward in the church, in life, if I were unequally yoked. If I went to ceremonies regularly, and my wife didn't, our marriage would fail. It would be like two horses pulling a wagon, both going two directions; the wagon would break apart. Likewise, my wife must come in, or my marriage would break apart.

I didn't dare tell her that my marriage was already breaking apart. I didn't let on that my wife and kids would never come in this tipi, that the wagon was already pulled apart, by far more than a missed ceremony. I nodded in agreement. Suddenly I understood I was at a major crossroad. I had been delivered to this location, this juncture, partly by me, mostly by fate. If I really wanted to live much longer, if I had any vague hope of saving my defunct marriage and alienated children, I needed to commit to this ceremony wholeheartedly, believing that I could be changed. Tonight was it, the last hope I had in the whole world. I either walked out of this tipi tomorrow whole, or I crawled out, tail between legs, a beaten and conquered man. A dead man.

The dedication ceremony was short. Not that we had a lot of spare time. We passed around the water bucket full with the water from the faucets in the camp, which tapped into the pristine aquifer deep in the granite below us, local water known for its excellent quality, a real rarity in this part of the country. After drinking the water, Johnny passed around the sacred food in order: first the fire roasted corn cob halves, some canned fruit, followed by the traditional pieces of unsalted buffalo meat heated by the campfire and shredded into strips, all pulled from the motor home and creatively prepared by the Navajo Elders. We stood up and followed Johnny outside, circling the tipi clockwise, reaching over and touching each pole through the canvas to complete the dedication.

Lilly-Ann was disappointed more people hadn't shown up for the dedication. I don't know where she thought they were going to come from. She was two days away from home, and none of the local Indians I knew would come to this type of gathering, not without some beer for refreshments. I told her I thought it was great, and I didn't care if any more came for tonight's ceremony. I certainly didn't expect any more to show up. I would be quite content having a tiny group in my first meeting. I was nervous enough as it was, and didn't need a big audience to make a fool of myself.

Johnny, Franco, Steven and I took off in two trucks in search of the elusive "perfect" firewood for tonight. We made several stops on Reservation land, looking at downed trees, burnt wood, rotting wood, and gnarled wood. Each time, Johnny looked at our enthusiastic find with disgust. After over two hours of fruitless searching, where he had turned down what we thought was some pretty nice firewood, I began to wonder if the wood he was after really existed. I started to believe he was being unrealistic, no, ridiculous. We were only hours away from the start of the ceremony, we had two empty trucks, and we were running out of places to look. I told him we had no more options, we were on the last stretch of the mountain that was Reservation land. The landowners beyond the Reservation were not known for their neighborliness and did not take kindly to trespassers or firewood scavengers.

We were up about 4,000 feet in elevation, the fog was turning to pea soup, and rain was starting to fall. Cold, wet and tired, I pulled into a turnout overlooking a steep ravine. Steven and Franco pulled in behind us, got out and walked to the edge of the ravine. Through the thick fog far below we could see a good section of pine forest that had blown down some years before. We grabbed our chainsaws and slid down the wet slope, crashing into the first row of toppled pines. Johnny scoured the trunks and branches for rot, termites, or signs of fire damage. Finally, he announced it would have to do. The branches were nicely seasoned, between 5 and 8 inches thick, and straight as arrows. It really was a great find, and none too soon. The day was growing old, and the rain was overruling the fog, and we were all getting a little cranky. Naturally, my mind was starting to obsess over how warm a shot of tequila would feel just about now.

I informed everyone it was possible we were not on Reservation land. It could be National forest, where woodcutting was illegal, or worse, private ranchland. Getting shot at with salt rock was a huge possibility. If we were going to get this wood, speed was of the essence. And chainsaws were hardly stealth tools to work with. The advantage we had was fog and rain. Fewer people would be on the road to wonder what we were doing.

Johnny showed us the exact pieces to cut, where to cut, lengths, sizes, details beyond obsessiveness. He demanded we only cut right where he pointed, acting as if we had a few weeks to gather the necessary wood. We ran two chainsaws continuously for over three hours, in the steady rain, almost cold enough to snow. We piled up our harvest and began hauling it up to the trucks. The steep climb up the wet ravine was bad enough, carrying armloads of long pine branches made it that much more treacherous. We hauled at least 40 five-foot-long pieces up the slope, loaded them into the trucks, and headed back to the tipi site.

When we got back, exhausted, wet, and filthy, we were met by Sonny and the women, along with about ten strangers that had arrived. They helped us unload, then went to work, stripping the bark off and chipping any tiny branches away with axes. It looked like a pretty nice pile of wood. I was about to sneak over to my truck and search under the seat for a tiny airplane bottle of Jose Cuervo, when Johnny announced loudly that we needed at least another truckload to make it through the night. He was concerned about the change of weather, and didn't want to have to settle for a small fire. Franco laughed out loud, thinking Johnny was joking. Steven, always up for adventure, argued in Johnny's favor, and off we went. Just thinking about sliding back down that hill and dragging more wood up made me thirsty. By the time we cut, hauled, and returned with another truckload, I would be ready for a bottle of tequila, a bag of chips, and a good night's sleep, certainly not an all-night ceremony.

We returned to our secret fallen forest, cut what we could, loaded up and drove back. When we pulled down the washed out dirt road into the camp, I couldn't believe what I was seeing. There were at least 40 people there, cooking, cleaning wood, laughing, and chattering away. There were a handful of guys drumming and singing by the small fire inside the tipi, beating a water drum with a hand carved drumstick while one singer shook his decorated gourd rattle to the sound of the drum. What had been a lonely campsite a few hours earlier now looked like a bustling Indian village. The women cooking by the campfire near the motor home were huddled beneath a big beach umbrella they had found inside it, laughing loudly about something one had said in a language I had never heard before. The men cleaning the wood definitely understood her, and they started laughing louder than the women.

I didn't recognize anybody there, and I couldn't figure out where they had come from. This was my first exposure to what I would come to know as the Native American Church underground network. When there was a ceremony coming up, word got out, and as many as could, would come, if they were in traveling distance. It could mean anywhere from one hour to two days drive. Many would drive all night to attend a meeting, depending on the reason for the meeting, the sponsor, and the Roadman running it. They all went for one reason: to support the sponsor. To pray for that person. To help. And in doing that, they helped the Roadman, his wife, everyone at the church, and themselves. Everyone who attends a meeting is helped in one way or another. In their giving, they also received. I didn't know it right then, but everyone was there to pray for me, for my sobriety. Helping in my sobriety helped them in theirs, and helped relatives they had with the same problem. My asking for help to quit drinking was uncommon, so they wanted to be a part of the miracle. I didn't have the faintest clue how intense this was going to be.

As I stood there watching this drama unfold, Steven announced he had to head home. Franco yelled at him for wanting to leave, and they started a loud argument about adventures and home life, so I quietly tried to make my way to my truck unnoticed so I could take the edge off and take all of this in. At one point, the atmosphere shifted abruptly. The activities stopped, and everyone started changing out of their casual work clothes and into nice outfits. Many wore more traditional Native wear, moccasins on the women, nice boots on the men, jewelry of turquoise, silver, beads, and the church symbol, the water bird, displayed in many fashions on both men and women. Wash rags and baby wipes were passed around for superficial clean-up. People moved in and out of the motor home and their cars and trucks. Those with long hair were braiding it, or tying it up neatly.

The casual mini-ceremonies that Chino and I had had up on the high desert by the cave were fairly primitive in nature. Nice clothing was never a part of it. Once again, another detail I never read about or was warned about, I had nothing appropriate to wear to a fancy church meeting. Who would have guessed we had to be dressed up to sit on the ground around a fire in a tipi all night? I had brought a shirt I had worn many times up by the cave, but it was worn out and torn. I realized how ridiculous I was going to look as sponsor of this ceremony, center of attention, in scraggly, torn clothes. What I had on now was muddy, smelly, and not an option. Lilly-Ann kept asking me when I was going to go get ready, but I had no intention of driving all the way home, so I was very embarrassed about not being better prepared. Things were going from bad to worse. Certainly someone could sit in for me as sponsor, while I slept off this exhaustion in the motor home. Realizing these people were here to support me gave me no options. This was church, and like all churches, one dressed up out of respect. I wish I had known. I went to the river with a towel, washed up as best as I could, found some clean Levis and moccasins in the motor home, put on my torn shirt, and buttoned up a red plaid Pendleton over it. People started eating the bread and light food prepared for the evening meal, as even more cars pulled into camp. I had never been this nervous, and didn't like the feeling.

As the light slowly disappeared, the campfire got brighter, fighting to survive the steady raindrops. The tipi was glowing from the fire inside, silhouettes of people inside creating an eerie scene like an old western painting. Now that Steven left, I was surrounded by total strangers, other than Franco, who was busy getting to know everyone, whether they liked it or not. People would congratulate me, thank me, and tell me how brave I was for sponsoring this meeting. If they only knew. And they were all so proud that I had bought the tipi, what an honor, a privilege, and even a great responsibility. I nodded as they praised me, not knowing what in the world they were talking about.

One man confessed he wasn't ready for the huge responsibility of owning a tipi and doubted he ever would be. Here was this mature Indian veteran of the Native American Church, calling himself unworthy of owning a tipi. I was confused. What was the big deal? With each positive comment I got, the smaller and more confused I became.

I had begun something I was definitely not ready for. I was determined to get to my truck and down as many shots of tequila as possible so I could either talk my way out of this ceremony, or have the courage to go in. Whatever the result, I would live with it. I just needed to calm my nerves. As I was reaching desperately under the seat of my truck for a bottle, Franco came running over, hooting and hollering all the way, making sure all eyes were on him and then me. I pushed my arm way under, not finding anything. I reached all the way back, sliding my forearm under a seat spring, the end of the coil slicing my skin as I pushed harder, frantically searching for that familiar plastic shape. I pulled out two empty bottles, now getting angry. I rushed to the passenger side, threw open the door and thrust my bleeding arm under the seat, flailing it back and forth, trying to get my fix.

Franco yelled at me, "What the hell are you doing? Mellow out!"

I stood back, breathing hard, now getting desperate. It was bad enough abstaining for this long, but once I had made up my mind I was going to drink, all bets were off. There was no stopping, I could get real ugly. The psychology behind the act of drinking is truly addictive behavior, and once my mind had passed the point of abstaining from the drink, and now was preparing for the physical and mental rush of the alcohol, it was almost as if I had already taken the drink. But if I went into drink mode, and for whatever reason didn't follow through with the actual act of drinking, violent withdrawal symptoms kicked in. I pulled the seat as far forward as it would go, and yanked all of the trash and junk piled behind it out, poking my hand under the back of the seat. I felt a tiny bottle, a sense of relief came over me, and I pulled it out, totally hiding it in my palm in the dusk light, ready to run to the Porta-Potty and gulp it down, then return and search for another. As soon as my hand was free of the seat, I realized it was another empty. "What the hell!" I cried out, pushing the bottle back under. I threw the junk back behind the seat and headed back to the driver's side.

Franco was tugging on me, barking loudly, "Let me wrap your arm, brother, you're bleeding pretty bad." I knew I had put many more bottles under the seat, and couldn't remember when I had drank them, not that that was unusual, but I was pretty good about never totally running out. I knew I had a few stashed in there somewhere, I just needed to find them.

Suddenly Lilly-Ann was right behind me. "Whatever you're looking for will have to wait until tomorrow," she said calmly. "Sonny wants us to line up to go in now. Everyone is ready, we're waiting on you. What did you do to your arm? Clean that up and get over to the tipi. It's getting late. Sonny likes to get started just after sunset."

I would find out the next day that Franco had found six little bottles of tequila under the seat that morning looking for his camera, and had thrown them away, thinking I was quitting drinking and didn't need any unnecessary temptation. I was frazzled, convinced I had to have alcohol or I would get sick. My heart was pumping hard and fast, sweat dripping off my forehead in the cool, damp evening air. I spate at Lilly-Ann, "I'll be there in a moment!"

She grabbed my hand and pulled me from the truck, "Don't you go getting cold feet. This is what we have all been praying about for weeks now. Sonny doesn't like to be kept waiting. Anyone who shows up late can come in after we have started. You come stand in front of me in line by the tipi. It's prayer time. Lock your truck. Franco, get me a Band-Aid from the back of my truck, he's staining his shirt, as if it's not bad enough already. He doesn't need to look like he's been in battle."

Franco laughed loudly, "How did you cut yourself, brother? What were you doing, anyway? Are you okay? You look sick, man. You look like you really need a drink, man!"

Lilly-Ann yelled at Franco, "Don't even joke around like that, Franco. This is serious. We don't make jokes about stuff like that. You be quiet and get in line behind the sponsor. No more talk like that, do you understand?" She surprised both of us with the power in her voice.

Franco backed down. "Yes, ma'am, I'm sorry, just kidding, you know. I'm sorry. Robert doesn't need a drink, he's fine. He doesn't have a problem. I'll bet I drink more than him," he lied.

Lilly-Ann replied quietly, "I certainly hope not, Franco. Any drinking is too much drinking. You can't drink and use this medicine in a good way. You'll get sick every time. No more alcohol talk, that's what we're here to fix. You can't even kid around like that, or we'll all get sick like that. Let's talk about good things from now on, in that way."

"Okay, Lilly-Ann, no more talk like that, I promise."

Then Franco leaned close to me and tried his best to whisper; "Who is the sponsor I'm supposed to stand behind, brother?"

All I could think about was where I had hidden those damn bottles. If I could remember, I could come out later and drink them.

CHAPTER 10

THE NATIVE AMERICAN CHURCH CEREMONY

The Bright Flame in a Dark Life

Everyone was already lined up as we walked to the tipi. The Roadman, Sonny, first, then a gap for me and his wife Lilly-Ann, then the Cedarman, Duane Wilson, next, the Drummer, Orlando Crashing Thunder, then everyone else behind. The line wound up the dirt road to the camp entrance. Where had this huge crowd came from? It was still a big mystery to me.

Johnny, the Fireman, went into the empty tipi and swept it out, cleansing it of the day's activities and of any spirits that didn't belong. Silence fell over the whole camp. The rain stopped, the sound of the rushing river seemed to drop far away into the background, no more vehicles passed by on the road above us, a moment of silence was granted for us to begin.

Sonny started praying in his tongue, Navajo. This was when the tipi turned into a church. No longer canvas and poles, it became a sacred entity, free of all of the filth of the world around it. He prayed out loud for cleansing, for a good ceremony, for all prayers uttered inside this church to be answered. He thanked the Creator for this ceremony, for the opportunity to once again be a part of it, and the chance to serve Him again. He prayed for nearly ten minutes, and I occasionally heard him mention my name in English, along with sobriety and other words relating to my problems. Then we all walked, single file, around the

165

outside of the tipi, clockwise of course, then around the big stack of beautifully cleaned, straight, firewood just outside the door. Then, bowing our heads to fit in the low door, we filed clockwise into the tipi, everyone taking their prepared seats.

Many carried ornate or simple cedar boxes, like fancy fishing tackle boxes, containing a variety of personal ceremonial effects: gourd rattles, eagle feathers, fancy fans, drum sticks, medicine, many with photos of family--both living and dead--pasted to the inside top, tobacco, cedar, and sage. Many boxes contained artifacts of the church from hundreds of years ago, family heirlooms, relics of the past. Entering this meeting were not just those folks I saw, but also hundreds of years of tradition, the prayers of generations of ancient medicine people, the love, the hurt, tears, and joy of thousands of ceremonies exactly like what was about to happen, all from long ago. It has taken me years to appreciate what it took to have this one ceremony, not just then, but everything that had to happen centuries ago for it to be as it was that night.

The tipi didn't look the same as it had when we set it up hours ago. The fire, directly in the center of the tipi, had about eight pieces of our hand-selected wood on it, stacked up in the shape of a wide 'V', the open end spread apart about 4 feet at the door end, the 'V' pointing to the west, at the Roadman, Sonny. The wood was carefully stacked intermittently, like the old ranch fences, equally piled one on another, only burning the tips in the front of the pointed stack. The west end of the stack of wood burned brightly, nearly smokeless, a tiny plume of clear smoke drifting straight up and out the slightly opened flaps at the top of the tipi.

Considered a great honor and privilege to be asked to participate in this ceremony as an officer, the job of fireman is the hardest, just behind carrying the drum. Nobody ever turns down when asked to serve. The fireman works hard, and is completely worn out the next day, yet gets so many blessings by performing this selfless duty; he is honored to be asked again. Johnny loved this uncomfortable job, and it showed in how diligent and attentive to every minute detail he was, and how perfect his fires always were. Years later, I helped him with fire in a ceremony, and I barely lasted to midnight, fried and exhausted. Until then, I never appreciated how miserable this service was, yet how rewarding it could be.

Johnny's prediction proved correct. Every so often, throughout the ceremony, I would recognize a piece of wood going into the fire. Something would be familiar about it; that I remembered cutting it, or hauling it up that wet slope, or cleaning it with strangers around the campfire only hours before. He recommended praying over each piece of wood. As I remembered certain pieces, I understood why.

I began to see the validity of Johnny's obsession with the perfect wood that drove Franco, Steven, and me crazy earlier in the day. His desire for clean wood made sense as I watched this fire burn bright, hot, and practically smokeless all night long. Experience and tradition has taught Johnny that the more blood, sweat, tears and prayers put into the ceremonial wood, the smoother the meeting runs, with gracious and positive feelings all the way through. The seasoned participants have also learned to look into a well prepared fire's embers deep enough to read them like a nicely written book. The fire, interpreted correctly, can reveal information about the sponsor of the meeting that isn't readily volunteered at first, freeing them up to face those hidden truths that must be confronted so they can be properly addressed and taken care of once and for all. If a sponsor truly wants healing, nothing can be hidden or it won't be dealt with, and the fire is consistently able to flush out those unpleasant facts that, left unchecked, will hamper even the best intentions, and prevent a positive outcome. You can't fake anything in here. There is no hiding of anything in these ceremonies, inevitably everything boils to the surface, no matter how painful or shameful, and that is the key to true healing, facing the facts so they can be evaluated and cleared up. All of the heavy baggage that is dragged into the tipi is eventually thrown into that fire, left to be burned to fine ash, never carried back out again. Giant bags of garbage that people have been lugging around their entire life eventually get pulled out of that hiding place behind them, put directly in front of them for all to see, then thrown into the fire piece by piece, bag by bag, until it is all gone. And if it is done right, they won't pick up another bag and start filling it up again. They walk around standing straight and tall without that heavy garbage hunching them over ever again.

A good fire does an incredible job of shining its bright light into every nook and cranny of the tipi and of our minds, revealing all kinds of garbage bags strewn everywhere so they can be burned. Even people who had no intention of letting anyone see their trash can't push those bags around anywhere long enough to keep them hidden. The fire is too bright, and the absolute ingenious beauty of the design of the tipi is that there are no corners to hide in, no place to stash your trash. All of our humanity, defects, blemishes and all, is there for all to see, in a neutral, nonjudgmental environment, so it can be burned away. Everything comes out. It is always spotless and clean once that sun peeks its eyes over the eastern horizon, no matter how high the trash heap, no matter how much must be burned.

In my case, any desire I had to hide anything pretty much disappeared once I accepted the fact that I wasn't going to get out of this ceremony. Any and all thoughts of leaving soon vanished with the sunlight, and I made up my mind to go waist deep into the muck and mire, let everything out and see what happened to it all.

I didn't know any of these new people, never saw them before, and figured I would never see them again, so there was no reason to pretend about anything. I was putting every drop of faith I had left into this ceremony, this medicine, this Roadman, this God. If faith truly could move mountains, tonight I wanted a volcano. I was going to tell everything and ask for it all. I wanted everything that was possibly available, and I wouldn't be bashful about it. If the answer to my problems was here somewhere, I wanted to find it, at any cost. I wanted what they had. And, at that point, I was going through alcohol detoxification, physically and mentally exhausted, so any fight I might have left in me was gone, drained out. It was patently obvious I had lost all control over alcohol, and of my life. That was the first step. It was also very apparent that something much more powerful than me was needed to save what was left of my life. That was my second step in the right direction. Tonight, the time had come to reestablish that connection I once had with my Creator. Step three, it was time for me to just let go.

Although I hadn't spent weeks preparing my firewood, thanks to Johnny's exacting requirements, along with all of the unexpected help I got preparing that wood, it looked like I had. That particular type of pine, unfortunately, is rare around here. Unfortunate, because it burns so nicely. To this day, I've never found that downed grove of pine we raided that evening.

And while we were crawling around that rain-drenched mountainside, Sonny was hard at work inside the tipi. He had dredged up some clean white sand in the outer shallows of the riverbed and formed the beautiful half-moon altar around the fire. About 6 inches wide at its base, sloping up nearly 4 inches high to a 3 inch wide top, the carefully compacted sand was shaped into a large half circle, maybe two and a half feet away from the tips of the stacked firewood in the back third of the center of the tipi. Starting at exact south, it curved around the fire with its middle at due west, continuing around to end at exact north. It created a half circle area that would eventually be completely

filled with pulsating red hot embers emanating waves of welcomed heat, especially warm to the Roadman, the Cedarman, and the sponsor, all sitting just beyond the burning coal pile at the west section of the tipi, facing the east.

On the flattened top of the moon Sonny had carved out a groove all the way around the altar. This was the Road of Life, the Red Road of Sobriety, the Peyote Road. The beginning of the road was at the south, and represented the beginning, one year old. The center of the curve was 50 years old, halfway through life, the end of a sober and productive life was 100 years, the northern tip of the moon. The inside of the moon, the fire side, is the spiritual side, all about God and good. The outside, where we all sat, is the human side of life, with its trials, troubles, and temptations. Sonny would explain later how we must stay on the top, living a good, clean life, never falling too far either way, staying balanced and centered, and if done well, expecting to live at least to the end of the moon, one hundred years, in good health and happiness, as a reward for clean living.

At the 50 year mark on the moon sat four tiny sage leaves, forming a cross. Once we were all seated, after the tipi had been cleansed and blessed, Sonny would stand and pray the opening prayers, throw a handful of dried cedar from the Cedarman's bag into the coals, and as the sweet smoke wafted up, he pulled his Peyote Chief, the holy cactus, from his sacred box and waved it four times back and forth into the smoke to bless it, then set it on the tiny sage cross on the altar. This signified the absolute beginning of the ceremony, where all words, thoughts, and actions had to be done in reverence and with respect, all joking and superficial talk ended then.

The Peyote Chief is the focal point of the ceremony. It is usually very old, and unusually big, even in its dried state. It is the actual cactus in its entirety, minus the roots. Called a peyote button, often times people think it is a part, or berry, or fruit of the peyote cactus, but it is in fact the whole plant. Extremely slow growing, a typical button the size of a tiny tangerine can take 15 years to mature. A ceremony usually involves using at least 100 buttons, usually many more, in dried, fresh, or tea form.

Each Peyote Chief normally has a long history. It has been used and passed down from generation to generation, father to son, and Roadman to Roadman, usually passed along with a style of fire, or fireplace, to continue the good work and miracles of the church. All blessings, prayers, instruments, and cedar are passed over the Chief, symbolically picking up the prayers and blessings of the ceremonies the Chief has been a part of, sometimes actually centuries ago. Not to be confused as an idol or substitute for the Creator, the Chief is merely a symbolic icon as focal meditative point, something worshippers could focus on other than the fire, to avoid wandering eyes and drifting minds, keeping all prayers centered on one purpose, to help the sponsor. Not unlike the crucifix in a Catholic church, the Chief is no more a god than the crucifix is actually Jesus himself. Misinformed strangers to this way of prayer mistake it as idol worship. The only thing worshipped in this ceremony is the Creator, nothing more, nothing less. All good power comes from Him alone, although He does use certain items to pass His power through, be it the medicine, eagle feathers, tobacco smoke, cedar, even the Chief, if he so chooses.

From the Roadman's position, looking east towards the door, to his right, sitting next to the moon was a white metal bucket, with a white lid and small clear glass tea cup upside down on top. Inside it was about two gallons of freshly brewed peyote tea, made from boiling and simmering dozens of dried peyote buttons until it was dark in color, resembling black tea. Sitting next to the tea was a ceramic bowl filled with freshly harvested bright green peyote cactus, all roots, dried skin, and flower buds cleaned off and the remaining green fruit cut into tiny dime-sized chunks. In a matching shallow bowl next to that was a mound of finely ground, light brown dried peyote with a tiny ornate sterling silver spoon.

Between the medicine bowls and the Drummer sitting to the south of the Roadman sat the water drum, an old cast iron kettle, actually an all-black Dutch oven the size of a volleyball with three tiny offset legs. Inside was about a half quart of water and four coals from this fire, and tightly stretched over the open top was a thin piece of deer hide, strapped down and over and back again in an ancient rope pattern, with seven boulders from a child's marble collection wrapped over with the hide and rope to create handles and tension on the drum skin at the same time. When wet, the drumstick pattern pounding on this unique traditional ceremonial instrument sounded hauntingly like a heartbeat deep within a cave, the sound of the heartbeat of Mother Earth. Leaning against the drum, rested the hand carved hardwood drumstick.

The man who would carry the drum in my ceremony sat to Sonny's right, as he looked east. Orlando, a young, strong Navajo who had served in Desert Storm, was a recovering alcoholic who had traveled some distance to come to this meeting after hearing it was a sobriety ceremony. Sonny had chosen him to drum tonight only hours before the beginning of the meeting, when I was still gathering wood. He had spent the last hour tying the drum as taut as was possible, taking pride in his ability to tie it up the way his grandfather had taught him as a child, honored to be selected to take part of tonight's miracle. Another difficult and demanding position, the Drummer beat out the heartbeat on his drum all night long, kneeling to the right of each singer, keeping the steady beat to four songs for each person. Starting with the Roadman and his four opening songs, he would rotate clockwise one at a time as many rounds as time would allow, stopping only for Midnight and Morning Water.

Always aiming for four rounds of the drum around the tipi in a ceremony, every meeting had a different dynamic. The amount of rotations was determined by many factors, including how many people, how many of them sang, how long the songs were, and how much time was spent on teaching, talking, praying and crying, gentle chastisement and emotional forgiveness, and rebirth. Even though all ceremonies are exactly the same ceremony, they are all completely different. As the spirit leads, and as the attendees follow, the direction varies every time, depending what the occasion called for, the ancient formula always followed diligently, while the spirit of the night changed the outward course of events as needed to accomplish whatever had to be resolved. A lighthearted birthday meeting could be upbeat and happy all night, while a healing or teaching ceremony could take everyone places they've never been before, no matter how many years they have been going to meetings. By the same token, a birthday ceremony could change direction 360 degrees at a moment's notice if unresolved issues came bubbling up to the surface. The medicine has an uncanny ability to clear the air and clean the tipi while cleansing lives, no matter what the perceived intentions might be, especially if the sponsor or someone close is not completely forthright about all of the issues in their life. Subconsciously they want help, but are afraid or unwilling to ask for it.

The universal symbol of the Native American Church is the water bird. This bird lives mostly in flight, but to eat, it dives down deep into bodies of water from high altitude to spear a fish and brings it back to the sky to devour it. In the ceremony where someone is unable or unwilling to honestly deal with the real issue hindering their spiritual growth, the medicine becomes that water bird, diving deep into the soul of the wounded heart, isolating that problem, bringing it to the surface so it can be washed clean or devoured by the fire. Unless one is a master of deception so strong they fool even themselves, or in such overwhelming denial they are preventing help from coming to them, that help does come, in one form or another. Sometimes the disorder is so stubborn, so resistant to recovery, the medicine will force the issue, causing that person to vomit, often very violently. Rather than consider this act as a negative, it is welcomed by those who know it is the only way this person is going to rid themselves of their personal demons. Throwing up, while often rumored to be a common and expected result of consuming peyote, does happen, but always for a reason. Nobody is shocked by it. In fact, it is called getting well, not getting sick, as it apparently is a necessary action for this particular situation. Many sponsors who resist help are often relieved after the act, because inevitably he is freed of his problem, and the prayers begin to work as needed.

Also, the medicine will remove itself from those who use it improperly, outside of a ceremonial setting, without reverence and respect, usually those who ingest it seeking some sort of drug-induced mind altering state. One of the many reasons the hippie movement gave up trying to include peyote in their repertoire of drug abuse is they consistently got sick, as the medicine will not work for any other reason than what God intended it to do. The reputation for inducing vomiting has managed to keep it safe from those wishing to use it for purposes other than spiritual growth. Unless the situation calls for radical solutions, "getting well" is not a common occurrence in most peyote ceremonies. Nonetheless, rarely does anyone come into this ceremony openhearted and open-minded and not walk out fully changed and fully cleansed. If they wanted help yet didn't know how to ask for it, the medicine brings it all out of the dark and into the light. For me, this night, at this point, finally, I couldn't be any more willing and ready. Nobody had to force me anymore.

Placed carefully on the ground in front of Sonny, next to the moon, was the staff. It was intricately beaded with the plumage of tiny fluffy eagle breast feathers surrounding the long, jutting horsehair tip. Lying next to the staff was the gourd to be used by all of the singers tonight. Mistakenly called a rattle, Johnny didn't pass up the opportunity to chastise me gently with his signature line: "Babies have rattles, we use a gourd." The sound of the tiny precious stones inside when shaken by experienced hands would sound more and more like tiny bells on Santa's sleigh as the night wore on. Each singer would hold the staff in their left hand, base on the ground, with the fancy tip leaning toward the fire, with the bundle of broomtail sage that is passed around in the beginning so everyone can brush themselves with it to cleanse away the thoughts that didn't belong, and the large eagle feather or fan used for blessing throughout the night. The singer kneels, facing the fire, and shakes the gourd until a beat is established for their four songs. Then the Drummer, seated to the singer's right, joins in, tipping the water drum occasionally to drown the deerskin in water and deepen the tone of the beat.

Next to the gourd lay two fans. One is ornately detailed with multicolored beads on the handle holding 12 long feathers, some Macaw and parrot, and some smaller accent pheasant feathers softening the base. The other fan is a majestic family heirloom, as old as it is rare, made of solid white Bald Eagle tail-feathers. Near them is the big black and white eagle feather that will accompany the staff around the tipi, along with transferring blessings from Sonny and the sponsor during the night.

Centered in front of Sonny, leaning up against the side of the moon, nearly touching the Peyote Chief, rested the 6 inch long, hollowed out eagle bone whistle, used to call for water, to pray to the four directions, and accent certain sacred songs during the long night ahead.

This was the collection of sacred instruments, ready to be taken up as needed and put to use, the same way they have been used for centuries.

CHAPTER 11

INVENTORY, ADMISSION, SUBMISSION, AND HUMILITY

Steps 4, 5, 6, and 7

With everyone situated, settled down, set up, and the Peyote Chief in his place on the altar, Sonny began. First, he welcomed everyone. He started at the doorway and worked his greeting clockwise around the crowded tipi, addressing each person individually, introducing himself to those few who didn't know him, and greeting those he knew with particularly personal attention, along with relatives and close friends. He spoke in his limited English, and conversed in Navajo with those who understood, which was many of them. Even some other tribes represented understood a lot of the similar words from their tribal language. The occasional English words gave clues to his meaning. Throughout the night, he would speak in English enough for me, the sponsor, to understand what he was talking about. But with English as his distant second language, it wasn't easy, for either one of us. I had to listen very attentively to every word to know even remotely what he was saying. For ease of understanding and reading, much of what Sonny taught me, and spoke to me all night, has been re -translated to me by his wife, Lilly-Ann, and presented in a coherent and fluid style so the reader can grasp all of what he is trying to express.

He began explaining the reason for this ceremony. While many there had a good idea, his job is to clarify it so the prayers could be directed accordingly. He mentioned that he had dedicated this new tipi today, that it was now my tipi. Several men made grumbling sounds, sounds of agreement, I would later learn. Many times throughout the night I would hear "MMM", "AHAHH", and, especially "AHO". These were the only common words spoken by many there all night, but were all positive reinforcement to whatever had been said or was being prayed. This deep, almost primitive groaning was completely new to me, but familiar to everyone else. I had to do my best to act like I had heard it all my life. Naturally, before the night was halfway through, Franco was grunting and moaning along with the best of them, often out of order and just to be part of the action.

Sonny went on to tell everyone that I had requested not just a tipi, but also this meeting. He said I wanted to stop my drinking, and he thanked me for the courage to do this. He told us how he appreciated the fact that I chose these ancient ways to address my problem, stating confidently that he knew this way would work, as it had for him, his wife, many of those present, and thousands of others whom he had helped. He said the key was to first admit it, then turn from it, then to have the faith to know that God would take that alcohol away for good. He said that we all have it within ourselves the ability to get sick, and the same ability to get well. It was all about choices and faith. He spoke of the incredible power the mind has, how most of our problems originate in our minds, and likewise, can be cured by our minds.

Sonny spoke directly to me, and reminded me of what I already knew, but had been conveniently forgetting, or, more accurately, denying. "You chose to put that alcohol in your body many years ago. You continued to make that choice. At some point, Robert, the alcohol started making that decision for you, and it is now time for you to start making your own decisions again. The medicine will clear your mind of all of the years of garbage so you can make that decision clearly. Alcohol is a distilled spirit," he explained, "a distilled evil spirit, and when you drink it, you take on that distilled, evil spirit. That spirit is insatiable, always wanting more, taking a piece of your true spirit every day. As that evil spirit grows inside you, the Great and Holy Spirit leaves you, and you slowly become that distilled spirit, more and more miserable, no longer a remnant of your old good-spirit-filled self. To become clean, you must get rid of that evil spirit. That is where the medicine does its work, like the water bird, it dives deep into your soul, spearing that evil, distilled spirit, and carrying it up and out of you, into the fire."

Sonny once again thanked me for sponsoring the meeting. Repetitious gratitude is one of the hallmarks of these gatherings, constant and repeated positive affirmations. He explained that while the ceremony will help me, it also will help everyone here tonight, each one benefiting in their own way by helping me. Then Sonny turned to me and said, "Tell everyone here, Robert, in your own words, the reason for the meeting. What kind of help you want. What we are all to pray for tonight."

At first I was going to go into elaborate detail. Then, as I looked around at the faces of these strangers staring at me, their eyes sparkling from the orange and white flames dancing on the tips of the firewood, I quickly decided to keep it simple, only to the important facts. Nobody wanted to hear the travails of a very sick person down to the gory details. It wasn't necessary. Most of them had been where I was, and they knew the sickness well.

"I own a fairly successful pool building company, at least until recently. I have a wife and three children. I have been drinking excessively for over 25 years. I am a functional drunk, I can maintain a life...or so I thought. It has become very hard lately. I have a real problem with tequila, I no longer enjoy it. My kids hate me, my wife is leaving me. I don't even know what it is like to be sober. I don't know what it is like to think without something clouding my senses...Forever...I'm either drunk, hung over, or both." I took a deep breath. "My last drink was about 20 hours ago, and that is the longest I've been sober in so long I can't remember. And I want a drink right now. I'm done lying, denying, pretending, hoping. I really, really want to quit. I want to stop drinking. I want to be sober. I want to live again, to enjoy myself. I want my family back. I could pretend I am okay, maybe to get your approval, because the truth is, I am very intimidated by this whole ceremony, by all of you here, and everything to do with this tipi. I just wanted a tipi, but I also believe right now that maybe I really wanted more, much more. I want your help. I don't understand this ceremony, but if it can help me, then please just show me what I need to do. I have come to the very end of my rope, and I am ready to hang myself with it. So... if there is any way this ceremony, this medicine, can help me, then please, God, let it happen."

I started to shake from head to toe. I was overcome with emotion. Tears came to my eyes; a huge lump in my throat choked me. I took a few long, deep breaths. I tried to regain my composure, feeling like a fool. I heard the groans, and several "Aho"s, from around the tipi. Still not used to these affirmations, I wasn't sure if they were agreeing with me or completely disgusted with me. I looked down, trying to hide the tears streaming down my face. This was no time to fall apart. I breathed deep and held it, wiping my eyes with my dirty sleeve. I looked back up, then around. Many were looking down, tears coming from their eyes. Lilly-Ann and Sonny were smiling at me, tears on their cheeks.

"I need help," I cried. "Nothing else has worked, I've quit a thousand times. This is my last hope. If it doesn't work, I'll lose my family, my work, my house, probably my life. My doctor tells me my liver is swollen and hard, twice its normal size. My kidneys hurt. I've burned a hole in the lining of the back of my throat from gulping straight tequila morning, noon, and night. I really want to see what being sober is like again, I don't remember. I am so tired of fighting, screaming, yelling, all about nothing. I'm in a rage, a drunken rage, I hate everything and everyone, for no reason...Please, I want your help." Everyone was silent, only the sound of crying, people wiping their eyes, and sniffling. I hoped I hadn't gone too far, as I always seemed to do.

I found out later the significance of what I had just said to this crowd. Everybody there that night was affected by alcohol negatively in an intimate way. Some were still struggling with drinking, afraid to ask for help. Some had quit only very recently and needed the stark reminder of its evil. Many had lost family and close friends to alcohol through poisoning, abuse, car accident, suicide, even murder. All but maybe two or three had prior problems with their abuse of alcohol. They gave me a lot of credit for admitting I needed help. They called me very brave. I didn't think I was brave. I was a mess. I had been brought to this point by forces way beyond my understanding. I had no control over what I was doing. It just happened, pieced together like a puzzle, and I was not the one putting the puzzle together. I certainly didn't plan what was taking place right now. My life was day to day, bottle to bottle. I had an overworked and underpaid guardian angel. I never crashed my vehicles, hadn't been to jail since Father's Day decades ago, never killed anyone, at least not directly, that I could remember.

To think that I was brave, that I had actually put a lot of thought into this moment, that I had meticulously planned out this ceremony so I could bravely come forward and repent of my sins in front of total strangers was not even remotely accurate. A much higher power beyond myself, beyond my comprehension, had brought me to this place, this time, this moment of truth. It may have looked brutally honest, honorably brave, fiercely noble. In reality, I was a crumbling shell of a person ravaged by alcohol and drugs since my early teens, sitting all alone at the end of a rotting tree branch, high up in the air, waiting for it to come crashing to the ground. The party was over, and I really wanted it to be, one way or another.

I gave up, gave it all over to God, whoever He was. I did have old memories of God when I was a child that were pleasant, and memories of contact with an Almighty Force Chino had called the Creator in our humble ceremonies up in the cave. I knew deep down He was there somewhere. I had simply given up hope that He had any personal interest in the day to day activities of people, His great experiment run amuck. Now I prayed that I was wrong, that He did care. I asked Him to forgive me for all that I had done, and asked Him to take away this drinking problem, remove all of the negatives in my life, and put me on that Red Road of Sobriety carved into the top of the moon altar on the floor in front of me. I dropped all illusions I could help myself. I knew my fate was in "God's hands", so I turned it all over to Him right then. I put my complete faith in this illusive God, in the Roadman, Sonny, running this ceremony, in the prayers of the people there, to the power of this ancient ceremony, and the power of this sacred medicine that I was about to take. There was no bravery in any it. None. Just complete submission.

CHAPTER 12

SACRED TOBACCO

Here Long Before Marlboro or Winston

A few people spoke, although I remember very little of what they said. Sonny opened his big cedar box, pulled out two blue and red cloth tobacco pouches, and what looked like two cloth wallets, with dried corn husks folded up inside each one. Johnny walked over and took one pouch and one wallet back around to his seat by the door. Both men carefully chose a particular corn husk from its packet, licked it and moistened it in their mouths to get the husk damp. Then, holding it open in the left hand, used their right hand to pull fresh, pungent, tobacco out of their pouch and fill the husk like a giant rolling paper, creating custom Indian cigars. When done, each passed the tobacco kit to their left, so everyone in the tipi could follow suit and make their own 'smoke'. Totally new to me, like everything else, I watched carefully, making sure I wouldn't look like the complete amateur that I was. I was taken aback by the wetting of the corn husk to make it rollable and stick together, but made sure I did exactly as everyone else was doing.

Between me and the Roadman, Sonny, was the Cedarman, Duane Wilson, a tall, thin Indian from the northern part of this state, very friendly, and well aware of my ignorance of all aspects of the ceremony. He would lean over to me and whisper explanations, warnings, advice, and interpretations throughout the night, a real lifesaver. He carried the cedar bag, filled with dried flat leaf cedar, to be thrown on the fire at many different occasions as the ceremony unfolded, as blessings, prayer,

185

and to clear the air of bad energies. The smell of the smoldering evergreen was like nothing I had experienced--fresh, pungent, sweet, sometimes overwhelming.

Earlier, one of the Elder Navajo women had climbed to a spot on the hillside near the river and pulled up a dead yucca cactus flower stem. She cut it to about 18" long, smoothed its skin, and made a 2" thick lighter stick. Often the lighter stick was very ornate, carved and colored, sometimes beaded, a work of art. She had decided we needed to get back to the basics in this meeting, and insisted we use this traditional yucca lighter. Lying in the center of the firewood V, between the Fireman and the fire, facing east to west, Johnny slid it on the ground and into the base of the flames burning the ends of the wood. He then pulled the lighted stick out, blew on it until the flames were gone, only burning embers crackled at the end of the yucca. He handed the stick to the Doorman to his left, who then blew on the embers, put his newly rolled smoke on the coals, and smoked it to life. The process was repeated by everyone, passing to their left once the smoke was lit.

As the lighter went around, Sonny encouraged anyone who wanted to express themselves to do so now, to ask for prayers, or offer encouragement. Some spoke up, greeting old friends not seen in a long time, some asked for help with their relatives with alcohol problems, and others thanked me again for the meeting, and for my openness. I sucked intently on my poorly rolled smoke so it wouldn't go out, looking down at the ground in embarrassment, not feeling worthy of any compliments or praise, having being delivered here by unknown means.

The smoking of tobacco is integral to history of prayer life of many tribes. Not to be confused with cigarettes or cigars, they use pure tobacco from the plant, often a favorite blend of dark robust tobaccos, mixed with some mild herbs like mullein, anise, spearmint, sage, and others. Used in a pipe in some ceremonies, or rolled in corn husks in the Native American Church ceremony, and hand rolled in cigarette papers for casual smoking outside the ceremonial circle.

Tobacco has been used by North American Indians since the beginning as an instrument of prayer. The prayers are carried to the Creator inside the smoke. The offering of tobacco to the four directions, the placing of tobacco on the deceased, in the tracks of the enemy, spreading over water for fortune, and many other customs are all part of long held beliefs in the power of tobacco. A common blessing is blowing the first exhale on the ground, blessing the Mother Earth, thanking her for the bounty she provides. The second exhale is blown up, to the Creator, in thanksgiving for our life. The third exhale is blown in front and across the smoker to the air, that it may always be pure. And the fourth is blown onto the left hand, then the hand passes that smoke over the body and over the head, blessing one's left side, that we may humble ourselves before the Creator, that our prayers may be answered. The fifth is blown onto the right palm, passing that smoke over the right side of the body and the head with that hand, blessing ourselves that we may always be awake, aware, and sober, remaining on that good Red Road of Sobriety. After that, the smoker then prays about the subject or request of the moment.

Many tribes have varying traditions related to their tobacco smoking and customs, many offering tobacco to one another as a greeting or sign of respect or honor. Usually when someone wants to sponsor a Native American Church meeting, that person will offer a bag of tobacco to the

Roadman that they want to run the ceremony, asking them for help, and explaining the reason for the prayer service.

With everyone's smoke being lit, the Fireman, Johnny, returned the fire stick to its position in front of him, on the ground by the fire, just far enough away that it would go out and not burn all the way down, yet ready to be pushed forward and lit again when the next smoke was called for. The Roadman then encouraged everyone to pray out loud, in their own language, with their smoke as the vehicle to carry the prayers to the heavens. He asked us to pray for me and my request for sobriety, and for any other needs that anyone might have, and to pray that all of our prayers would be answered in the way we wanted. He cautioned us to be very careful in what we asked for, because it would probably be granted, and often people do not fully understand the consequence and responsibility of what we desire. If anyone wasn't sure of a need, he recommended that they simply pray for the sponsor, because that was what we were all here for at this time, and that prayer was going to be fulfilled.

This is a solemn time, the opening prayer. Some prayed loudly, others in a whisper. I could hear at least five completely different languages, none of which I could remotely understand. The confusion of differing words, decibel levels, and intensities was almost chaotic. For me, it was difficult to concentrate on prayer, something I rarely did anymore, and really didn't have a set way of doing it. I knelt there, eyes closed, and tried to eavesdrop on other prayers, those that I could comprehend. Many got very emotional, pouring out their souls, petitioning God for their needs, thanking God for this fire, this church, the Roadman and his wife, this meeting tonight. They prayed for the sponsor, asking forgiveness and mercy, hoping for healing and restoration through this medicine. They cried out for help for friends and family, for relatives dying from drug and alcohol abuse. They were praying for an end to the cycles of abuse among Indian people, for a successful ceremony, for those who died that this ceremony still lives. And that, come sunrise, everyone here will walk out of the tipi completely new. Some simple requests, some complex and confusing, all seemed to be sincere and to come from the heart. I would sneak a peek around occasionally to watch people pray, tears pouring down their faces, genuine sadness and brokenness is what I saw and heard. Everyone was so real. So sincere.

And I saw what I could only describe as faith in action, as these people truly believed God was listening and He would answer them. Based on their past experiences with this ceremony, they knew it to be true. And I wanted to believe, I wanted their faith, I wanted what they had, their humility and conviction. But, as much as I had told them and myself that I was surrendering it all to this night, I was still suspect; my skepticism ran deep. I really wanted *something,* but had been disappointed so many times before, I was afraid it could happen again. But as I watched and listened to these prayers, I did have hope. What I was seeing was an outward manifestation of faith, hope, love, and charity. So I latched real tight to that glimmer of hope, and settled in for the ride.

Over the years I had seen and heard people pray at different venues and circumstances. Churches of every flavor, revivals, gatherings, funerals, weddings, communes, I had seen it all. So many people pray loud, use great flowing prose, long words, practiced phrases, impressive

189

words, telling stories to God as if He needs to be filled in on our activities, sounding too much like the dreaded family Christmas letter from the relative that relates every sordid and mundane detail of their life over the last 12 months. For some reason private communication to Our Maker has become a contest of poetic phraseology, and the incessant need to include everyone within yelling distance every minute particle of our life, and to inform God of these uninteresting factoids as if He has never heard of us before, like He has been on a vacation in a foreign galaxy and needs to be updated on every tiny aspect of our boring lives. They do not mean what they say, and have no expectation of any results from their so called prayer. It is all for show, it doesn't come from their heart, and it falls on deaf ears.

I saw no sign of that tonight. Not one. I was the only phony there, as far as I could tell. I was the only one looking around at others; nobody was watching to see if they were getting an audience. All were engrossed in their personal communication with the same God that had answered their prayers and ultimately led them to this ceremony on this night in my tipi. Maybe some were loud, but not for any other reason than that's how they prayed. The prayers weren't eloquent, fancy, or poetic. They were simple, and their simplicity revealed their sincerity. They were praying from the depths of their souls, their humility was genuine, and that humbleness before God was refreshing, so much more powerful than the prideful prayers I was used to tolerating. The opening prayer smoke set the tone for the whole ceremony, and it looked like everyone was in tune.

As the smokes got smaller, the prayers slowly got quieter, until, gradually, the last person ended with an "Aho" and an "Amen." Then the Roadman instructed the Fireman to collect the dead smokes on the north side of the tipi and put the collection, ash toward the fire, at the very end of the moon, at the base of the 100 year mark, while the Doorman collected the smokes on the south side of the tipi and placed them at the base of the beginning of the moon, at year one.

CHAPTER 13

PEYOTE, THE SACRED SACRAMENT

Good Medicine for the Soul

The Drummer brought the three containers of medicine and set it in front of the Roadman. Sonny took out a fresh bundle of broomtail sage he had picked back home in New Mexico, wrapped together with a red thread at the bottom like a bouquet of flowers. He put it to his face and inhaled deeply the strong sage smell, then brushed himself off with it: arms, back, head, legs. Then he took a tiny leaf off and popped it into his mouth to chew up, all a cleansing ritual everyone would copy as the bundle was passed to his left. He then took four tiny spoonfuls of the dried peyote powder into his hand, dumped the pile from his hand to his mouth and began chewing. He took a small handful of the cut-up pieces of fresh picked peyote cactus and tossed them into his mouth, munching away with a big smile on his face. He dipped the clear glass antique tea cup into the peyote tea bucket, scooped up a cup, finished chewing the other, and swallowed the still warm tea, drank three more cups of the tea, then passed the collection of refreshments to his left, to the Cedarman, who repeated the process.

While I was sitting there anticipating ingesting the medicine, I got this sudden sense of irony about my trepidation. And not just my preconceived notions about peyote, but more how society at large has been conditioned to have severely negative prejudices about this mysterious cactus, while millions are addicted to various forms of psychotic and narcotic drugs, and it is culturally acceptable, as long as it is prescribed by a physician. I thought of plenty of so called "pillars of the community" that abused their prescriptions constantly, yet I never heard of anybody that abused this Sacred Sacrament. I shook my head at the sadness of it all, then glanced over to study Duane as I awaited my turn.

As Duane, the Cedarman, my new mentor, ingested his medicine, I leaned toward him and, trying to be as nonchalant as possible, quietly asked if I had to take as much as he and Sonny had taken, or could I start off slow. As he ate and drank, he discreetly let me know that it is all up to the individual how much to take, that the number four is very important, yet not mandatory, and four did not necessarily mean four full spoons, four full pieces, or four full cups of tea. The motion and intention of four was really the only issue, and even that was subjective. He told me the medicine itself would dictate how much to take. I would know when it was enough, and if I overdid it, it would come right back out. Relieving words, but not comforting, and hardly definitive. It was all I got.

I put four half spoonfuls of the powder in my hand, then added four of the tiniest pieces of fresh cactus I could find. I tossed the handful deep into my mouth, and started chewing. After watching Sonny smiling ear to ear while he ate his medicine, for some bizarre reason not based in any reality I was aware of, I thought the medicine was going to taste good, despite years of experience I had with it; there was no way to disguise or improve the physical reaction to its incredibly bitter taste. As soon as the tiniest bit of the gritty powder hit my taste buds on my tongue, I had an uncontrollable urge to gag that started in the base of my abdomen, pushing up against my diaphragm, sending waves of nausea through my entire body, choking me as if I had thrust two fingers down my throat. I clamped my mouth tight and consciously pushed the vomit back down with my mind, breathing deeply and trying hard to think of better things. I managed to stop the convulsions enough to save face, and even cracked a fake smile to make me look good. I had to keep chewing, as the fresh cactus was just the right size to get stuck halfway down, and the powder was closer to grinding gravel in an old blender. There seemed to be no way to clear it all out of my mouth without more gagging and backward hiccups. The involuntary physical reaction to the many alkaloids and extreme bitter taste was nearly impossible to control.

Trying to maintain composure, I took the little glass cup and dipped it into the tea bucket, attempting to only scoop up a small amount, I managed to slop some over the cup. I brought it to my lips, pretending it was going to be delicious, and poured it in. To my amazement, it wasn't horrible, not even bad. And because it was still a little warm, having been boiled a short time ago, it felt good in my mouth, and soothing to my throat. I dunked it again, topping it off, and swished it around in my mouth, rinsing out all of the tiny bits of gravel and chunks of bitter cactus stuck in and behind my teeth, then swallowed it down. Two more cups managed to fully clean out my mouth of all of the fresh and dried peyote. It was surprisingly refreshing. I treated it like a cocktail, and it worked. I had swallowed much more shocking and revolting drinks over the years, this was hardly unbearable. It was warm, soothing, and infinitely better than eating the powder or chewing the fresh cactus, so I was fine.

I was going to take another cupful when Duane nudged my arm, signaling me to pass it on. I sent the medicine to Franco, who was chomping at the bit to have a turn. Naturally he loved it all, and kept telling me all night how the powder reminded him of almonds, something I will never understand. Duane then warned me to be moderate my first time, this was a very strong tea, and undoubtedly Sonny would be fixing up a special powerful healing mix for me after midnight to deal with my alcoholism. I decided then I would only drink the tea, and pass on the other two versions of the medicine.

CHAPTER 14

PEYOTE SONGS

Ancient Healing Prayers of Worship

After the medicine had made it all of the way around, the Drummer put it back in its spot by the moon, took up his drum and stick, and sat down. He blew into the ridge of the drum, forcing air through the skin, and trapping it inside, tightening up the drum head for a more forceful beat. Sonny stood up, gathered up his staff, feather, gourd, and the bundle of sage, and knelt down. He announced to all of us he was going to start singing. He encouraged everyone to sing, and when the staff and drum were passed as far as the doorway, he would decide if it would proceed, or if it was time to begin another part of the ceremony, depending on how long it took to get to there. He once again thanked me, thanked everyone, and recommended that we all relax and enjoy ourselves, and let God dictate the flow of the meeting. He put the sage, the feather, and the staff in his left hand, pushed the base of the staff into the ground and leaned it forward, shaking the gourd vigorously to start, then slowing it down to a one/two beat, signaling the Drummer to follow his lead, and proceeded with the first of the four opening songs, songs from long ago and not far away.

The opening song that started the worship, *Hayatinayo*, was obviously well known to all but me and Franco, and set the pace for the next three. After he was applauded with the customary groans and "Ahos", he then traded his instruments for the drum and stick, so the Drummer could sing his four songs. After that, the Drummer kneeled in the Roadman's seat, the Roadman in his, and the Drummer, Orlando, kept the beat for Duane, the Cedarman next to me, for his four songs. Normally, I would be the next singer, as sponsor, and the next person in the circle. However, this being my first meeting, with virtually no remote familiarity to any of the vast and endless amount of beautiful Peyote songs that have been sung over the past hundreds of years, obviously I wasn't even tempted to fake it, being overly self-conscious enough as it was.

Duane passed the staff, sage bundle, eagle feather, and gourd to me, quietly instructing me to keep all of that in my left hand, and make sure I didn't drop anything. On his lead, I put the staff in front of me into the ground, leaned it toward me, then ran my right hand from the base of it, straight up the staff, brushing the horsehair tuft sprouting out the top, and in the same flowing motion, brought my right hand over the top of my head, then touched my chest over my heart, then my stomach, then my knees, then gently tapped my chest again two more times, a symbolic gesture bringing the blessings of the staff and its songs and prayers to me and into my heart. As I did this, Duane set the drum on the ground in front of me, and rested the drumstick on the top, steadying it so it didn't roll off onto the ground, a major taboo.

All eyes were on me as the staff was handed to me, everyone curious to see if the newcomer who owned the tipi knew any of the songs since it was highly unusual to own a tipi and to never have been in one. It was even more unusual to sponsor a meeting that is also your first meeting altogether. Many go years, sometimes their whole life, never sponsoring a meeting for themselves, but go to support those who do. But I took the cake on this night, not only did I own the tipi, I had never been in a tipi before, never been in a peyote meeting before in a tipi, never been in this ceremony before, was the sponsor of my first meeting, and didn't know the first word of any of the traditional songs that make up most of the ceremony. So when I blessed myself with the staff, indicating that I was passing and not singing, their amazement grew, probably their confusion and possibly disgust or mistrust, at least that's how I felt in my twisted mind. But my heart was fully into it now, and I think they could see that. I wasn't a pro, and didn't pretend to be. I wanted help, and it had been offered, so there I was, beginner of beginners.

I passed the staff to Franco, number two beginner in a row. He whispered in his loud voice, "What the heck am I supposed to do? Try singing?" Too many words for me to grasp at the time, knowing full well everyone was staring at us and could hear his feeble attempt at being quiet. I told him to do exactly as I had done, and pass it on. He took the staff and accessories, nearly dropping everything, while I blushed bright red with embarrassment. He snickered just enough to get a look from Lilly-Ann that we could almost hear and feel without even looking back at her. He put his head down, his tail between his legs, and told me, "Sorry, man, so sorry." I just nodded and passed the drum and stick in front of him, keeping my hand on the rolling drumstick until he had passed the staff and grabbed the drum to pass it along.

The man to Franco's left held the staff and motioned to Orlando with a nod that he was going to sing, and needed a Drummer. Orlando walked to Franco's seat, and stood there. Franco was still looking down like a dejected puppy, so I nudged him. "Franco, the Drummer needs to sit there to play for the next guy. You gotta move."

Franco looked up, smiling ear to ear and announced, not quietly, "Hey, brother," he practically yelled, "I'll move over, man, there's plenty of room for you here." Then he added, "Move over, brother, let's give the man some room." The entire tipi erupted in laughter, first muffled, then loud. I looked over at Sonny and Lilly-Ann; they were both grinning widely, while Johnny just shook his head. Duane bumped his arm against mine, leaned close to my ear, and told me that Franco had to walk around to Orlando's seat while he drummed. I knew Franco had to move, and assumed Franco understood what that meant. Whenever someone sang, the Drummer sat in the seat to their right, and the person whose seat he was in went to sit in the Drummer's original seat, between Sonny and Lilly-Ann. This not only opened up enough space for the Drummer to be comfortable, it also enabled the Roadman and his wife a few seconds of time to share some words in confidence, humor, or just encouragement with nearly everyone in the tipi.

I explained to Franco where he had to go, and he jumped up like a jackrabbit and started walking to his right directly to Orlando's seat. Immediately, several people spoke up at once, "Stop! Other way!" they ordered. Duane reached out and grabbed Franco's arm as he was scurrying past us. He turned him around and sent him clockwise around the whole tipi to his new seat.

Franco waltzed around, laughing all the way, enjoying every second of his popularity. "I'm sorry...again!" he said, as people chuckled with him.

He spun around and sat down. Again a group of people shouted at him, "Turn around!" Franco looked at me, then at everyone, confused. He turned to face the wall of the tipi, when Lilly-Ann tried to set him straight. She told him to stand up, then spin in a counterclockwise circle, one time, then sit down. Franco spun around like a clumsy ballerina, then sat down, to everyone's relief and delight.

Duane explained to me that Franco had turned around in a complete circle in his walk around the tipi, as he was sitting down. He had to be unwound, or he would get all spiritually tied up all night. Not only must you always move the correct direction, you never turn your back to the fire or the medicine, and you never complete a circle when coming or going from your seat...if you do, you must turn back, restoring your orientation to the fire. That moment of lighthearted humor disappeared faster than it appeared, and it was back to the serious business at hand.

The drumming and singing had started. I watched Franco talking to Lilly-Ann across the tipi as the Drummer pounded away, and saw her face go from smiling, to anger, to smiling, so rapidly I worried what Franco was saying. Soon the four songs ended, and she sent him clockwise to his seat, everyone watching to see if he would circle again. He didn't. The staff moved on, along with the drum and Drummer, four songs per person, on and on it went. In about one and a half hours of singing, it made it to the door. The Fireman held the staff as Sonny announced he would let it continue on back to him, then decide if it was time to call for water. As Johnny passed the staff across the doorway, Sonny rolled another smoke. The Fireman brought him the fire stick. He lit it and prayed aloud, passing it to his wife, then Duane, then to me, continuing on with his loud and passionate prayer until the smoke was tiny. Then he placed the smoke against the moon in front of him, to the right of the Chief.

The songs and drumming continued on. It amazed me how each singer was so different in tone, style, language and intensity. It was obvious who had been singing for a long time, although this ceremony really didn't have any inexperienced singers. If they held the staff and called for the drum, they knew their stuff. Fortunately for me, this meeting was filled with seasoned veterans of this method of prayer, so there were no distractions or problems. Everyone knew what to do. Many of the songs were very special, some were passed down for generations, sacred songs of worship, prayers of healing that have been sung for centuries, bringing with them history, tradition, and ancient words no longer used except in holy prayers of requests for help from God.

The first round of songs was usually simple, single or double chorus basic songs to start the ceremony. As the night wore on, the songs got stronger, and after round one, they also got longer. At first, they sounded like chants to me, words without meaning, and a lot of the same chants just switched around a little. As I listened closer, really paying attention, I realized how complex and structured they really were. Duane occasionally explained a few words to me, and alerted me when someone was singing a song of healing and help meant only for me, the sponsor. Most of the primary words are used solely in Peyote songs. The words *Heyowicheeniyo*, *Wicheeniyo*, songs named *Heyowinniho* and *yanahiano*, and many variations of them are said to be sacred spirit-calling words and songs unique to the peyote ceremony, universal among all tribes, and used only with holiness and respect. The exact meaning of each is slightly different to each fireplace. Many songs are sung in the Navajo, Winnebago, Comanche, Pawnee and Apache language, and some are sung with Indian vocals in a very high pitched style with English words interspersed in such a way I almost can't recognize them. Many of the songs have English phrases about Jesus; "He is the only way", "Jesus, our Lord and Savior", "You are the Son of God", and other Christian words in them that completely took me by surprise, but in a good way.

Deep in my subconscious was an unwarranted fear born of my early years in Catholic school, especially reinforced by one certain nun that used to teach the religion class. She was a red haired, red faced traditional ultra-conservative nun with a strong Irish brogue who was adamant about warning all of her students about hell, and how most of us were destined to wind up there, fire and all. When I was in first and second grade, she used to scare me so badly with her descriptions of the devil, I sometimes could not sleep alone and had to crawl into my parents' bed. She was detailed and graphic, and loved to see children terrified. And she hated boys, and made no attempt to hide that fact. For whatever reason, she had a special loathing of me, and constantly used me as an example of who was most likely to end up burning in Satan's fire, as the demons whipped me and screamed at me day and night. She burned a fear of paganism deep into my young, impressionable brain, and her idea of pagan was anyone not devout Catholic. She screamed about the heathen Indians who still were surviving somewhere in the United States despite her church's best attempts to convert these savages and their hideous forms of idol worship, evil witchcraft, and native rituals.

Even though this was the ranting of a lunatic who eventually wound up in a sanctuary for the mentally insane, she caused a lot of damage to many innocent ears, mine being two of them. Way inside me was a fear of the unknown about religious taboos, even though my rational mind knew better. So much so, that just hearing the word Jesus in some of the songs and many of the prayers gave me a sense of safety and assurance, truly a guilt ridden, Catholic response to a holy and sacred Indian prayer service. Rather than try to analyze it, I wisely let it go, all of it, feeling safe and secure in the absolute knowledge that this was a real, true, spiritual experience, and not about to let a repressed memory of a disturbed psychopath ruin it for me.

There are four standard sets of songs in the ceremony sung by the Roadman, usually Esikwita or Mescalero Apache songs. *Hayatinayo*, the opening song, *Yahiyano*, sung before midnight water, *Wakaho*, for Morning Water, at sunrise, and *Gayatina*, the closing song at the end of the ceremony. These are the only required songs. All of the rest are randomly chosen by the singer at the moment they begin to sing. Most singers know many, many songs and practice them during the week, at regular sessions where members gather, tie up a drum, and make it an event, while others only sing when they can, while driving, between jobs, or other spare moments. Some sing only at ceremonies, yet attend so many ceremonies they sound like they work on it day and night. Many have songs ready to sing, then when the staff is in their hand, can't remember one word. They shake the gourd and sing a recall chant, "Hey ney hey ney. hey ney, hey ney", as the Drummer thumps away, waiting for the song to begin. Soon enough, the spirit puts a song on their lips, and they open up. It is always a song relevant to the moment, to the ceremony at that hour, and to the struggles the sponsor might be going through. Rather than try to set up songs for each round, the regulars don't even think about what they will sing. They just join in, in full force with the other songs, creating a loud and beautiful chorus of voices that sound like this group here and now has practiced together daily for months. When their time comes, they allow the medicine to choose the songs, and they comply. The result is phenomenal. The singing and drumming improve all night with each song, and the sound is like nothing I had ever heard. More than 40 people singing unknown songs, loud, fast, and perfectly, never missing a beat. Songs of power and healing from a different century, reverberating in front and behind me, the fire crackling in the center…an experience of true power in itself, and only the beginning of what was about to happen.

Occasionally the singer with the staff would pray aloud after finishing his songs, and express himself with thoughts about the meeting and his experience with alcohol, and its devastating effect on his life. Just when I thought I had heard the worst story, a middle-aged Indian shared his recent experience that left us all in tears. He had three beautiful daughters, one with a new baby, his granddaughter. On a recent evening he was returning from a visit with friends with his wife, their three daughters and the new baby, when a drunk driver fell asleep at the wheel, crossed over the center divide, and hit his car head on, with no warning and no way to avoid it. His wife, three daughters, and granddaughter were all killed in the crash, in an instant. Sobbing as he continued, he tried to find a reason. One minute, his life was better than it had ever been, everyone was happy, home life was good, his son-in-law had a great job and had just started running ceremonies. In fact, that night his son-in-law was taking care of fire in a meeting when it happened. He had felt it happen, when he couldn't get the fire to burn;

it would only smoke. He knew he had lost someone, but didn't know it was everyone. The Indian wept as he lamented, "Why did I live, and God take my family home? The distilled spirit has another win, and humanity is dealt another loss, and all for what?" he begged.

The staff was passed, and the songs continued. As the first stages of the effects of the medicine kicked in, there was a feeling of sadness and melancholy, almost sleepiness. Immobilized in our seats, the singing got more intense, old songs came out, songs of cries for help, songs begging the Creator to have pity on us, to save us all from the ravages of life. Some were in primitive Indian dialect, rarely used songs, prayers from another time. I listened intently, watching the singers give their all, holding back nothing, certainly not their tears. I passed the staff again to Franco, who by now was curled up on his blanket, sort of kneeling, sort of bowing down, rocking back and forth, grunting and moaning with every "Aho" and affirmation that went around.

When the drumming first began, I had hoped it wouldn't last long, and was disappointed when Sonny said it would go around again. If this was the bulk of the ceremony, I was going to go insane listening to it. But by now, it was sounding so good, each new song was better than the last. Figuring out the basic beat, and some of the standard chorus and response words, soon all of us were involved with every song, including me. After it had passed the door for the second time, it was late into the night. Sonny got up and brought the medicine bowls and bucket to me, and told me to have some more, so I wouldn't get tired. Not the least bit interested in taking more, it didn't matter. After taking a minimum of powder and fresh cactus, four more cups of tea went down slower than last time. Duane then signaled me to pass it to my left, so it could follow the staff back to the Roadman.

Only a few songs later, the medicine hit me completely differently, my mind shifting into full gear as my body faded away. The songs took on meaning; the words became clear and understandable. I could hear the drum behind me, and the gourd in front of me. Faces were lit up by the dancing firelight and looked hauntingly familiar, as if I had been here with these people before. The shadow of the staff against the tipi looked like a single feather on the head of each singer. I stared into the coals of the fire, and started seeing details of entire villages, cliff side dwellings, hundreds of people scurrying around, doing their daily chores. The scene would change as a liquid was poured over the village, and the people melted. I looked up to see where the liquid came from, and there was nothing. Looking back, the coals were changed again. Thoughts of alcohol devouring entire communities filled my brain. Not wanting to think "hallucination", I looked around at everyone. They seemed to nod at me in agreement, as if they, too, had seen the melting village. I began to think of the years my life had been devastated by alcohol. Everybody's story was the same, just varying degrees of destruction. Why was I participating in the total destruction of my marriage, my family, my job, and my life? Finally I was letting myself think this through, allowing my mind to stop denying reality. This was suicide, and it had to end.

I looked directly through the flames and at the old Kiowa Medicine Man. His name was James Red Hawk, full blooded Kiowa from Oklahoma. He grew up in this church, his grandmother was born in a tipi, and he was proud of these ways. Stubbornly traditional, he hated anything slightly different from the way he was taught. He had told me he had a bout with drinking, but decided over 20 years ago it was giving in to the white man's curse, and returned to this church, in honor of his ancestors. He came to this ceremony because his mother was dying, and some of his relatives were so drunk they didn't care. He was brutally honest with me, saying in his mom's day they wouldn't have allowed a half breed like me in this ceremony, but he understood my need.

As I watched him sing, his appearance changed. It was if he took on the spirits of his ancestors. His songs in Kiowa came thundering out of his soul, singing more intently and louder than anyone. In between choruses he would let out a sort of scream, or howl, like a war cry. As he did, others would answer him, and the entire tipi erupted in a yipping, like distant coyotes. I could feel a huge change in the air, as he called on the spirits in song. Sonny leaned over, picked up the eagle-bone, and belted out four sharp whistles, followed by loud groans from many of the men. Duane pulled out a big handful of cedar from his bag and tossed it into the coals. As the smoke swirled up out of the fire in a snakelike coil, sweeping clockwise up the center of the tipi, the canvas started shaking violently around us. A strong wind had just descended on the river valley, and was whipping around us, tweaking the tipi back and forth, separating the canvas from the poles and slapping it back against them. The wind dropped down the open flap, and scattered the cedar smoke all around, engulfing us in a cloud of sweet incense. Red Hawk, sensing the energy, sang that much louder, bringing everyone into the intensity of the moment. I looked around, trying to read everyone's reaction, making sure we weren't going to fly away. All eyes were on the fire, and the smoke played games with their faces. Looking at Franco didn't help. He was glaring up at the top of the quaking tipi with fear in his eyes. I was not afraid, but I could feel something in the air, something powerful, something good was coming, but I couldn't put my finger on it.

The drumming stopped after he sang his fourth song. Instead of passing the staff to the next singer, Red Hawk began to tremble, tears falling down his face slowly, then he started to sob. He cleared his throat and prayed loudly in his native tongue, the few English words sprinkled into his discourse exposing enough of his intense sadness that the few of us who didn't understand his language still clearly interpreted the gravity of his plea to the Creator. I tried to sit up, realizing I had slowly slouched to a very unacceptable position. Finally accepting that I could not move a muscle, I gave up trying and mentally sat up at attention and listened.

In the years to come, it seemed I played this segment of the ceremony over and over again in my mind. I could recall it so easily.

When the Kiowa finished praying, everything went silent. Dead silent. The rain let up, the wind stopped howling, the fire burned soundlessly, even the river seemed to stop flowing. All I could hear was the subdued crying of many of the people in the tipi surrounding me.

The Roadman, Sonny, stood up to speak. I could hear his joints cracking as he straightened up, his body complaining about sitting still for hours being warmed in front by the fire and chilled behind by the frigid and uninvited air sneaking under the canvas. The night was slipping into early morning. He directed his words to nobody in particular, more to all of us, spread out in that tipi on the mountaintop, and all of humanity crowded on the planet around us. The fire heated his words so they became seared into our hearts.

"We, as humans, have lost our way. We have gone off course, floating uselessly with the wind. We have no center, we have no balance. Our past, present, and future have become one straight line going nowhere. The circle is broken.

"Because we are no longer in touch with the Creation, we have lost contact with the Creator. Our souls cry out for peace, for harmony, for balance, for love, and we ignore the cry, getting farther and farther from the earth, the animals, this beautiful, wonderful world that God created for us, neglecting, rejecting, destroying, and we are paying for it in our own miserable existence. Using drugs, alcohol, sex, anything and everything to hide from ourselves, from God, from each other, trying to fill that God-shaped hole in our hearts. We have forgotten the simple solution written in our souls that can restore us and our world back to sanity.

"It is time to take our shoes off, run barefoot on the earth again, to feel the dirt and grass between our toes, the water from the creek cooling our throats and soothing our souls, the air from the wind in the trees refreshing our lungs, to get back to the basics, to what we really are about, to restore our connection to the Creator. To live every day like it matters, like we matter, that everyone matters. Helping everyone we can, giving back more than we take away, remembering our close ties to the earth, and how to live on it. This used to be normal. We didn't talk about it, it just happened. Now if I say these things, people think I am strange, crazy, someone out of touch with reality, when, in fact, that is the only true reality. All of this distraction and technology is pulling us away from that which is real, and confusing our spirit into thinking we don't need God or His Creation anymore.

"All of us--red, white, black, and yellow--we are all native to this earth, somewhere. We have forgotten that. Some of us by force, some by ignorance, others by convenience. But we are suffering from this forgotten fact now. All of us. We have to return to the basics now or we will drown in this rising sea of ignorance and isolation, becoming so intelligent we have lost all of our common sense and forgot how to survive in the real world, which is still there, just beyond the gated community and city limits.

"No other solution will work. Not another invention, not another law, not a better politician. We have to return to what has always worked for all of our ancestors, no matter where we come from. What we are doing now isn't just failing, it is destroying us. We are all dying from the inside out. The generations yet to come are relying on us to get back on that good path, that red road of sobriety."

His eyes connected directly with mine when he said "sobriety". A sudden self-induced feeling of shame came over me when that word connected with my conscience. That conscience that until this moment had been drowned out with alcohol. Lots of alcohol. I looked away from him and around the tipi only to find all eyes on me. I closed my eyes, a big mistake, as that started the movie in my head with me as star villain. I watched a short clip of my wife and three children watching my latest drunken rage in confusion and terror. Not a physical rage, but an equally devastating verbal assault against anything and everything my pickled brain could muster up. Ashamed and embarrassed, I opened my eyes, convinced everyone had just watched the same replay. Perhaps the

Roadman did. When I looked up at him, he nodded as if in agreement with my self-disgust.

The words he had spoken went deep into me, even though I had heard this type of talk many times before. Almost too simple, too cliché. But deep inside I knew that as basic as what he had said was, it was all I needed, all we needed. Everyone. Not just users and abusers. All of us. It was simple, yet truly was more profound than anything I had heard or read to this point. It suddenly made sense, because I wasn't trying to analyze it, parse his words, find fault in what he said, or look so deep I went right through it.

"What we have done is complicate and confuse life, trying so hard to improve it we have completely lost sight of what it is all about. We want more. It is never enough. Happiness has been replaced with consumption. The more we have, the more we want. All problems can be remedied with a pill or a drink. We've even created nonexistent problems so someone can make a pill to fix it. Alcohol is only the obvious addiction we use to fill our spiritual voids. People are addicted to everything. Moderation is laziness, obsession is ambition, excess is success. Yet this formula, like all imposters, is failing. People are dropping like flies. Marriages are falling apart, the economy is collapsing, society is morally imploding trying to survive on tolerance of all, and relativism for absolutism. Humanity is isolating itself through indirect contact with new inventions, and government claims to be the answer to everything as it methodically takes control of every aspect of our lives. The solution is not more of the same. The solution is where it has always been. Far from the maddening crowd away from cement and asphalt. Hidden under every rock and leaf, coursing through the rivers and streams, at the mountaintops and on the valley floor, deep inside God's ultimate dream made manifest in His Creation is the secret, the solution to all of our ills. Return humbly to the simple beauty only found in Creation, and we will once again find ourselves, and once again find our Creator."

The Roadman threw a big handful of cedar onto the hot coals and sat down in silence. The cedar crackled and burned, sending a swirling cloud of sweet smelling perfume in clockwise circles over the fire, spreading out among all of us and pouring out the open flap at the top of the tipi. But it wasn't the smoke in my eyes that made the tears run down my face. It had been decades since I had felt my heart break, and it actually felt good. At least I could feel something.

Sonny announced that when the staff returned to the Drummer's seat, he was going to go outside and pray to the four directions, blowing on the eagle bone whistle at each of the four prayer locations. As he walked around the tipi in prayer, at this sacred hour, he was going to ask God to help me with my problem, to end the hold alcohol had on me. When he returned to his seat, as the Drummer sang, anyone who needed to be excused could go outside at that time. When the Drummer had concluded his four songs, everyone needed to be in their seat, so the Fireman could sweep up the tipi and prepare for the Midnight Water.

Then it hit me like a rock. I got a glimpse of where I was, what I was going through, and why. Why so many Indians had come to this meeting for a stranger in search of sobriety, why they came to support me. Everyone was in the same boat, not just this group, not even all Indian nations as a whole, but all people who fight this problem; everyone wanted answers, help, guidance. We all have a common enemy. It is no longer the Spaniards, not the Europeans, not the new Americans. This enemy is unforgiving. It is relentless, strong, and surrounds us all. It is a spiritual battle of unimaginable power. It seems as if it cannot be killed, or even wounded, yet it will kill us. Many of us are already wounded. And we are ready to convince ourselves it is okay to give in.

Everyone here was hoping this meeting might be the one at which the medicine will show us the way out, once and for all. This wasn't about me, it was for me. To everyone else it was bigger than that, this was about an enemy so strong it seemed invincible. Many had been to sobriety meetings. But this one was different. I had opened a door, I had put all of my cards on the table. My naiveté, my ignorance of this ceremony was my saving grace. I hid nothing, nor tried to make it trivial. I knew I was dying, and I was willing to say or do anything to change. That was what would open the door to solutions heretofore hidden. The pride and, ironically, the shyness of Native people along with cultural taboos, prevented them from really admitting how bad things were, even if everyone already knew. Total repentance and submission were necessary for real healing to take place. Tonight, I, of all people, had the chance to bring on a long awaited miracle only because of my total ignorance, forced humility, and absolute desperation.

Sonny walked outside to pray to the four directions as the next to last singer poured out his heart in song and prayer. The possibility that something truly amazing was going to happen felt so strong, I was shivering with anticipation. My faith was so strong, nothing could suppress it, and this was a beautiful feeling, a confidence that was so overwhelming it could conquer all demons, I was certain of it now. I prayed out loud as he sang, begging God to complete this belief, to conclude this desire, to free me and all of us of this evil repressive spirit, and fill us again with His Spirit. I was nearly yelling my prayer as the Drummer stopped, but I didn't care. I continued my cry until I was done, then looked down at the ground in front of me. The affirmative moans and grunts gave me a feeling of belonging right where I was, at that very moment of my life, finally.

As the staff was sent to the Drummer, the last man to sing placed the drum in front of himself so Orlando could conclude the second round of songs. Nearly everyone stood up, stretching, moaning, and taking deep breaths, putting on their jackets or wrapping blankets around themselves, and headed for the door, single file, clockwise, one after another, ducking out into the cold, damp midnight air.

As I followed Franco out the low tipi door, from the warmth of the fire into the chilling darkness, I got an overwhelming sense of being alive, truly alive, a feeling I hadn't had for more years than I could remember. The moonless night was clear of the storm clouds enough to expose millions of stars winking at us. The brisk, freshly cleansed high mountain air filled my hungry lungs. The river gurgled and rushed by, sounding restless and aggressive with the new rain runoff adding to its strength. Someone threw a handful of dry pine needles and twigs into the nearly dead campfire, bringing the drowning coals back to life. Then more wood was added to restore its flames to their earlier glory. People gathered around it and lit cigarettes, talking softly as others went into the darkness to relieve themselves, myself included.

As I stood far away in the darkness, eliminating the water I had guzzled earlier in the evening, I stared at the tipi and could hear Orlando singing loudly inside to the drumbeat. I could see the eerie silhouette of the remaining people kneeling inside the tipi against the canvas, lit up by the flashing fire in the middle. This scene brought to me ancient memories of a similar scene I had not before witnessed, yet was oddly familiar and comforting, as if I saw it every night of my life. I watched it with fascination for what seemed forever, but was only a few seconds.

Wandering back to the campfire, a woman approached me from behind. "You are a very powerful man, and very brave. It takes a brave and humble man to admit his addictions as you have done, and the help you are going to get will free up that power you have inside you. You have more power than you know. You only need to recognize it and use it. You are taking the first step now by regaining power over yourself and your destiny. You can no longer relinquish your power to evil spirits...you have to claim it as your own."

For some reason, I couldn't bring myself to turn and look at her. She was behind me, and her words went into both ears like a surround sound theater. Her voice was even-toned, not deep, and certainly not shrill. I tried to detect a defining accent, something familiar, as there were only a handful of women here tonight. I could not respond. I didn't know how.

She walked back into the darkness, and I returned to the fire, where I found Franco entertaining everyone and getting much too loud for the mood of the people gathered. I stood back in the shadows so I wouldn't stir him up more with my presence. Orlando finished his last song, and we all filed back inside, going to our left and clockwise around the fire, each person dropping out of line at their respective seat, until the door rolled shut once again. Duane stood up and threw a big handful of dried cedar onto the coals, announcing that it was for all of us who had gone out, meaning we all had to bless ourselves with the smoke spiraling up the middle of the tipi. It involved us reaching with both hands toward the fire, and symbolically pulling the smoke back to our body, splashing the smoke on our face, torso, and legs, repeating it for a total of four times, cleansing ourselves from anything unwelcome we may have accidentally picked up while outside.

As I was pulling the cedar to me, I glanced around at everyone, using the freshly stoked flames for bright light, focusing at the women sitting down. I could not pick out who had spoken to me outside, not being familiar with any of them, even the process of elimination turned up nobody. The voice was so strong, yet culturally neutral, and fit no face I was searching, not that I had a clue what I was looking for.

I thought about what she said, but not too deeply, because I knew I wasn't brave, and I definitely didn't feel powerful, so for now I just let it go. All of a sudden it occurred to me I forgot to search my truck for the missing bottles of tequila I had to have earlier. Not only did I forget to look, I forgot how badly I needed a drink. The odd part was that at this moment, I had absolutely no desire to drink. In fact, if I thought about it, it had no appeal to me at all. It felt incredibly liberating not to want to have to drink, no matter how temporary it might be.

CHAPTER 15

MIDNIGHT WATER

The Water of Life

Johnny swept up the whole floor. He moved every instrument and utensil, bowl, and bucket. He fanned those areas clean with the eagle feather. His slow, methodical sweeping with the short, decorated peyote broom erased all footprints and traces of activity. He gathered up the remnants of all of the smokes everyone had prayed with, at both ends of the altar and a few near Sonny at the center of the moon. Duane gave Sonny the cedar bag and he stood near the front of the fire, said a silent prayer, threw a big handful of evergreen into the glowing coals, then tossed all of the handmade smokes into the burning cedar, creating a temporary burst of bright flames. When he did this, Sonny explained he was putting our prayers into this location, this fire, and one day, in the future, others will sit here by the fire and pick up our prayers again where we had left them. Johnny was cleaning away the first half of the ceremony, washing away my past, freshening up for Midnight Water, a very sacred part of the night that was coming up, preparing the church for the miracle about to happen. He was finishing out the day, ending its problems, and beginning a new, fresh, and pure morning.

As Johnny cleaned, Sonny elaborated how the tipi was the inside of the woman. The poles were her ribs. When you come out of here the next morning, you are being born again, leaving the Mother Earth's womb, all things become new. The floor around the moon was her hair, and as Johnny swept, he was grooming her, brushing her hair.

After he was done sweeping, Duane drummed for Sonny, who sang three of the four Midnight Songs. When Johnny went outside, Sonny whistled his eagle bone four times. While Sonny sang the Midnight Song, Johnny ceremoniously came back in with the beautifully airbrushed, multicolored water bucket, sat it right against the fire stick, moved his blanket to the bucket, and knelt down.

As the drumming ended, as if on cue, the silence was broken by a loud down pouring of rain, beating on the canvas and sending several stray drops through the open smoke flaps and into the airspace above the fire, turning to wisps of steam as they descended. I looked at all of the big smiles on everyone's face, and knew it was more than coincidence. I was rapidly losing faith in the concept of coincidence. Midnight water had more than one meaning.

Sonny spoke, then repeated his words louder, as the rain increased. Even as close as I was to him, the rain was so loud it drowned out his words. Lilly-Ann yelled something at him, and they both laughed. Soon, everyone was laughing. Franco yelled something to me, most likely it was fortunate I couldn't hear what he said. For what seemed like a half hour, but was probably about five minutes, all of us just sat there in the tipi, looking around and up through the smoke flaps in amazement at the intensity of the rain. Small droplets would fall from various sections of some of the poles, and we wrapped our blankets closer to our bodies. Eventually the rain slowed to a light sprinkle, then stopped completely. Only a breeze was left to make the wet canvas ripple and drip.

Orlando said something in Navajo that caused almost everyone to laugh out loud again, then Sonny spoke. He repeated his earlier greeting to everyone, one at a time, again introducing himself to strangers, acknowledging old friends and relatives, some with joy, some with past sadness, all with genuine friendliness and love. He once again spoke to me at length about how happy he was that I had chosen this way of worship and healing, how pleased he was that I now had my own tipi or "home" as he called it, and how I must bring in my wife and children into my home to make it complete. He assured me that the rain at Midnight Water was the best of signs, that everything was on schedule, and help was here. I didn't have to suffer any more. He spoke with confidence when he said that I was finished with alcohol and was headed safely down the peyote road, the Red Road of Sobriety.

When he was finished talking, Duane, the Cedarman next to me, followed suit, greeting everyone all the way around, laughing with those he knew, which seemed like almost everyone. He picked on Franco, asking him if he was all wound up, or if he needed to spin around again. That got the crowd laughing, and for the first time I could remember, Franco was completely speechless; he just sat there grinning ear to ear. Then Duane loaded me with positive reinforcement about what was happening, and encouragement about the ultimate outcome of this ceremony, reminding me we had only just begun, the night was young, the miracles were still in the making.

Then Orlando, the Drummer, talked to us all, and reiterated how brave I was for coming forward with my problem and asking for help, because it wasn't my problem, it was everybody's problem, and he wished he and others had the courage to ask for the same help I was going to get tonight.

I was embarrassed at all of this attention I was getting. I was not prepared for so much positive reinforcement. It was bad enough being so inexperienced, so completely unaware of the next phase of the ceremony, not knowing what to expect, and feeling far too much credit was being given to me. In fact I had little or nothing to do with where I was now at this exact moment. Somebody or something far more powerful than me had set up this grand meeting, and I was strapped in for the ride. But I could not honestly take any credit for what was going on, and felt more and more self-conscious and unworthy every time someone tried to praise me and set me up as some kind of hero.

Johnny was kneeling in front of the fire, rolling the tobacco in the husk Sonny had just given him. He started to greet everyone just as the other officers had just done. He used some very personal words for a select few, especially his mother and father, who he hadn't sat up with in a long time. After re-establishing old connections with many of the people here, he addressed his parents, mostly his blood mother. He told them he missed them deeply, and missed the old days, running meetings all over the country, helping so many suffering people. He said his life had so much more meaning then, that his job was necessary for survival, but he was getting tired of it, and really wanted to join them again in the ceremonies more often. It seemed the more money he made, the more he needed to break even, whereas when he hardly worked at all, he was never hurting for enough money to live on. Many people appeared to agree with this paradox, judging by the amount and volume of the groaning and "Ahos" that erupted. He went on for quite some time expressing his love for his mother, and I had to strain to hear what he was saying because he spoke to her so softly. He started to get choked up as he reminisced, and stopped talking altogether for a few seconds to regain his composure. Lilly-Ann was crying softly, piling up the tissues beside her, but very happy to be reunited with her only son. Even though it would only be a short visit, I can't think of a better way to get the most time and emotion out of a weekend.

Then Johnny turned to me, and spoke with intense seriousness. No longer talking softly, he returned to his stern way of communicating to me, complete with an abundance of the use of his signature phrases--"like that" and "in that way". He reminded me of how he had insisted on the perfect wood for the fire this morning, of how much trouble we went through to get it, and the reason he was so relentless in finding this straight, seasoned pine, cut to perfect lengths, and why we spent hours cleaning it and stacking it up neatly outside the tipi. He revealed he was aware that we were getting impatient and frustrated with him as he turned down tree after tree. Impulsively, Franco sprang to life and grunted loudly, out of turn, out of place, and embarrassingly off cue, at least in my mind. Once all was said and done, the only problem Franco had the whole night was my personal shame that I tried to lay at his feet and force him to absorb all of my failings. As I was busy worrying how "embarrassing" Franco was, I didn't realize how sincere and real he was...or how insecure and self-conscious I was, projecting my embarrassment of myself onto him.

Johnny continued on, unaffected by the outburst. He told me I was very fortunate that I still had two real friends willing to help me get that wood, and I should appreciate them, too. He said he wished Steven had stayed, but he was glad Franco was here to support me, and that they were true friends, and that was precious and rare.

The fire before him was smokeless, crisp, clean, bright, and warm, a living testament to his dedication to this fireplace, and the result of excellent wood and diligent care. He again explained the importance of the fire, the need for clean, straight wood, the careful stacking, rearranging, and fixing of the wood, and the precise art of spreading the coals inside the moon altar. Just before Midnight Water, he had reloaded the fire with wood, and shaped the hot, brightly luminous coals into a giant eagle, with the tips of the wings touching the moon altar, and the claws reaching into the fire. A good fire paid off during the meeting, he explained, and even more so after the meeting was over and life had to be lived.

He told me my life up to this meeting was exactly like the wood I had collected at my house, the campfire logs he immediately rejected. Gnarled, twisted, broken, dirty, inconsistent, diseased, rotting. That wood was me. What sense did it make to put the same unhealthy rot I was living into a ceremonial fire that was supposed to help me? He wanted to use wood that represented how he expected my life to become--straight, clean, pure, healthy, spiritual. He wanted my life to become bright, strong, warm, and powerful, like this fire he had been planning to build for me all night. He said he was only choosing the best of the wood we had prepared, and he wanted me to get well. He did not play games, and when his dad ran a meeting to help someone, he knew he meant it, and he did his very best to help out. He said this beautiful wood burning in Grandpa fire would help me, also. He said this immaculate fire symbolized my future; out of the jungle and into the forest, out of the forest and into the trees, out of the trees and into the meadow, out of the meadow, and up to the mountaintop. At midnight, we were leaving the forest and into the trees. What he meant, I had no idea. He apologized for any mistakes he might have made earlier with the fire, humbly asked me to forgive him if he did anything wrong from here on out, and assured me he was doing his very best that he knew how to do, and hoped his best was good enough for me. He ended by saying that we had a long way to go, but at the end of this ceremony, everything was going to be good. I would be whole again. He had seen it many times, and he could feel it happening tonight. He quietly and humbly thanked me for allowing him to sit at my fire, in my tipi, and help him get better also.

As Johnny was talking, the Doorman and the man on the other side of the door had re-arranged the wood on the fire, added some new wood from outside, and spread out the coals so the Fireman could remain kneeling by the water bucket. The fire was burning big and bright again, but watching the two stand-ins freshen up the dying embers and the resulting semi-bonfire that left Johnny politely shaking his head and smiling, definitely made me really appreciate his talent as Fireman. Tradition tells them they must do as little as necessary to refresh the fire while he is talking. They want to disrupt his speech as little as possible, as fast as they can, without totally changing the quality of the flame, so it is a challenge no matter who helps out. But the difference was dramatic, and everyone noticed. Orlando walked around the tipi and knelt in front of the fire, pushed down firmly on the loose stack of fresh wood, pulled one or two pieces out and restacked them, pushed and prodded here and there, and in a matter of seconds had the wood tightened down, the very tips burning smokelessly, and the flames small yet bright. Johnny thanked him as he walked back to his seat. Obviously he had taken care of fire many times before; drumming wasn't his only talent in the tipi. While slightly embarrassing to the two who had tried to fix the fire, it was nothing more than a learning experience for them, and was not taken the wrong way. They both thanked Orlando, also.

When Johnny was finished talking, the Doorman handed him the fire stick. He lit his smoke, and began praying. He begged God for forgiveness for himself, and for all of us. He asked Him to have pity on us, we were only human, and had a hard time doing what we should. He apologized for his past use of drugs and alcohol, and thanked his Creator for taking away those obsessions right here in the tipi so many years ago, and implored Him to do the same for me tonight. He prayed for everyone here, some by name, others by inference. He thanked God for taking care of his mom and dad, and all of his relatives. As he prayed for himself and his job, he started weeping, describing his long hours, the days without rest, the lack of friendly human contact, the inherent dangers he faced daily on the oil rigs off the coast. He was grateful he had a good paying, steady job, but was afraid it was taking up his whole life, reducing social and spiritual time to almost nothing. He begged God for endurance, guidance, and protection. Once again he thanked God for this ceremony, this sacred medicine, the sponsor, and for another opportunity to be a part of this sacred rite. He asked God to forgive him if he forgot anything, if he left anyone or anything out, and that he would do his very best to make a nice ceremonial fire that the Creator could use to make His presence felt, and heal the sponsor of his problems. Slowly, in between deep inhales of his smoke, he wound up his prayer with humility and honesty, ending it in a litany of Navajo words and the usual "In the name of Your Native Son, Jesus, I pray, Amen and Aho". Then Johnny put out his smoke. Sonny walked around, took the smoke, put cedar on the coals, then dropped the smoke into the fire, and sat down.

Johnny tipped the water bucket forward and spilled a small amount of water on the ground, an offering of water for refreshment to Mother Earth. He then passed the cup to the man behind and to his left, followed by the bucket. The man set the bucket in front of himself, put the handle on the fire side of the bucket, dipped in the cup, and drank up. He had one more cupful, then passed it to his left, setting the bucket in front of the woman next to him, again tipping the handle to the fire side. As the bucket of water made its way around the tipi, different people expressed themselves about various themes, all somehow related to alcoholism and addiction.

Some took this time to introduce themselves to new people, greet those they knew, and relate something about alcohol problems. Once again, Red Hawk, the Kiowa who had prayed earlier during the drum rounds, looked through the fire directly at me and spoke.

He was serious. There was no kidding around with him while inside the tipi. This ceremony was holy to him; there was no mistaking that fact. He again reminded me his grandmother and his mother were born in a tipi. This was his heritage, unlike many tribes that held this ceremony in a tipi. His tribe historically survived centuries using the tipi as their home and church. His family, his relatives, all of them were Peyote People, he proudly announced, in his deep, raspy Oklahoma accent. The irony of a proud, strong full-blooded Indian sounding like a redneck cowboy because of his Okie roots was rich, but I doubted many people ever mentioned it to him.

His family lifestyle, his upbringing was centered around this ceremony, this medicine, this way of life. His father had been diagnosed with cancer many years ago. He refused the standard treatments: chemotherapy, radiation, painkillers, slow death. He was certain he got it from the white people once his family was forced to relocate to the Reservation, so he wasn't about to try their remedy, especially after watching too many others rot away from the cancer treatments faster than the cancer itself.

Instead, he did what his family had done with disease for hundreds of years. He ate this peyote, morning, noon, and night, for years. He fasted and prayed, and sponsored many ceremonies. After living far longer than any doctor could predict, he finally walked on to the next life or, as Red Hawk declared, went back to be with his family, among the buffalo, the tipis and where there were no white people telling him how to live. To prove a point, Red Hawk's father had requested an autopsy, and his family honored his wishes, against all tradition. He claimed the autopsy report made waves with the local Indian Health Council because the results concluded there was no explanation for his body living so long. The coroner who performed the autopsy described him as "completely empty inside, virtually impossible to have survived as he had, with only a shell without vital organs, like nothing he had ever seen or read about." He had been kept alive and functioning solely from the "power of the sacred medicine of his ancestors", far beyond what common sense and medical science tells us is possible.

Red Hawk then described the harassment he and his tribe had endured to keep their way of life alive. He talked about the importance of keeping everything as it has always been, or it wouldn't work anymore. He told how his dad used to perform miracles daily, how all of the old people were always performing miracles, and how they are getting rarer all of the time. It was because too many people are falling for the miracles they think alcohol brings them, and they are all fooled, and we are all losing our personal power and giving it to alcohol. He used me as an example, how I had no power over it anymore. "That's how it works. It starts slow, seduces us, promises us happiness and fun. If we just relinquish our power, it will give us all we desire. Then, before y'all know it, our power is gone, and the alcohol ruins us, then kills us. I done seen it too many times. That's why those in AA say they are powerless, cuz they are, only becuz they gave it away...but they can have power again, everyone can, if they really, truly and forever reject this alcohol, and mean it!"

Then he was quiet, but everyone knew he wasn't done. He shifted on his knees, the only position he used all night long. He stared through the shrinking flames of the fire directly into my eyes, penetrating through me. I felt nervous, self-conscious, as if he was about to yell at me for being so weak.

"I was the town wino 20 years ago," Red Hawk confessed. "I drank continuously. Ruined all my things, cars, houses, my guitar that was signed by 'Ol Willie himself. Hurt a lot of people, wrecked a lot of lives. Then, I realized I was being taken over by the curse. I was losing my own power. I had a moment of clarity, just as I was going over the edge. And I done quit."

He then said something I've never forgotten. "Y'all don't keep quittin', drinkin', you don't keep saying 'no'. You quit one time. You say 'no' to the alcohol only once. Then you're done. Don't say 'no, yes, no, yes, no.' Once. Tonight. And y'all don't use this medicine and drink. You are either a drunk, stay that way, don't pretend otherwise, don't waste nobody's time, and don't say 'no' - or get real, and then y'all really are on this Red Road of Sobriety. You use and respect this medicine and this way of life, you say 'no' tonight, and you're done. Forever. Never mix the two again. This ain't no game. I don't know how much you understand about this way, but now that you have chosen it, be a man, stand up and be counted among those who reject the curse, and demand that your power be returned to you. Tonight you can make the choice that has eluded you, so don't miss that chance, a chance most nobody never gets."

Of everything said to me that night, these words, reaching across the fire from somewhere in the distant past, rang true. Without diminishing anything else said or done to me that night, to this day I consider those emotional, angry, sad, strong words, in his Southern drawl, perhaps the most powerful and effective because of their clarity and simplicity. And because of the authority that he put forth as he spoke. I hear them in my head all of the time. And I have repeated them to other struggling alcoholics.

It really isn't profound, or earth shattering. In fact, it is very basic, at best. So simple, that at first glance, it is so obvious it goes without saying. Alcoholism and addiction are as basic as it gets. We try to make it far more complex and complicated than it deserves. It is a real dichotomy, though, because we have come to understand that it truly is a disease, yet it is the only disease you can purchase in a bottle at the corner market. But it requires more than a simple cure, and, unfortunately, that cure can't be bought in a jar at another store.

Overall, the professionals and programs are sincere and honest in their diagnosis and treatment. But when that Kiowa Elder from Oklahoma spoke across Grandfather Fire that night, he brought forth an ancient wisdom that cut through every excuse modern society has created to explain away personal responsibility. He explained it this way:

"You can use all of these new answers to the age old problem. And for some, they work. The problem, or the catch, is, you are powerless. And as spiritual beings, we are not created to be powerless. We are to be powerful, in control of our destiny, by walking that Red Road of Sobriety and Responsibility. Do you think all of the civilizations before us that came up against a formidable enemy just gave up, deciding they were powerless against whatever came against them? If that were true, none of us would be here today. It is a new concept to be powerless, and it can be self-defeating."

Red Hawk went on to say, "The ancient, time proven model is simple, basic. It takes self-control and self-determination. You say 'no'. Once. You quit. You never say 'yes' again, therefore never having to say 'no' again. There is no longer anything to say no to. Done. Finished. Simple.

"You give it all to your Creator, to God, let Him control your destiny. He is, anyway. You just get into His will, learn where He wants you to go, and follow. Let God take away any cravings and desire to drink. Let God do what you can't, let Him take over where you have always failed. That is not powerlessness. That is availing yourself to God's power, allowing Him to empower you to do what is right. Alone we have no power. With God, we can accomplish anything. We think we are in control, that we are running our lives. But God has a plan for all of us. If we understand what that plan is, if we grab a hold of it when He shows us the way, that magical moment, we have easy sailing all the way through. But if we know where He wants us to go, and we deny Him that right, and try to direct ourselves in some temporal, pleasure-now, ego-centric, self-focused aberration, He lets all of the obstacles come before us, allows us to become addicted, drunk, crazy, whatever we think is the best direction. But we know deep down inside we are wandering down our own, private road to destruction. And the results are always the same. Addiction, alcoholism, and all of the other "isms" that we dive into, they are all our feeble attempts to direct our lives where they don't belong. We sink deeper into our disease of choice, thinking we have no way out. We convince ourselves we have no escape. It is too hard.

"And the moment you say it is too hard, too powerful, too overwhelming, then you have lost. You have no faith in God, no faith in yourself, and you have defeated yourself, even without taking one sip of alcohol. Life is too precious, the greatest gift the Creator has given us, and we have no right to throw it away. With God's power, with His help, all things can be accomplished. Left alone to our own self-induced diseases, we will fail.

"We must remember that what has worked for eons hasn't suddenly stopped working because we somehow decided to ignore it. That God isn't watching us because we quit seeking Him. That ancient wisdom, traditions and warnings are no longer true, or relevant, because we pretend they never existed. We believe we can bend and break timeless rules and get away with it because they no longer apply to these modern times, or that their situation is different, special, that God will continuously forgive and forget, and there are no repercussions to all of our repeated wrongdoings. To every action, there is a reaction, whether we want to acknowledge it or not.

"Traditional ways, societal mores, community values, all of these guidelines that have worked since the dawn of time when followed, are such for a reason. Some rules are obvious. Others are so old we don't remember the original intent, but that doesn't negate their importance. What has worked until now, still works, if respected and followed. Why do we tinker with what works? We think that in our sophisticated, modern, and self-important life we know better and can improve or improvise those 'silly old ways'. But it isn't true, and only brings regret. We must drive down that good Red Road, stay to the right, don't weave back and forth, stay out of the middle, no parking, no backing up, don't test the guardrails, and don't drive drunk. Obey the signs, know the rules, and if you do, you will be rewarded with happiness and longevity, and never go hungry. The rules are for our safety and health; the shortcuts and detours only bring trouble to you and everyone you love. Follow this road, don't change directions, respect those who built this road, straightening it, posting warnings, setting up rails, using signs to show the way. It is an old road, yet it is smoother, cleaner, and far more user-friendly than any of the new high-tech, well-lit freeways that beg us to travel on. This road is proven over time to guarantee we reach our destination in one piece, whole, and fulfilled.

"The answer to the seemingly contradictory message about alcoholism, or any "ism", is in the timing. We admit we are powerless over alcohol, that our life has become a mess. We turn our life over to our Creator, and avail yourself to His power. Yet, we constantly announce, almost proudly, that we are still alcoholic, that we could fall back into its power over us at any given second. We affirm our victim status, that we are still powerless, still sick, and subconsciously invite that bad spirit to hang around and wait, after all, we may not be totally through just yet. So the door remains open, ever so slightly, barely cracked, in case we need a back-up plan. In case we think maybe, just maybe, this time we can handle a drink, or two, maximum three, and off we go.

"How many recovering alcoholics do you know who went back to drinking, maybe only temporarily, often permanently, and fatally, even after being in a "program" for 10, 15, 25 years? Worse yet, many just keep repeating the cycle, getting three months, six months, maybe a year, then back in the gutter, finally one day taking one guzzle too many. It is because they are still 'in recovery'. They are still affirming mentally and verbally they are still alcoholic, they are never recovered, never an ex -alcoholic. The closest I have heard is 'a recovering alcoholic', or 'a grateful recovering alcoholic' - Yes, the logic says, keep reminding yourself so you never forget. If you really, truly, from the depths of your soul, want to quit, if you finally admit this is not for you, you must be certain, you must be firm, you must believe yourself, accept the power God can give you, and slam that door shut, tight, nail it shut, and find another door to use. Better than that, get out of that building, into one that doesn't have such a door, so the option is gone.

"The concept of timing is this: You admit you are powerless, you allow God to give you the power to never take that first drink. You can have that power, if you want it. It is available to all that ask for it. Then, you do have the power to not drink. Ever. You have all of the power in the world to never touch your first drink again. That is all you need. Nobody can force you to take that first drink. For it to reach your lips, you will have had to make many bad decisions in a row, many actions that lead to that moment, hundreds of thoughts that should have been shut down at any given time during your freefall. One day, you don't wake up, and a drink is floating in the air, and it dumps down your protesting throat mysteriously. The process for someone who really does not want the effects of alcohol to overtake their being, is long, and methodical, and can be stopped at hundreds of different junctions along that bad path. At any point in that process, from the first flirtation of the idea, the first romance of the thought, to the next step of physically aiming in the direction of obtaining or finding the drink, to the actual pouring of the drink and finally of lifting it to your mouth, every step along the way you are conscious, aware, and cognizant of what is happening, you are not in a trance, even if you think that makes a great excuse. It is a lie, and you have all of the power in the world and beyond to stop, drop, and think.

"The whole process of relapse can and has to be stopped at some point in the process, the earlier the better. Nip it in the bud, at first light. Pray. Call on God for His help, which He will give plenty of if you dare to ask. The power to never drink again is right then, at that moment, when you first let that evil whisper enter into your psyche. That is the timing, the moment the power you have been given is needed, and therefore used. Best at the very early stages, but imperative at some juncture in the sickness process. Bring down the whole army of angels from heaven, all of the good spirits, everything that is righteous and pure. Now is the time to call on those forces, while you still have the ability to ask, and the desire to receive, not later, when the power is gone from you, after you have given it back to the enemy. The prayers of a righteous man can move mountains. And if you are in the will of God, and doing what He requires of you to live wisely, those prayers will be answered, loudly.

"The sound of thousands of angels coming to your rescue is something that everyone must experience and hear. To be on the right side of the battlefield, where victory is guaranteed, is a wonderful feeling, something that can never be felt when in the clutches of the evil, distilled spirits. And this is all the same with drugs, the first pill, first shot, first puff, first snort, all have to be cut off at the very tiny beginnings of the return to sickness process.

"Once you understand that simple concept, you truly can shut that door, you are done, because without the first drink, alcohol has absolutely no power over you. Power is there for those who use it wisely, but, spit in the face of the Creator, and watch how well your life goes. It seems harsh, but it is so simple, so basic. Close that door, no more back-up plan, no more leaving even the slightest chance that you will return to this pig vomit you are wading around in now, and start fresh, and mean it. Now is your second, and possibly only chance. Take it, embrace it, and live it. All good things will follow."

As he finished speaking, the water bucket came to the Roadman, halfway around the tipi. He stood up, moved the bucket next to the Chief on the moon altar, and laid the handle on the opposite side of the bucket. The Cedarman tossed a big handful of cedar on the fire, smoke billowed up and circled the fire. Sonny picked up the eagle bone laying against the altar, waved it four times over and into the cedar smoke, then blew into it for four sharp, high pitched whistles. He set the whistle down, picked up the eagle feather, and dipped it into the water bucket, east to west, north to south, the sign of the cross, and the four directions. Then he pulled the wet feather out and splashed it in the four directions against the tipi and over the fire. He then dipped it again, and blessed everyone inside with the water, starting at his left, and working around, reloading water at the doorway, then continuing on his baptism all the way back to the Drummer seated at his right. As the water came to us, we reached out and let it fall on our hands, then blessed ourselves with our wet hands.

Although it was barely a few drops, more symbolic than anything else, I looked up at the feather while he was shaking it towards me. It appeared as if the top of the tipi had opened and a steady rain was falling down on me and everyone else. I felt like I was getting soaked in a downpour. I thought I was completely drenched, but when I looked at my arms and legs, I was bone dry. Sonny blessed himself with the wet feather, handed it to Orlando, who blessed himself with it, and his drum and stick. He handed it back to Sonny, who then handed it to Duane, so he could bless himself and the cedar bag. Back in Sonny's hand, he walked over to Lilly-Ann, blessed her, then back to me, and fanned me with the wet feather, my hands outstretched and palms up to receive the blessing of the Midnight Water. After doing the same to Johnny sitting by the fire, he sat down, picked up the bucket and drank directly from it, spilled a few drops on the ground in front of him, and passed the water to Duane, setting the handle on the fire side of the bucket once again.

When he drank a cupful, he handed the cup to me, then passed the bucket directly in front of me, careful not to slide it on the ground, or turn it at all, so the handle and the beautifully airbrushed water bird faced the fire. The red carved parrot was staring at me. Suddenly, and without reason, I was overcome with thirst. Up until that second, food, water, especially alcohol, meant nothing to me, and did not even enter my mind. But as I looked into the bucket at the crystal clear water, I was suddenly parched. My lips were at once dry, and I had no saliva. I took the cup, dipped it in until the water was spilling over, then poured it down my throat. It was ice cold, tasting like the best spring water I had ever had, and incredibly refreshing. I took another cup and gulped it down fast, savoring every drop as it soothed my parched throat. I wanted more, much more, but realized there was still half the tipi yet to drink. I stopped myself and handed Franco the cup, then placed the bucket in front of him so he didn't have to move too much. He grinned ear to ear, whispered "thank you" louder than if he was talking, and dipped the cup all of the way in, smacking his lips and grunting as he loudly slurped away, completely incapable of doing even the most basic of things without causing a scene. I could hear the snickers and chuckling of those who were entertained by his whole performance. I tortured myself needlessly all night worrying he was out of line, when the reality was he was quite harmless, innocent, and well-meaning, in spite of his gregarious personality. There was probably a total of one or two people that he slightly annoyed, and he eventually was loved by everyone, once all was said and done. I nudged him after his fourth cup so he would pass it before the bucket was empty.

They called this the Water of Life. Holy Water. As it went down, I tried to think of the last time I had really enjoyed drinking just water. When I was 18, going to art school, my good friend Bob Jones, got me hooked on running on the beach. We would run at least eight miles a day for months, another extreme obsession, although it did counterbalance a lot of the abuse I was doing at the same time. I remembered how we used to drink so much water when we were done running, and how refreshing it was, how great it tasted. It had been that long since I really appreciated water as much as I did right now. I drank alcohol to get drunk, not because it was refreshing or tasted good. Water was only good for a hangover, to ease the dehydration, nothing else. Now, this early morning, it brought back that healthy feeling I experienced drinking water after a good run. I felt as if it was healing me. For once, I wasn't drinking it to relieve my dehydration from alcohol. Maybe I was, but it didn't feel like it right now. It tasted so good, so fresh, so real.

As the bucket moved around the tipi towards the door, someone else started to express their thoughts, but I couldn't hear them. Their words became distant and soft, far away. Suddenly, all I could hear was the river behind me, rushing over and around the boulders and down the mountain.

The river became louder and louder, almost as if someone had opened the weirs at the dam, and tripled the water flow. It was an overwhelming sound, almost as if I was laying right beside the water. I was mesmerized by the sound. It was all I heard. I found myself thrown into my past, sitting on a boulder by this river not 15 feet away from where I was sitting in the tipi. Somehow, I was 14-years-old again, looking into the rushing river, waiting for my new friend, Chino, the Cahuilla medicine man, to return. And, once again, the river started talking to me, as it had done right here so many years ago.

The water communicated to me exactly as it had when I was a young teenager, fresh into the world. I still could not understand how it could be talking, nor could I apply any logic to it. I just knew that words formed from the foam and spray of the cascading, turbulent water, and somehow were sent into my ears as audibly and clearly as any words spoken to me all my life.

It spoke to me of lost, wasted years, of ignoring what it had tried to tell me 26 years ago, of throwing my life to the wolves, even though I knew better. It lectured me on the damage I had caused, of losing my battle with alcohol, of being no different than all of the others who never cared about anything, how I strayed too far from the stream, how I was being washed down to the ocean to drown. It was now almost too late, it was my last chance to come clean, no more polluting my body, my temple. My polluted veins were the same as the polluted river, as I polluted myself, so did I pollute the river. We were all the same, and all choking from the pollution. I sat on that boulder motionless, listening to the river chastise me for straying so far for so long. I really felt like I had returned, that I was a teenager again. I understood what I was being told, and started crying, tears pouring down my cheeks, onto the riverbank, streaming into the river, barely realizing how far I had gone, now understanding I had betrayed myself, and also betrayed the river, rejecting the wisdom it had dared to give me so long ago.

I washed from the boulder to the tipi and back again, through time, from childhood innocence, to adult depravity, tossed from past to present and back again, as the water slowly faded into the background, until I was solidly back in the tipi, crying out loud. All eyes were on me when I opened mine, wondering what had happened, many knowing I had left for a few minutes and fell into my past.

I was overcome with emotion, and spoke up. I told everyone that for the first time since I was very young, I could hear the river speaking to me, and I understood what it was telling me. My emotional announcement flowed out of me and was met with enthusiastic grunts and groans of approval. Sonny concluded it with a loud "Aho". Duane stood up and tossed some cedar into the coals, as if to sanctify what I had said. Only in this place could anyone reveal they were in close communication with a river of water and be met with total understanding and approval. Either we were all crazy, or something monumental had just taken place. I leaned heavily toward the latter explanation.

The water bucket had reached the door. Johnny picked up the cup and bucket and walked clockwise all of the way around the tipi, then took it outside. When he returned, he brought in a big load of wood. Then he set about completely redoing and rekindling the rapidly dying fire. Soon it was bright and hot again, and we could once again see each other's faces, smiles radiating from all of us as the midnight hour faded into history.

Typically, at this time, the Roadman would call for the staff and drum again, and begin the singing cycle from wherever it had left off before Midnight Water. Then it would continue as far as possible before he would announce the Main Smoke. The Main Smoke is the highlight of any ceremony. The peak. It is when the sponsor rolls himself a smoke, and asks for all prayers to be aimed at his plight, his reason for the meeting, and it is when he prays only for his one, solitary request, so that all focus is on the whole reason why everybody was there, without distraction or generality. The subject is defined specifically, leaving no question about the intention, no prayers for "peace on earth" or other ambiguous and wide ranging generalities, only one purpose, one accord, one cry. And only one answer is expected, and it is expected in the affirmative.

CHAPTER 16

MOMENT OF HEALING

The Medicine and the Miracle

Instead of resuming the songs of prayer, Sonny announced a slight change of schedule, due to the gravity of this night's purpose and the importance of success with my prayer request. Tonight he was going to do some "doctoring", a healing in his own style, as every Roadman has a different way of bringing about healing. After that, in the interest of the time involved, he would call for Main Smoke, and resume the drumming and songs that filled much of the night.

He spoke to the many Navajos present, in their language, then translated briefly for the few of us who did not understand. Judging by the amount of time he spent talking in his language, and the few words in English, he had told the Native speakers considerably much more than those of us limited by language about what was about to happen. I felt all eyes burning into me. He told me he was going to fix up some medicine for me now that would heal my ravaged organs, and also end my desire to drink alcohol. He said he would mix up a special concoction, filled with all of our prayers, and full of power from the fire and the stars above us. He explained to me in his limited English, the relationship of the pulsating coals surrounding the fire, and the sparkling stars in the sky above us tonight. There were certain hot coals that represented, or were related to, the stars directly in our line of vision through the open smoke flap above us. The way he transferred that star power to the coal, then into his medicine cup, was how I would be healed tonight of my sickness, giving me a second chance. Without going into detail that would make even less sense than he was making now, he told me that the extra power from the heavens only assured that the medicine would succeed, and he wanted to be sure he did everything correctly.

Sonny poured a small amount of liquid from his box, into a new ceramic cup in front of him that had a crude, handmade inscription on it that read "Jesus Loves You". His mix was a thick, gritty and bitter soup of at least 30 mature peyote buttons, with the texture and look of fresh avocado guacamole.

He set the cup down by the moon, close to the Chief, and stood up to pray. He prayed in Navajo with some English words tossed in where his language could not explain the situation, and mentioned me by name. He prayed for almost a half an hour. As he prayed aloud, everyone prayed silently, facing the fire. His prayers became more and more intense, nearly desperate, as he cried, literally, pleading for help for me and all of us who struggle with this evil substance. Listening carefully, I was able to discern enough English to understand why he was crying. And, I was also able to comprehend enough of his language to fully grasp what was being requested, even though logic told me I knew not one word of Navajo, and could not possibly know what he was saying. This was the language of the code talkers who, during World War II, had saved the United States from losing to Japan because their best decoders could not translate one word of this complex language. But for some reason that I simply could not grasp right now, many of his words entered my consciousness as English, and I could understand his prayers. I shouldn't have been surprised, only because I had just translated words spoken by water, and that was impossible enough, in and of itself. At least Navajo was being spoken by a human. For the briefest second I questioned what language the water had spoken, whether it was actually English, or some universal words everyone could grasp. Then I stopped, realizing I was over analyzing something that was already incomprehensible, and I didn't need any more confusion.

Sonny's prayers continued, stronger and louder. He called out for help for me, for those he was related to, and unknowns who struggled with sobriety. As he mentioned certain names, the crying turned into wailing around me. His fervent prayer was for all people who were losing the battle against this liquid that had no respect for people, races, or nations. I got on my knees and bowed down to the ground, crying like everyone else. I could feel the ground tremble beneath me as we all prayed. I got nervous, like maybe we were going too far. With both palms completely flat on the dirt floor, the earth definitely rolled back and forth gently, and I glanced up at the fire when some of the top logs dropped into the coals from the trembler. My fear quickly turned into deep, deep humility, feeling so small, so totally out of control, just a tiny dot in an enormous universe, not remotely worthy to be in this close contact with the actual Creator of All Things. Suddenly, I could feel His presence all around me, all around all of us, a warm, pleasant energy that completely enveloped the entire tipi and brightened it up so much I had to close my eyes it was so vibrant and bright. This prayer wasn't just for me, it was for everyone who was drowning in this morass. And it was big, real big. I was in very good company, everyone present was affected by the ravages of alcohol, to one degree or another. We were all there for help, all on the same sinking ship. We all needed and wanted help. This was my last hope, and maybe was true for many others present. If this ceremony didn't help me, all the more helpless everyone here would become. I wanted badly to be healed. I was no longer in denial, tonight, now, I begged for an end to this insanity, this sickness I that had consumed me. If someone who wanted sobriety as bad as I did right now could not get help, then those who stubbornly held on to their addiction had absolutely no hope at all, and everyone was aware of that fact. I thought of my prayers, and felt a huge load being lifted from me, from within me, and around me. Indescribable in words, it was like being washed clean from the inside out. Everything filthy, dirty, and evil was being slowly pulled out of me - even my guilt washed away - and as it left, I felt light, weightless, clean, pure, new. In a moment of freshness, like a newborn baby, my mind and all of my thoughts were white, glowing, radiant, almost like I was floating away.

Sonny slowly ended his prayers, wiped his eyes and face with a cloth, picked up the cup of medicine, and Orlando's drumstick. He walked to the side of the fire, near a wing of the eagle-shaped coals, tossed in a big handful of cedar, and knelt down, setting the cup next to him. As the dried cedar burned, it woke up that section of coals and they flashed bright red and orange, looking just like a string of tiny Christmas lights tangled up on the ground, flickering on and off. Sonny's eyes followed the thick smoke up through the opening at the top of the tipi and looked far into the stars sparkling in the midnight sky, as just enough of the clouds cleared directly over us. He looked back down at the coals, searching for something, then looked back up into the sky.

He took the drumstick and deliberately poked it into the hot coals, touching the very tip of it against a particularly bright and pulsating charcoal, then methodically brought the stick to the ceramic cup next to him. The silence was deep and everyone was following his every move. I watched carefully, and as the drumstick went from the coal to the cup, there was an unmistakable trail following it. The tip of the stick was bright white, and the trail was like lit to a sparkling brightness close to the tip. It got fainter as it fell away, leaving a misty trail in the air resembling smoke, or maybe steam. It disappeared as fast as it appeared. I knew it was some form of energy, but my logical and skeptical mind tried hard to dismiss that notion. He moved the drumstick slowly, and the energy trail behind it fell away to the ground even more slowly, as if it was shedding millions of tiny dandelion seeds with a bright penlight refracting off of it. I glanced at Franco and could tell he was seeing the same thing, along with everyone else, just by the size of his mouth and eyes as he gaped at the spectacle.

Sonny dipped the glowing stick into the mixture, stirred four times, then made the sign of the cross in the cup with it. The cup lit up almost as if he had dropped a small flashlight in it.

Some months later he tried his best to explain to me how he finds a star in the sky, then locates a certain coal in the fire that is related to that particular star. When he touches that coal he picks up the healing power innate in that star and transfers it into the medicine. He says the medicine and his faith alone will work miracles if it is the Creator's will, but occasionally, when the situation calls for it, he uses this secret. His grandfather taught it to him to help take away any chance of failure. The alcohol spirit is strong, one of the worst enemies he faces, but it cannot withstand star power. When Sonny told me these details, he said it all matter-of-factly, not apologetically or timidly, because he had seen God do so many miracles, just as his ancestors had done. It was not intimidating or unusual to him, and in his sort of innocent, or pure, way, he considered it to be quite normal, and to be expected. He has no idea how far most of society has fallen away from this type of reality, and how incredible and special it is. He's heard about it, and is somewhat aware of the fact that relating stories like this only make him and those who believe him look delusional, or downright insane. He still has the attitude of expectancy and faith that nearly does not exist anymore, and it is that clear, directed, reliable faith that has the power to effect miracles, without the pride and arrogance that drowns those who only wish they had his abilities. When I saw his faith perform this miracle, I became an instant believer.

I was so immersed into the process Sonny had just gone through, I nearly forgot that the magical mixture he had just concocted was for me. It hadn't seemed very long since the Peyote had made its last round, and that distinct taste was still floating around in my mind, and it wasn't a pleasant memory. The tea in the bucket had the consistency of creamy milk. I had watched Sonny pour his mix into the cup before he added more powder to it, and it had gone in reluctantly, he had to persuade it by shaking the container it came from as it slowly blended in, with the consistency closer to a thick batch of oatmeal, green oatmeal at that. All of a sudden it occurred to me that there was a good chance that I couldn't get this cup of "guacamole" into my stomach without violent protests. Not only would I not want to vomit in front of all of these well-meaning people and prove to be the weakling that I was, if the key to my cure rested in this magic potion, it was very possible that it would not stay inside me long enough to do any good. In fact, the more I thought about the reaction I had with the last round of medicine, the more the taste returned to my mouth, and the involuntary gag reflex actually started a faint reaction in my stomach and throat. Franco could see I was turning pale as a ghost, and leaned over toward me and did his special version of whispering, affirming my thoughts, "Man, you look really bad, brother, are you all right?" I nodded, lying to him and myself.

Even though I knew that throwing up in this ceremony was not totally unusual, and certainly not discouraged, I truly did not want to participate in that part of the process. My brief education on the subject covered the fact that sometimes it was necessary to clean out the problem in one's life in a literal sense during the ceremony as the medicine physically removes the disease, whatever it may be. I had read about many healings of cancer and other maladies as the patient vomited out the actual tumor or clot, or whatever was killing them, and I even witnessed it later on. But, as with everything, I returned to my control issues, and was busy making up my own rules for self-healing, letting my stubborn ego try to dictate how I was to be cured. I thought I had submitted, thought I was done trying to control God, and myself, finished with fighting against what was good for me. But there I was, this far into a miracle, and my overbearing self was putting on the brakes, directing God and everyone here how it was supposed to happen, putting my special limitations on fate.

The reality was, and I knew it, despite my stubborn mind going out of control, that I had no say whatsoever what I was going to do or not do, because I had surrendered long ago, and my mental masturbations were just that; I was trying to screw myself, but nobody here was going to allow that to happen. They call it "getting well", and if that was what

I needed, it was going to happen, and I had no chance of stopping it, or anything else, at this point. The Roadman, or at this time, the Medicine Man, had fixed up a special mix to clean me out, from the soul on up, and even though I didn't want to "get well" in front of a tipi full of strangers, my stubbornness no longer had any say in my affairs. And if I consumed all that he made, which was mandatory, and didn't throw it up in some reasonable amount of time afterwards, the dosage would be infinitely more than I had ever experienced, and could take me places I've never been, and maybe never wanted to go. At least I was in safe company, with one of the best guides, if I did go on an extreme adventure.

Sonny fully expected me to "get well", as did every single person in there. This was not baby food, and it had a job to do. I tipped the cup all the way back and swallowed it all down in three big gulps, attempting to send it home before my body had the chance to reject it. I treated it like an alcoholic drink dare at a party, without stopping for air. As if the taste wasn't bad enough, the texture and thickness made it beyond unbearable. Immediately every neuron in my body began signaling "poison" to every part of my nervous system. I instantly began to experience "purge" reactions so I frantically started taking deep breaths trying to hold back the convulsions. I could feel the back of my cheeks start to tingle, like hundreds of tiny needles poking my jaw. My throat swelled up and I gagged. My stomach and chest were having spasms on top of spasms. Every part of my being from sub-conscious to conscious was screaming for me to get rid of this stuff, to reject the "poison." Only my intense stubbornness held it in. I stared deeply into the burning wood and breathed deeply, concentrating on relaxation, against all reality. Franco wasn't helping by growling his own loud gagging noises. It nearly cleaned me out. When I closed my eyes all I could see was a vision of me projectile vomiting across the tipi.

I started to set the cup down when Duane nudged my shoulder and handed me a pint water bottle, motioning for me to dump water into the cup. He told me quietly that I couldn't leave a drop in the cup, as it all worked together, and was incomplete if unfinished. I nearly yelled at him how absurd that was if it was all about to be gushed all over the ground in front of me like a fountain, but refrained, mainly because I was afraid to open my mouth. I dumped some water into the cup, swished it around, used my fingers to loosen up any chunks stuck to it, and gulped it down, hoping again to complete the deed before my mind could acknowledge just how insane it was. That was almost the final blow, as it got stuck in my swollen throat on the way down. Knowing all eyes were on me waiting for the explosion, I dug deeper into my ego and refused to give them the show. My reasoning was if this medicine was going to work, it at least had to get all of the way inside. It didn't make any sense to me to throw it up before it could work its magic. I wasn't going to go through all of this and then chuck my hopes on the ground in front of me at the last minute.

After what felt like an hour of misery and deep breathing, the spasms subsided enough for me to relax just a little bit. The first alkaloids to enter the blood are calming in nature. I felt glued to my blanket, unmovable. Then it went to relaxed and comfortable. Before I knew it, the Drummer was back at it, and the songs had returned. The music sounded crisp, clear, and beautiful. The drumbeat was exactly in time with my heart, which for a second, seemed too fast, then it went into a perfect pace, with my blood pumping along with each beat. The fire took on a surreal appearance, and the villages in the coals returned, bustling with activity. I watched tiny, nearly invisible sparkles from the flames fly up and out of the tipi, far into the sky, heading for a reunion with the stars. Smoke around the coals was swirling around, dipping up and down, dancing to the sound of the music.

Someone was praying and crying out loud, behind the sound of the drum, gourd, and singing. Tears were once again falling from many peoples' eyes. Just looking at them filled me with a deep sense of sorrow. I began thinking heavily about my two sons, my little daughter, and my wife, how they deserved someone much better than me. They were sick of me. My wife was in the process of finding a new place to live. My sons hated me, my daughter was sad and confused. I had worked for years on the house we had bought together, but it was never a home. I started seeing hundreds of clips of my life, of drinking, yelling, fighting, anger, hurt, pain, and suffering. I thought of my mom and dad, so hurt by me over the years. I thought of that look I saw in my dad's eyes that first night I had run away drunk as he drove by my hideaway, unable to find me. I had a strong desire to drive home right that minute and hug my family, to apologize. To beg for forgiveness. I felt as if it was too late, as if they were moving out as we sat there, never to return. Tears seeped out of my closed eyes. Maybe this ceremony was too late, I had waited too long to change. Even if I sobered up now, yet lost my family, was it worth it? Had I thrown it all away, waiting too long to try to fix it?

I had a beautiful, loving wife who stood by me all of these years, hoping, waiting for me to wake up, now, had finally had enough, along with my children. It wasn't remotely fun anymore, and they were tired of faking it. I sat there, eyes closed, reflecting on the damage done, wondering how I had gotten here, and if it could be reversed this late in the game. My mind went through fast rewind, until I was once again back on that boulder a few feet from where I sat right now. A little earlier, when I had heard the river talking again, I still had blocked out what had occurred right here so long ago. It came pouring into me now like a flood, that Sunday morning nursing a hangover when I was still fairly innocent, before I had jumped face first into this cesspool of alcoholism and addiction. Chino, the local medicine man, had introduced me to this medicine that was now gurgling throughout every capillary of my being, and predicted this very moment 26 years ago. He had warned me about the problems I would face, even helped me throughout the years. Chino told me I would one day sit in a tipi right where I was right now, and learn the ceremony I was deep into right now. He foretold how it would be my last hope, that I would need it to save my life, not just my sanity. And I had laughed at him, to his face, and told him he was crazy. What was the chance of me sitting in a tipi in a Native American Church ceremony not four feet from where he had mentioned it, clinging on for life, in the company of total strangers, learning the ancient truths from a seasoned medicine man? Maybe if I had stayed on the straight and narrow all of these years, and had entered into the spiritual community long ago, and planned and diligently set up this ceremony with this group of committed, spirit-filled people, maybe then it might happen. But, instead, I had broken every natural law, every civil, state and federal law, ruined my life, tried to kill myself slowly with excessive drug and alcohol use, and wandered right to the end of my life. And still, somehow, his prediction came true to the last detail. Here I was, as he had said, not only had I forgotten about it, nothing I could do would stop it from happening. I thought about the process that fell into place, then remembered the rest of his prophecy. I was going to get better. My life was going to return to me. The hard part was over. I had passed the test. Not willingly, not the best way, I had slipped and fallen way too many times on way too many levels, but I had made it! I remembered his analogy of the staircase, the steps I had to take, the hard journey I must endure, but I also remembered that if I made it to here, to this tipi, I would make it. And life would become good, from here on out. I felt it, now. Why would his prediction come true to this point, then drop me like a rock? On top of all of that, I was once again on that elevator he had put me on with his medicine that morning long ago. The glimpse of truth, the trip to the top, so my faith could be renewed. And this morning's elevator was going way up, it was still going up now, I hadn't reached the top floor yet. I got excited thinking what awaited me up there this time, now that my hard climb was finally over. I felt that cosmic Presence of God Himself again, just as I had a few moments ago, when Sonny was praying over the medicine.

However, the ride wasn't over, nor was my education. They had called this an educational meeting, among other things. My lessons were still in session, I had not been excused from class. The morning was young, very young, yet there was still much to do, even though I was perfectly willing to end school right now while I was feeling victorious. Not for me, not this early…much more had to be revealed, and the hurting wasn't over yet either. I wasn't getting off that easy.

I felt an unusually cold blast of air over the top of me, like a downdraft had blown through the top opening of the tipi. A thundering, loud familiar voice reverberated into both ears, vibrating through me: *"Look at what you are doing to yourself! Look at what you have done to yourself!"*

I opened my eyes and somehow found myself at the very top of the inside of the tipi, suspended by the upper part of the poles, against the open smoke flaps, directly over the fire, smoke swirling to my left and right trying to sneak past me. I could feel the freezing night air on my back, and the heat of the fire coming up from below. I could see everyone in the tipi sitting up, watching the fire, one man shaking the gourd, Orlando sitting next to him furiously beating his stick on the drum in perfect rhythm to my heartbeat, as it started racing from fear and confusion. The song was a Navajo flight song, and I understood every word, as if it were in English. I was the proverbial fly on the wall, watching an ancient ceremony. I looked down at the sponsor seat and saw myself. I was slightly laid back, half sitting, half lying down, feet outstretched, looking up at me looking down. I could see Franco rocking back and forth, all balled up. Duane was singing fast and loud, staring deep into the fire. Sonny looked up at me, right through me. He looked at me sitting down, then back up at me hanging from the top of the poles. He smiled, then went back to singing and staring at the fire.

When I looked back at myself on the ground, my torso had a giant hole in it with blood oozing out, like I had been hit by a shotgun blast at close range. I was breathing normally, blood flowed through the vessels around the wound, and wasn't pouring out anywhere. I was definitely alive. It looked like a war wound, but wasn't messy with blood or parts spilling out. The loud, all-encompassing voice bellowed again, repeating the same command, *"Look what you are doing to yourself!"* two more

253

times. As I looked at the gaping wound in the middle of what used to be my body, I saw my parent's faces, my wife, each of my children, all of them were crying, as I had never seen before. Somehow, I knew they were crying for me because I had died. It was like watching a 3-D movie inside a disgusting hole in my body.

I looked up, and around, to see who was up there with me yelling at me and found nobody. Nobody below acknowledged the loud voice, or me up here, or my torn apart body sitting among them. Far from being subtle, like some kind of interactive hologram, this experience was scaring the hell out of me.

Then, suddenly I somehow lost my connection to the tipi poles and started to slowly but surely drift out of the top of the tipi, while below, my wounded body tried to pull me back down. All I could hear was the wailing of my family, individually, and all together. From above, I could still see them intermittently in the wound, while from below, all I could do was hear them cry. Sonny said something to Duane, and he threw a handful of cedar into the fire. The smoke came straight for me, while the heat of the fire was carrying me up and out of the opening. I could feel myself heading into the sky, the stars coming at me fast. I tried to scream, but couldn't, I was so unbearably afraid. I was rapidly losing sight of the tiny tipi far below me. The cedar smoke was wrapping around me like tentacles on an octopus trying to pull me back to my body inside the tipi, now just a tiny, white dot lost on a dark mountainside.

Suddenly I heard Sonny ordering me to sit up straight. When I opened my terrified eyes, I found myself sprawled on the tipi floor, no longer remotely resembling a sitting position. Elated to be back on earth,

I sat up fast. I put both hands all over my stomach, feeling for blood or missing parts. I was still whole, just a little swollen over my liver. This was too much reality for me to take all at once. I didn't want to look up at the top of the tipi. I didn't even want to close my eyes anymore. I was relieved, but still petrified. Try as I might, there was no convincing myself that what had just happened was not real, and I felt fragile, humbled, and unsure about what was coming next, and whether I could handle it. There was no chance of throwing up any more, and it would make no difference if I did. I was on the elevator ride, and it was what we used to call an E ticket, the best ride at Disneyland.

Sonny began telling me about the Main Smoke, coming up next.

CHAPTER 17

THE MAIN SMOKE

The Reason for the Whole Night

The Main Smoke is the culmination of the whole night's prayers and songs, some call it the main purpose of the ceremony. All focus is on the sponsor, why he has called for this meeting, and what he wants to come out of this prayer service. He (or she), prays only for himself, nobody or nothing else, for the specific reason he set up the ceremony. Everybody else in attendance also prays for that reason, and nothing else, keeping all other thoughts and requests silent so as to not confuse the outcome.

Whoever ended up with the staff at the end of the last singing session passes it to their left, and that is who will resume singing once the Main Smoke is lit by the sponsor. It is never planned out who will sing, as it is pure chance where it ended before the last break, depending on the duration of the songs and time of night. One of the many miracles of the Main Smoke is that the person who ends up singing while the sponsor prays is invariably someone whose songs and style fit perfectly into the sponsor's character and prayer request. Always an intense singer, full of powerful songs and talent to compliment the moment.

It is a great honor, and also a huge responsibility, to be the one who ends up singing during Main Smoke. At this time, the Roadman advises the sponsor to concentrate long and hard, to isolate his ultimate prayer request, and not to squander the opportunity to obtain the final result and outcome he desires from the meeting. Everything from the selection of the wood, to the location of the tipi, the gathering of this certain group of special people who have somehow come together for this meeting, all aspects, all prayers, all trials and tribulations leading up to this very moment all come together here and now, during the Main Smoke.

The sponsor is counseled on the magnitude of what is about to happen. He is warned to be very careful, very selective, and very brief. Three, four, maybe five or six words out loud, that's all, don't get all long winded or over-encompassing. Express yourself if you want, but be very careful with your vocal request to everyone listening. What you say out loud at Main Smoke will follow you for the rest of your life. Keep it simple, keep it pure, keep it honest, and be sincere. No time for "peace on earth" or a "kinder, gentler government". Only a realistic, personal, answerable, direct request for immediate help from the Creator to you in your life at this time, right now.

This prayer at this time is answered. One way or another. That is why one doesn't ask too much, or talk too much. That Main Smoke prayer follows you out the tipi door at sunrise and stays with you forever. You must be very certain what you want following you for the rest of your life. Thinking about the ramifications of this all important prayer, I thought of the lyrics of a Willie Nelson song; "Be careful what you're dreaming, soon your dreams will be dreaming you."

Sonny reiterated the value of brevity while vocalizing the Main Smoke. He advised, "Too much said, too much revealed, too much asked for, too much to be accountable for." By this time I was more or less completely incapacitated. My mind was crystal clear, thoughts, questions followed by answers were flying through me, while my body seemed detached and uncontrolled. I really felt like a spirit. A lost soul, filled with light, separate from my physical being.

For me, right now, for once in my life, I was totally speechless. No words really needed to be said. Everyone was of one accord this morning. There was no secret, no mystery, We all knew what I wanted, what I needed, what everyone needed.

Normally, the Roadman gives the sponsor tobacco and a husk to roll his Main Smoke. Again, Sonny spoke in Navajo at length, then in English to me. He wanted me to concentrate on my prayer, not on rolling the smoke. In a rare move, and one of honor for me, he handed me an already tightly rolled smoke, ready to be lit. Because he wanted this prayer answered, because this cause was so great, he did not leave it up to me to roll it. I believe also that he saw the sad attempt I made at rolling my first smoke at the beginning of the meeting, not being used to using a corn husk to roll giant cigars, especially without the standard sticky part on one side that kept it together. That, combined with the fact that I had never thrown-up the strong medicine he had fixed up for me earlier, left me virtually immobile, and probably incapable of commanding my fingers to do anything at all. Regardless of the reason, I was very thankful that I didn't have to physically deal with it. Just getting on my knees and holding the smoke and fire stick steady was a major accomplishment right now.

I held the smoke and fire stick, unsteady and trembling, and just sat there. Tears welled up in my eyes while everyone was looking at me. I began to sob uncontrollably. Finally, I just cried out, "Sober me, God! Sober me!".

That was my prayer, plain and simple. My grammar was all wrong; it would have made no sense under any other situation. But everyone knew exactly what I was requesting, and responded with loud and varied groans and noises of affirmation. I put the smoke to my lips, the fire stick to the smoke, and inhaled deeply, taking everyone's prayers inside me with the rich tobacco smoke.

One of the very talented Navajo singers who had just quit drinking a year ago in a ceremony, shook the gourd fast, signaling Orlando to start the drum, then slowed the gourd down to the one, two heartbeat, and sang his first of four long, loud, and intense prayer songs, with everyone singing along word for word, verse by verse, as I sobbed and smoked, begging God to make this the last time I had to ask for sobriety, to allow me to once again be a human.

The singer was one of the best here, and had everybody fully involved with his incredible talent, singing all healing songs from long ago. His songs went on forever, I lost track of everyone and everything, immersed in tears, smoke, and repentance. Right then, I knew deep down that a miracle was taking place. I felt it. I knew I was done drinking, once and for all. I understood all of the unexplainable coincidences that led to this exact moment in time, this place, this tipi, these people, this medicine, everything made sense and came together like planets aligning for a new season. Meeting Chino decades ago at this very spot, him foretelling me about sitting in a tipi in a ceremony at this very same location, at this very time in my life, all that led up to it, at this second in time, this position in space, I was fully aware, fully cognizant of my life, past, present, and future. Where I had been, what and why I had done everything, and where I was heading, flying headlong into the future, sitting alone yet surrounded by destiny, at one brief, instant my whole life made sense. The bondage was broken. Purpose and reason surrounded me just long enough to know it was all real, all for a reason, and life was once again worth living.

If only for that fleeting moment, the revelation I had was powerful enough to sustain me. I had quit hundreds, if not thousands of times before, but it never felt like this. The words Red Hawk spoke to me earlier about saying "no" just one time became very clear. I had an intense, deep-inside feeling of finality, like nothing I had ever felt before. Always before when I quit, I kept a tiny reserve door open, a small, yet visible crack in the door, leaving a way out "just in case". For the first time, I slammed that door shut and locked it. Then, I came back and completely removed the door, so it couldn't be unlocked, it was no longer there. It was me I had been fooling all along, nobody else. And I wasn't going to fall for my own tricks anymore.

I rapidly went from being helpless, powerless, and hopeless, drowning in my own self-pity and sorrow, to a very strong sense of power through total submission to God's will. A will that had been there all along, I had just been rejecting it, thinking I didn't need Him, I could do it all alone. Through humility I gained power and strength. God had been directing my path all along, I just took the worst detours I could find attempting it on my own, still ending up in the same destiny, in a painful and roundabout way. But rather than wallow in shame wondering why I gone that route, I gained an empathy and understanding for those who also ended up on that terrible road of addiction. And a desire to help them get off of that wrong-way street, and also prevent others from even starting in that direction. Being judgmental of myself flew out the top of the tipi, and I became humbled and forgiven, restored and renewed.

I understood that weakness, self-pity, sorrow all lead to defeat. I chose the option of absolute surrender, self-powerlessness, submission to my God. The result was total power, absolute strength. I inhaled the smoke, slowly, deeply, filling my lungs, then letting the thick, blue smoke out even slower. With the smoke, the negative, fragile feelings of a defeated person left me forever. I felt a strong surge of power and pride engulf me, the unmistakable knowledge that God was on my side, and I was once again back on His side.

My Main Smoke was almost out, and the singer was ending his fourth song. I knew my prayer had been answered. I think everybody else did, too, just scanning their bright, smiling faces blinking with the flashing flames. I looked over at Sonny, wiped the muddy tears from my face, smiled at him and nodded my head, signaling the end of my prayers. He walked over to me, took the last remains of the smoke, and offered his hand for the customary one-up, one-down handshake. His hand was warm, almost hot, and it felt like his blood crossed our palms and penetrated into my hand, through my arm, directly to my heart. I could feel the joy he emanated, that deep happiness he seemed to carry with him all the time. It was like a blood transfusion, feeling his heart in mine.

When Sonny sat down, he addressed me only. He assured me that my prayer was answered, and I knew he was right. There was no doubt in his voice, and no doubt in my heart. Sometimes, rarely, you just know that something has happened, that a miracle has taken place. And this was one of those rare moments. And most, if not everyone present, knew it too. Because when it happened, it was earth shaking, and everyone felt it, sensed it, shared in the moment, and also shared in the happiness that I was feeling. They also had grasped the answer, not just the question. It all lay in the total submission to God's will, and the return to all that had worked for centuries before this disease had destroyed so many people.

Sonny explained in detail the process that I had just run through my mind, the power derived from submission, the strength in relying on God's will, and the rejection of weakness that came from excluding God and His Creation from my daily life. He then told me that I had just completed the twelve steps, that I was a graduate of the Native American Church's Twelve Step Program, also known as The Twelve Hour Program. I had walked through all of the twelve steps, even though until this moment I had no idea what the twelve steps were.

He went on to explain, "This isn't Alcoholics Anonymous, but it could be considered the same, as we all have the same result in mind, and, really, follow the same spiritual steps, only in a slightly different way. This was the crash course, with a twist. The main difference is the result does not leave you as a victim, still an alcoholic, still labeling yourself as a suffering victim. Rather, you are encouraged to accept that alcohol is a thing of your past, and is not invited to return, and will not be acknowledged as a factor in your daily life." He let me know he loved the AA program, only he loved this Church even more, and wanted me to be powerful against my addictions through the strength of God from now on, instead of powerless over alcohol for the rest of my life. Rather than some vague, unnamed, politically correct "Higher Power", we can be proud of our close relationship with a personal and empowering God.

He told me, "Robert, your Twelve Steps are completed."

What he said next was so important I will never forget. "Just before sunrise, it is going to snow. The ground outside will be covered in fresh snow. Where you sit, in the sponsor's seat, it takes twelve steps to get to the tipi door. When you step out of this tipi, early this morning, at sunrise, you will take your Thirteenth Step, into fresh snow. You will then make brand new tracks in that fresh snow, a new beginning. All of your old tracks will be buried, washed away, gone forever. You will make new tracks, take new steps, start all over, fresh and new. You will take the Thirteenth Step, and become a new individual, no longer an alcoholic, no longer a victim. You will be reborn, with no defects, able to start all over. It is your destiny."

Instantly I understood why he was a Roadman, why people asked for him specifically when they needed help. He had healing strength pouring from his very essence. His power was undeniable. His close relationship with the Creator and His Creation was obvious. Sonny's willingness to be an instrument for God's power and his deep compassion for mankind was unmistakable. Yet he did it all in complete humility, very subtle, low key, while totally confident and sure of his God-given healing powers. Here was a Holy Man, a medicine man, whose prayers were sincere, his unconditional love was true, and his tears were real.

He had never met me before, had trouble remembering my full name, and yet, his prayers and cries for help for me were not for show, certainly not for money. He truly wanted to help me, and truly wants to help anyone who really desires it. His life is a testament to who he is, who his parents and relatives were, his upbringing, traditions, introduction, and growth as a Native American Church Roadman. His connections to his ancestors, the Creator and His Creation, his ability to communicate with the spiritual realm, his ancient knowledge of healing prayers, medicines, and herbs, are all disappearing around him as his secrets of healing, knowledge, and wisdom passed down through the centuries are slowly slipping away. He is a living legend.

Sitting in that tipi, feeling alive again, listening to the river converse with the trees, the light rain starting up again on the canvas, frogs announcing the upcoming cloudburst, coyotes yelping up the ravine at each other, the crackling and popping fire, cedar smoke circling the tipi and exiting out the top, prayers out loud in an unknown Native tongue, then the gourd and drum resuming their haunting duet as backdrop for songs from a different century, it all became crystal clear to me.

Mine is not a lonely battle. It is one we all face, in one form or another. And the battle is for life itself. We are all slowly being separated from reality, from the natural way we are meant to live by our modern life and its excesses. We are being comfortably numbed by alcohol, drugs, and now prescription drugs, diet and abuse, and distracted by electronics, and obsessive internet and sex. The battle has nothing to do with Indian, black, white, brown, yellow, or any other race. This is a battle that we all must face, because we are all part of the great race, the human race.

Sobriety and a clear mind are but pieces to the puzzle necessary to retain those ways of life that are critical to our survival into the future. Without a firm grasp of the past, on our history and culture, on those rituals and traditions that kept us whole as a people, we have no chance of regrouping and moving ahead, able to be healthy, aware, strong, and spirit-filled. That bridge to the past has been broken, but it has not been destroyed. It can be rebuilt, we only need the pieces that the Elders hold, the Medicine Men, the Roadmen, the holy people, those disappearing keepers of the fire.

It became so clear to me that the solution was the same as it has ever been. Return to what has worked. Spiritually speaking. Although we can never return to the physical beauty that was America, on the grand scale that it used to be, we can definitely return to the spiritual miracle that was, the intimate connection of man and nature, of Creator and Creation.

I let out a long, leisurely breath, as I marveled at the miracle given to me, and uttered, "Aho."

CHAPTER 18

THAT WHICH CANNOT BE REVEALED

After the Main Smoke, and all that happened, I was mentally exhausted. The staff and drum continued its circuit, and I was ready for a spiritual break. As if on cue, Sonny got up and brought the medicine bucket, and the bowl of dried and fresh peyote, and set it in front of me to start a new round so everyone would stay alert. The thought of ingesting any more medicine made me nauseous, but there was no way I would let that show. Fortunately, Duane, knowing I had to be at the verge of total cleansing, leaned over and let me know that if I didn't want any more, I could bless myself with the medicine by touching the container, then bless my head, heart, and stomach, and pass it on. I passed the dry powder and what was left of the fresh buttons, then took one cupful of the tea, now very cold and even stronger than before. Once again, the spasms started up, deep within me. I questioned myself as to why I thought I could handle it more now than a little earlier, as I gagged and held back the uncontrollable convulsions in my stomach.

I passed the tea on to Franco, who now looked like a cartoon character. He perked up again and murmured how it was about time he got some, and loaded up on everything in his own special way. The songs got loud and even more intense.

This was the time that things happen that are never talked about, mainly because they cannot be explained in any language. Between Main Smoke and Morning Water, here is a period of time early in the morning, while the world is asleep, that there is a concentrated effort to meld all of the songs into one strong voice. It is a time to bring in the

266

good spirits, the guardian angels of everyone present and petition them for personal help. Also, help for close relatives that struggle with the same problems that are mentioned in the sponsor's prayer. This is another reason why certain people gravitate to some meetings, so they can also get help during the spirit hours, after the sponsor has been helped at Midnight Smoke.

I looked up through the open smoke flaps, into the partially cloudy sky, trying to catch any sign of morning light, knowing this had to be the longest night of my life, with no end in sight. It seemed it was several hours since Midnight Water, so the sun should be coming up by now. The sky was as dark, if not darker than before, and there was no indication that it was any closer to sunrise. I wondered if tonight would ever become tomorrow. Time was fast asleep, and I hoped the loud singing would awaken it, so it could return us to the natural schedule I was accustomed to, back to my now outdated concept of time.

As the songs progressed during this unexplainable period when the spirits are called upon, things happened that went far beyond any spiritual teachings I had ever known. Because I, and everyone present, knew for a fact that my prayer had been answered, the ceremony progressed into a spiritual realm that cannot be described in human words or with rational understanding, and has never been revealed before, and has no reason to be explained now, nor does it have relevance to the subject or reason for my ceremony. Certain elements of this ceremony, as with many others, must be kept in the spirit world, only to be experienced by those present, out of respect for the ceremony, the Roadman, and all of those who have suffered to keep this as it has always been. All things do not need to be revealed to all people. In deference to those who gave the ultimate sacrifice so that this ceremony could continue on, there is a certain amount of secrecy that must be kept so that all has not been revealed. Only those who have the generational and traditional right to experience this ceremony know what occurs during the hours after the sponsor has been taken care of, in the dark of the early morning, long before the Morning Water is called for.

This is the time the chorus of singers receive literal response to their prayers, when not only the spirits come to visit, even the Creator Himself makes His presence known.

CHAPTER 19

MORNING WATER

Nurturing and Rebirth, Time of the Woman

Many hours later I looked up through the opening and noticed the endless darkness was slowly getting a tiny bit lighter. Not much…it was barely discernable. I had been obsessing about it for what felt like all night, and it was a faint beginning that announced the sunrise. A new day, even though I knew it was still hours away. At least now I could relax, knowing this night was going to end sometime, it was not going to go on forever.

The sky was completely clouded over, no stars were penetrating the thick layer of what now appeared to be snow clouds, truly a rare appearance up here at this time of year. Yet, the clouds themselves took on a subtle change, hardly noticeable, the transition of night to morning, of darkness to light. A slow process on a normal night, this was going to take an eternity, as time itself had taken on a completely different expression, stretching way beyond anything usual or predictable.

As the staff and drum came closer to the Roadman, Sonny spoke up. He announced that once the drum reached him, he would call for Morning Water, in much the same way he had at Midnight Water. After he sang three of the four Morning Water songs, he would blow the eagle bone whistle four times, Lilly-Ann would enter with the water bucket, and then he would sing the morning *Wakaho* song. He tactfully said that the Elders had taught him long ago that this is a very reverent time coming up, the female time of the ceremony. All due respect and honor was about to be focused on the matriarch of the ceremony, the caregiver, the nurturer, without whom none of us would be here. It was time for tribute to the softer, gentle side of life, symbolic of Mother Earth, also a time to put aside all unhappiness, to be joyful, to feel good again. He said if at all possible, those who were able should sit up nicely, or better yet, get on their knees, in deference and respect for this solemn moment, the grand entry of the Water Woman.

In many tribal societies, the women are leaders, if not obviously so, definitely in a pragmatic way. Final decisions were made by the female Elders, even in matters of battle. While the visible Chiefs were often men, the women behind the scenes made the final and absolute decisions on all things important. The women did much of the camp labor, including set up and take down , game preparation, cooking, care of clothing, and bedding, while the men did the hunting, conducted the raids, and the heavy labor. Councils were run by men, but deep inside the hierarchy of decision making were the Elder women. The women gave birth and raised the children to a certain age. Great respect and honor was given to Native women prior to Spanish and European influences. Spousal and child abuse was non-existent; reason for banishment from the tribe. These were behaviors used on them and taught to them in the boarding schools and orphanages, all coming about and in concert with the advent of alcohol abuse, and diabetes and heart disease, all new, devastating results of the decimation of their traditional culture.

Sonny's wife, Lilly-Ann, bringing in the Morning Water, symbolized all things feminine, nurturing, caring, and loving. Birth and rebirth. During this time all thoughts focus on mothers, grandmothers, aunties, sisters, daughters.

As the Water Woman prays over the Morning Water, then speaks to the sponsor and all present, she completes the circle of life in a nonjudgmental, happy, loving, and gentle way. The Water Woman takes the edge off the harsher moments of the night, making everyone feel good, peaceful, and calm. Nobody interrupts. The fire is built up big and full before she enters so minimal attention has to be given it so as to not disturb her.

Lilly-Ann's life had not been an easy one, and is a constant reminder of just how out of control the system was, and still is. As a child in Indian boarding school, at eight-years-old, nobody had adopted her. Unwanted and in the way, the school took her and all of the other children who were eight-years-old, the cutoff point, put them in burlap sacks, and dumped them far out in the desert wilderness on the outskirts of the Reservation, letting chance and survival decide their fate. Many died of thirst, starvation, or were killed by wild predators. After a period of time, word leaked out of the barbaric practice, and certain Protestant families would search the known areas for children, taking in survivors they would find and raising them as their own. Lilly-Ann was one of the fortunate ones who ended up being raised by a white, Christian family instead of dying in the desert. It was only much later in her adult life that she met her real father, the father who was forced to put her in the missionary boarding school as a baby so they could "remove her savage tendencies". As it turned out, her father was one of the surviving Navajo code talkers from World War II. The sad truth was that what he went through during that war ended up killing him. It was supposed to be kept a military secret, including the fact that he had an Anglo bodyguard assigned to him during the war to protect him as a vital secret weapon. He found out later his bodyguard and friend was also sworn to kill him if he was captured, so the Japanese could not torture the code out of him. He died a hopeless alcoholic, haunted by the truth about how some of his best friends were killed during the war, and who had killed them.

So Lilly-Ann had many issues and one of them was her own alcoholism. Fortunately she had ended that curse many years prior to this night. She had been an alcohol and drug counselor on the Reservation before taking to the road with Sonny to help others with their problems in a traditional way. She knew all too well what drugs and alcohol do to a person, so her insight is valuable. Her first husband, Johnny's father, had left her long ago because of her uncontrollable drinking, a man who, to this day, she admires. She also has had endless experiences with far too many casualties of alcohol abuse.

The staff came to Sonny, so he started the four sacred songs. Everyone shifted from their somewhat relaxed position to straight up on their knees. The atmosphere abruptly changed from casual to intense. I could feel the change in the air, everyone was wide awake and alert to what was beginning to happen. Moments earlier Johnny had swept up the entire tipi, even cleaned the moon altar with the eagle feather, then put some cedar in the coals, tossed in all of the smokes left leaning against the moon, and rearranged the fire. He stacked plenty of new wood on to assure a bright fire. Most important, he had changed the coal's pattern from the Midnight Eagle to a giant heart, called the Sacred Heart of God. This huge red heart was pulsating and blinking from bright red to deep orange, beating exactly to my heartbeat. It felt like all of our collective hearts were made into one, receiving the love from the feminine side of the dawn. The drumbeat went faster, as did the pulsating of the red hot coals, keeping in perfect visual rhythm with the sound of the drum, and our hearts.

I was on my knees, not knowing what to expect. It felt like we were greeting a dignitary, and in reality, we were. All eyes and attention were directed at the tipi door. Sonny threw cedar into the hot coals of the red heart, blessed the eagle bone four times with the smoke, blew the whistle four times, stirring up the smoke and sending it in clockwise swirls around the air above the fire, calling in the water.

Lilly-Ann walked in slightly hunched over from a combination of the weight of the water bucket, the soreness from sitting all night, being tired, and also her age. Perhaps she was bent over from carrying the weight of the whole ceremony in that water bucket. The prayers about to be said, infused into the water with tobacco smoke and cedar, would turn each cupful drunk into soothing, healing holy water.

She leaned over, set the bucket in front of her, flipped the handle towards the her, put down her folded Pendleton blanket, and knelt down on it, close to the roaring fire. Like clockwork, as she settled in, I heard the faint yet distinct patter of rain falling on the canvas above her head. It started ever so gently, then rapidly built up into a major downpour, completely drowning out the last chorus of the final song. Everyone looked around at each other, smiling broadly. No words needed to be said to validate the miracle of this rain. It is common to have rain at this time of the ceremony, the heavenly acknowledgement of our prayers.

Rain in and of itself is a special blessing, bringing with it cleansing, renewal, rebirth, and growth. It's always considered an answer to prayer, it is especially powerful when it happens at the exact moment when the bucket is set inside the tipi during Midnight and Morning Water. People in need of rationalizing it as a coincidence have trouble with the lack of forecast, lack of clouds, wrong season, and often it is an intense localized cloudburst directly over the tipi site, and generally nowhere else. When we emerge from the tipi hours later, it is sunny, dry and clear. Rather than dwelling on it and making a big deal over it, it is accepted for what it is, a blessing, a sign, an answer to prayers, nothing more, certainly nothing less. It is no less exciting nor redeeming each time it happens, it is simply a matter of fact, and another of the many reasons why we continue on in giving thanks to our Creator for His many blessings and answers to our prayers.

Lilly-Ann beamed with joy as the rain pelted down on the tipi. Everyone joined together in one big collective smile. Nothing unites a prayer service more than a small miracle as the sky starts to lighten up, announcing the soon rising morning sun through the rain.

Just as quickly as the rain began, it subsided into a light drizzle, then mist, then silence, only a few stray drops falling from the top inside poles. The only sounds were the increased flow in the river from new runoff, and the early morning birds greeting the rising sun. Now that everyone was smiling, Lilly-Ann could speak. She greeted everyone in general with her cheerful "Good morning, Yah'ah'teh' ah'bin'eh!" in English and Navajo. Then she went on to personalized greetings, thanking and encouraging each person as an old friend, relative, or new friend. She spoke in her Native tongue to those whose first language was

Navajo. And she spoke in Navajo to relate to relatives and friends in a more personal and traditional manner, all the while interspersing English in her conversation so she didn't ever appear to offend those of us who could not understand a single word, keeping everyone comfortable. Over the years Lilly-Ann had developed a graceful balance of transitioning from Navajo to English and back again that kept everyone attentive and included in a loving way.

Sometimes during the more emotional conversations she would speak and cry with her Navajo counterparts for extensive periods, evoking a universal compassion that transcended language and culture. Just when it almost seemed like the English only attendees were overwhelmed with a distinct feeling of isolation, she would switch over entirely to English. She would quickly summarize the whole conversation and cause for emotion, instantly including everyone present in the crisis being dealt with, inviting the temporarily fractured group to unite emotionally, focusing everyone on one thought so fast and smoothly, all ideas of a language barrier disappeared as if they never existed.

As Lilly-Ann worked her greetings around the tipi, she spent more time with some for various reasons, bringing up personal stories relating to each individual. Tears flowed liberally as they revisited a recent tragedy that was all too familiar, all too Indian, one of the tragic occurrences that replayed itself ceremony after ceremony. There was a high incidence of sad tales involving death and dying not only from the distant past, but even the recent, immediate past, often happening between the last ceremony and the present.

As the Water Woman talked her way around the circle, she came to the two Navajo women who had come out with her from her hometown in New Mexico. She paused for what seemed forever, in silence, trying her best to hold back tears, controlling her emotions as much as was possible. These were women that had been in her life for many, many years, and they were getting older by the minute. Neither were used to travel anymore, but both believed so strongly in these ways that they sacrificed their comfort to travel days in the cramped back seat of a pickup truck to participate in a healing prayer service that was specifically aimed at sobriety. They wanted to come at any cost, fully aware that their opportunity to be at this type of ceremony was quickly disappearing.

The eldest, in her late eighties, Lilly-Ann called "Mom". Yesterday, as we were preparing wood by the tipi, Mom was sitting on the moist ground by our small campfire, a gentle mist slowly saturating her turquoise dress as she rolled ears of corn back and forth on the crude campground grill that rested on river rocks on the fire. She prayed in Navajo over the corn, blessing it for the morning sacred food yet to come in this ceremony. I distinctly remember thinking, in my semi-alcoholic stupor at the time, how certain tourists I remember seeing crowding the lookouts at the Grand Canyon in Arizona would have paid good money to photograph that traditional, ancient image I witnessed. As I thought about that scene, it seemed so far away now. Yet, those same tourists would die for a glimpse of this moment, right now, sitting in this tipi, dawn creeping up on us, the Water Woman crying as she greeted her companions, all of us bright and cheerful, sitting around this sacred fire.

I had a sudden, deep feeling of deja-vu. Not necessarily the classic deja-vu of personally being in this situation before, but this overwhelming feeling of this very scene, this ceremony, this whole night, being played over and over, hundreds and hundreds of years ago, and for all I knew, perhaps even right here. This was not different, or strange, only to the current society we happened to be in. This very meeting, in a tipi, in front of a fire, with the Water Woman crying with the participants, the prayers, the healing, the medicine, cedar, tobacco, drum, gourd, staff, Roadman, all of it, was a real life rerun. The people had different names, but it was all the same.

Perhaps the only thing that was unusual was the very fact that I even had this thought, this sudden realization, that this was real, when in fact, this was one of the few things in life anymore that is real. The ceremony wasn't odd; thinking it was odd was the weird part.

Society has changed so much, so fast, advancing beyond its own ability to adapt, and yet, this ceremony, this circle, this opportunity to sit together uninterrupted for 12 hours and be with each other's problems and solutions, to pray, to sing, to experience love and the love of the Creator, forgiveness and healing, sadness and joy, this was reality, this is reality.

To the fortunate few whose parents and grandparents grew up in this way of life, it is a part of their life. Just as outsiders find it impossible to relate to, so does the inner circle of those who have always known this way find it incomprehensible not to be a regular participant in this ceremony. It really wasn't that long ago that this and other traditional means of fellowship and prayer were normal, essential parts of everyday life. Religious practice was not an hour on Sunday, it was as normal as eating and sleeping. Only recently has the necessity of prayer and constant communion with God become like a switch to be turned on only in times of desperate need or sorrow, our Santa Claus in the sky.

Lilly-Ann talked to Mom very slowly, very deliberately, mostly in Navajo, interspersing English words here and there. As I stared at the fire listening to her words, I became immersed in the conversation. I don't remember exactly the moment it happened, not sure if it was gradual or all at once, but as I sat there listening, I understood her every word in Navajo, as if she were speaking in English. And I was so buried in the moment, it didn't occur to me until later that I understood her every word. When I thought back at what she had said, it was in English, but, in fact, the whole conversation was in Navajo. All of us around that fire right then were one people, one blood, one tongue, all sharing our intimate thoughts together as one family. Everyone present was part of what she was saying.

She went over their many trials and troubles, good times and bad that they had been through, old history and more recent situations, much of it relating to suffering and death and dying due to the ravages of alcohol on each other, their siblings, children, spouse, friends, tribal members. Only too recently Mom had lost two grand-daughters in an accident on the Reservation because her son was drunk and driving at the wrong place and the wrong time. She reiterated that part of the story, saying "when you are drunk and driving it is always the wrong place and wrong time, there is no right time to be drunk". They all cried together, as did all of us as part of the family.

There was an unspoken truth about both elder women that we all felt, yet nobody voiced it, because we all knew, and realized there was no reason to bring it up. Both women had already stopped traveling far because of their age and deteriorating health, and they had struggled to come here for this meeting. They sat there strong and proud, all night long, without moving or shifting around, just as they had done hundreds, if not thousands of times before. They did it because they believed in this way of life, this style of prayer. They had faith in its healing power, and loved to watch God in action. They were a remnant of a proud past of many, many people who had lived and worshipped this way forever. As children they had watched the persecution and hatred directed toward this church by the government, attacking their sacred medicine and way of praying, twisting the facts to insult and denigrate this holy sacrament. Yet they persevered, and were witnessing the return of the youth and the weary back to this special way of communion with the Creator.

They traveled hundreds of miles cramped in the back seat of a truck just so they could pray for a total stranger who put his faith in these healing ways, the ways of their grandparents' grandparents, and even before then. I thought of those who, in their cultural ignorance, mock and insult anyone involved in this peyote church, yet would probably change their attitude if they could actually meet someone like these two beautiful matriarchs, kneeling proudly in this tipi, radiating love to everyone they meet. But Lilly Ann knew, as they did, and as we could all feel, this would be the last trip away from home for them, and probably the last ceremony they could stay up all night for. There was a sadness that permeated the very air we were breathing, and it lay heavy on our hearts.

Mom leaned over to the other Elder woman and whispered something to her in Navajo. She smiled in return, and nodded her head. Mom said only a few words.

"If there was a good way to say good-bye, we would say it, like that, aaay. But we don't have that word in our language, because there is no goodbyes. In that way, we will always be in here, long after our bodies have quit working. Just as I saw my father sitting next to the sponsor last night, aay, we, too, will sit up with all of you again. And no better way to finish a lifetime of prayer than to watch the Creator heal one more drunk, to make a man whole again, like that, in that way. We are honored to have been allowed to witness a miracle once again, and because of that, we know God will have pity on many others who will ask for His healing, like that. Thank you, Mister Robbit Hayward, aaay, for having the courage to ask, and the grace to accept God's hand upon your life, like that. The only thing you have to do now is bring the rest of your family inside here, aay, and let them become a part of your miracle. Aho."

The tipi erupted in affirming grunts and groans, and "Ahos" all around. I looked down in humility and even shame, being reminded once again that my "accidental" freefall into this ceremony was not mine to claim. Rather, it was a collective miracle involving so many factors I couldn't begin to bring them into one thought. My inner ranting and whining only hours ago could have prevented this miracle, and ruined not just my chances, but also the hopes of everyone here. I was the only person in this tipi that didn't want to come in, and I was the reason we were all here. My shame was creeping over me, but Lilly-Ann put an immediate end to any negative thoughts because shame had no audience in this time and space.

Lilly-Ann returned to her greetings, with some generalities to lift us up. "What we have to do is encourage one another to continue on this path, this Peyote Road, walk that narrow path on top of the moon altar, help one another, keep each other sober, like that. Drum and sing together, eat and pray together, sponsor more meetings, sometime just to thank God for all of our blessings. And stay in nature, retreat to it when times are hard. It is deep in God's Creation that we will always find our Creator. He resides in his Creation, what is left of it. He created it for His enjoyment, in that way, long before He created us. So we can always get close to Him when we retreat to His Garden of Eden, like that. That is why we must always fight to keep what is left of His garden as pristine as possible. All of your problems can be brought into focus when you go far into the forest, in that way, high up the mountain, out into the desert. Like that, do not neglect that part of your soul that cries out for peace, that peace found only in nature, close to God. Jesus Himself left the crowds and confusion and went into the garden to pray and into the desert to fast and pray.

"Look around you. Everyone next to you, all of us here, are family, like that. We are God's family. He sits among us with favor. He is pleased with our effort. He will help anyone who asks, but we must ask. We must pray. We must live our prayer. Inside here in this tipi is the easy part. As we sit together here around this holy fire, in that way, we admit our mistakes, we cry out for forgiveness, we make amends, we leave our resentments in the fire, we are forgiven, and we promise to walk on His path. Talk is cheap, like that. This is not a religion, not a

Sunday prayer service. It is not even really a church. We have to call it that to satisfy the government. This is a way of life, not a building with a steeple that we attend one hour a week. We must live what we learn in here, and that can only be done by living in constant prayer and communication with God, to see how He wants our day to unfold. We are no longer our own, once we have been through this fire. We belong to the Creator, like that, and our happiness, our joy, comes from being in His will, doing what he has planned for us since the day we were born. Our satisfaction comes from helping others come to the realization that God is in control, and He will light our path if we focus on Him.

"As Daddy said hours ago, when you walk out of this tipi this morning, not just the sponsor, but all of us, you will be making fresh tracks in the new fallen snow, like that. Yesterday's sins, problems, addictions, faults, they are washed away forever. We will all make fresh, new, clean tracks in the white snow. Now comes the test, the hard part. As newborn babes, we are pure, yet easily tripped, easily fallen, unless we cling to the Father, looking up to Him every day, as spiritual beings. We are visiting here, spirits in a borrowed body, to spread the good word, help each other, and pass on a good way of living, like that.

"We must be diligent, clean and sober, or we will stumble again. As long as we stay sober and alert, the enemy cannot touch us. His way into our soul is through the distilled spirits, through the drugs that ruin everyone who uses them, like that. He is cunning like coyote, always blurring the lines between right and wrong, black and white, everything is a shade of gray. Nothing is bad, all is acceptable. What was right is now wrong. What has always been wrong is now right. All behaviors and actions are acceptable. The more perverse, the more destructive, the more acceptable it becomes. Confusion rules the day. Those who speak up for what has always been good, like that, are ridiculed while those who defend evil are revered, to the point that even those of us who know what is true, what is righteous, what is good, begin to question ourselves and even the Creator. For that reason, we have to be strong, awake, sober, able to discern good from bad without any question or doubt. Actions, thoughts, words, conversations that put time proven truths into question, arguments about such basic things as life, birth, death, marriage, family, and personal choices, all thrown into the bowl of utter confusion, blended together with nonsense and ambiguities, creating a bizarre culture of no right or wrong, like that, no left or right, just a haze of gray, obscuring all that we have known forever to be sacred and righteous to be blown away into a sea of mediocrity and lies, leaves everyone feeling completely empty.

"The reason this ceremony still works, why God still comes in here, is because we have never allowed any modernizations, adaptations, or compromises, like that. We will not give in to a society that believes nothing is sacred, that all things must adjust to the whims and desires of what is fashionable today. This political correctness and so-called inclusiveness poisons every institution that stands for good, every path that has discipline and tradition as its core. This new mentality believes God must adapt to man's perversities, not man follow God's goodness, like that. These ideas come and go, but we will always resist. We will never change, because we know that God approves, and that is all the affirmation we need. We do not need modern man to accept our time proven ways. If this current society continues in its dilution of all that is good and sacred, they will probably someday disappear, along with their immorality, confusion, greed, and emptiness. But we will still be here, praying in our tipi as we always have been. They may try to destroy our culture, but they cannot touch our souls, as long as we stay true to our ceremony.

"We must be the light on the hill we always talk about. Our lives must embody the righteousness we preach. All in all, we have to become those Elders we used to look up to as kids. We have to be as Mom and Grandma are here this morning, shining examples of what is good in this world, like that, people of integrity and honor, whose very presence commands respect, whose lives are examples of what it means to be holy, to live among the Creation and close to the Creator, never afraid to stand up for what we believe in, never ashamed of our life, no regrets, no need to apologize for being who we are, children of the Most Holy God.

"Lately I have been remembering the old days that were not really that long ago, but now seem like centuries ago. Sitting in a humble Hu-chunk Winnebago tipi in Wisconsin, we were surrounded by Roadmen and other holy men still physically and spiritually connected to the old ways, like that, unencumbered by the modern world and all of its addictions. Some of them were over 100 years old, and their minds were still sharp as a knife. They would talk about growing up in the wilderness, learning the old secrets from their grandparents, close to God and close to the earth. All of them were healers of one kind or another, it was in their blood. None of them ever drank alcohol or ate white sugar. In fact, they didn't like sweet things, something I couldn't relate to, because I was raised on sweets, and still love them to this day, like that, and my doctor tells me I have to stay away from them. They were natural born hunters and fishermen, and they spent many months threshing wild rice out of the lakes. When those old men spoke about living clean and pure, like that, it was from personal experience, not wishful thinking.

"When many of their families were rounded up and torn apart to be sent to orphanages and boarding schools, many of them took their families deep into the wilderness and separated from all society, living off of the land as best as they could in the increasingly limited space they could hunt and hide out. Once they were finally forced to live within the confines of the Reservation, they were outcasts, small groups whose social and spiritual lives revolved around all of the ancient ceremonies. Taught by their schools to reject them, the main people on the Reservations treated them as outcasts, outsiders, heathens, like that. They never assimilated into the new subculture of drinking, fighting, and dying.

"We used to go to so many meetings like that, surrounded by Elders that have now become a part of ancient history, we had no idea how fortunate we had been to have connected with that rich part of our collective past, learning from those who were still free as children. And before we knew it, they walked on to the other side, leaving the young ones to carry it on, as we have done, as best as we know how, trying our very hardest to help whoever we can in as honorable a way as we know how, like that. And as I look around this tipi filled with young warriors, I know I am looking at the next generation of Roadmen and Water Women, and it makes me proud. Sad, but proud."

Once again, her words brought tears to her eyes, and all of ours. I felt the sadness she spoke of, the rapid passing of time, and I felt an urgency, too. How much time had I wasted, how many years, chasing a bottle, when I should have been following my conscience? Time that I had to make up, and the only way I could do it was grab on to this moment, and remember. I had to be sober from now on, I had to focus on what God has for me, and I had to be real, because half of my life was already gone, thrown away. Now is the moment.

Lilly-Ann again turned to me. "As I told you yesterday, like that, we all become relatives in this tipi. We are a family, and we adopt each other as blood. All night I have prayed, asking God who you are to me, Robert. For Navajo, the Din'e people, a nephew is like a son, and a son is as a nephew. I am adopting you as my nephew, and you will always be related to me in that way. When I was your age, I, too, was a hopeless alcoholic. I related to your problem all night, like that, just as most of us here did. We are all bound together by our past, by our mistakes, and by what we do to overcome these mistakes. It is not so important the mistakes we make, what is really important is what we do about these mistakes. You are connected to me through that alcohol, but in a good way. You are now exiting on the other side of the abyss, finished with the problem. You have passed the test. Now you can use that alcohol in a good way, you can counsel others who are drowning in it, show them a way out, a way up. I was an alcohol counselor for many years, and helped many hopeless people see themselves for who they really are, not who the alcohol tells them that they aren't.

"Now that you have traveled that road and survived, you can better understand, better empathize with those who are seduced by the evil that is alcohol, like that, and help them escape a certain death. You can take that negative and now turn it into a positive. Now you know that it isn't a weakness, that even the strong and proud, who are in total control, can be destroyed by this wandering spirit. You are able to understand more fully what it is like to be completely consumed by that distilled evil. Now you can have true pity on those who have a harder time than you to overcome it. I can see, looking at you right now after my husband gave you that medicine, that you are through with alcohol. I've seen it before. I can honestly look at you this morning and see a different person than I met yesterday. I see clarity, resolve, and power, where yesterday I saw only confusion and defeat.

"You are one of the fortunate ones, like that, because you asked, and you also were ready to receive. Too many do not take that step of faith, like that, and struggle endlessly with this problem. This morning, as I look across this tipi at you, I see a free man. It brings tears to my eyes to see this miracle unfold this morning." Tears fell again, tears of joy, all around.

She continued. "You can answer that age old question with authority; if a tree falls in the forest with nobody around to hear it, does it still make a sound? You were there. You were nobody. God's Creation does not need the verification of man's ego to justify its day to day existence. God created the world before man, and does not need man to approve of His handy work, nor to witness its majesty, like that. And yet, God created us in His image, and He cares that much more for each one of us. He gives us free will, to make foolish decisions. But He also gives us an out, an escape for those bad ideas. All we have to do is ask, then return to His side, willing to do what He suggests, because He really does have our very best interest in mind. He hears every noise, sees every mistake, answers every prayer, everything He has created has His undivided attention, always."

I looked up through the open flap at what were stars, now as the morning was breaking, as the dawn was creeping up, it was getting ever so subtly lighter. But there was no sky, only what appeared to be clouds. I strained my wet eyes, rubbing them to clear them up, staring at what I finally recognized as thousands of tiny snowflakes mixing with the smoke swirling out. Some slowly drifted inside, and danced around the opening, melting as they fell closer to the heat from the fire below. I looked and looked, sure I was seeing things. It does snow up here, rarely, only in the dead of a very cold winter, never in September during a drought, that I could remember. I elbowed Franco to have him look, an idea I instantly regretted and tried to reverse, but it was too late.

Franco sat up straight, nearly standing up. I reached over to grab him in case he jumped up. He stared up into the snow flurry, and let it out, unconsciously for sure, being the Franco we all loved by now. "Man, oh man, check it out, dude. Brother, he was right. I thought he was crazy, but he was right, man. It's frickin' snowing right now, man! I can't even believe my eyes! Look, it's snowing. It doesn't snow here, never, man, never. I mean, it is snowing, and it's summer. Holy crap. This is a frickin' miracle, man. Look, man! We are gonna make fresh tracks. Maybe even a snowman. Wow!"

He would have carried on more, but the laughter drowned him out. Everybody was laughing out loud, even Johnny this time. And looking up at the snow, we laughed, knowing Franco was right. It was a miracle.

It snowed for at least an hour, and the temperature reflected it. Not only is that two hour period just before sunrise the coldest of the whole night, when it snows, it is especially frigid. Johnny went outside to get more wood, and we all peeked outside as he went. It was still very dark, that odd time of pitch black just as the light starts to show up. All I could see was white, solid white, in the darkness. It was coming down steadily and covering everything. As the door crashed down, it sent in a huge wave of ice-cold air, and floated it all around the room. Lilly-Ann got the worst of it, kneeling by the door, and she let us know, as she pulled her blanket over her prayer shawl, wrapping it tighter and reached her open palms towards the fading fire.

Under normal circumstances, the Fireman would not rebuild the fire as the Water Woman sat in front of it, but this called for more heat and light, and more wood was the only way to accomplish that. When he came back in, loaded with snow-covered logs, the freezing air came rushing in again. I could feel it at my seat, and knew it must be much worse at the door. I got off of the dusty blanket I had ground into the dirt all night, and wrapped it around my back, surely looking like a cave man more than anything else. This was the first time I actually felt cold, and it felt good, refreshing. I felt alive, and for the first time in forever, didn't immediately think of drinking tequila to warm myself up. It was a liberating feeling not to have to return to my devastating habits. The dirty blanket did the trick.

Everybody had the same idea, but they all had a separate, clean blanket, shawl or jacket, and all looked great in their new colors. Franco was like me, unprepared, so he wrapped a free part of his blanket around his back, and let out a long "Brrrr!", one that said it all.

Johnny quickly and smoothly added three sticks to each side of the fire, compressed it together, spread a few hot embers out over the darkening heart to liven it up, and sat back down. The melting snow hissed as it evaporated, refusing to let the wood fully ignite. Then he got back up again, took his broom and waved it fast across the face of the fire, until it suddenly leaped into bright white flames, pouring heat throughout the tipi and spotlighting everybody's smiling face. Lilly-Ann thanked him and asked for the fire stick, ready to light her smoke.

She addressed me one last time. "Nephew, you have won this battle, and we are all happy you did. Now you have to honor us by staying sober. If you want to, it will be easy, but you have to want it. You owe it to yourself, to your family, to God, to my husband, this medicine, this ceremony, everyone here, to succeed, or you disrespect all of us. You have a duty to spread the love and healing you have received in here tonight. We have all shed a lot of tears together, but a new day is here, and the time has come to wipe away those tears of the past, and greet the sun with happiness, and greet God's Son with happiness. It has been a long journey for all of us, but the sadness has to be replaced with joy. It is time to smile, because we have won. Healing has come here today in this sacred tipi, because we have faith. We are all going to make new tracks in this miraculous snow outside. The old has passed, the new has come. And the next time you come back into this tipi, you will bring your family, and the circle will be complete, like that.

"So I say to you, Nephew, and all of my relatives, from the doorway in to the doorway out; yah'ah'teh' ah'bin'eh, good morning, good morning, good morning! I love you all, and God bless you, like that. I will say a short prayer for this water, for my nephew, and for all of us here, and then we will drink this sacred Morning Water and become well, as the sun rises on this new and wonderful day."

The Fireman handed her the fire stick, and she lit her smoke, filling the entire area around her with the white, thick tobacco smoke. She prayed in Navajo. This time I couldn't understand her words, but I felt her sincerity. Then she switched to English, summarizing all she had prayed, asking God for forgiveness, begging Him to continue having pity on us all, thanking Him for His love, and thanking Him for healing her nephew, the sponsor. She pleaded with Him to keep me well, and keep all of us well, safe, and happy. She asked for special blessings for every person in the tipi, mentioning each person by name and their particular need, leaving nobody out. She even asked God to help her new brother, Franco, learn to speak without using those bad words. And she thanked God that Franco gave up his night to sit up with his friend, and asked that more people could be as giving.

She finished her "short prayer" just as the fire was again fading away, and the brisk predawn air started filling the tipi again. "Heavenly Father, Creator, God, please bless this sacred water, this precious water of life. Let it heal each person as they drink it this beautiful morning that You have allowed us to participate in once again. May it bring new life to our weary souls in a good way, and I ask this in the name of the Almighty Father, your Native Son Jesus, and the Holy and Great Spirit. Amen and Aho."

She handed the smoke to Johnny, who took four puffs, got up and walked it over to Sonny, who sat smoking it for a few silent minutes. The tipi was getting light; entire bodies were emerging out of the darkness, no longer just lit up faces and bright smiles. I was amazed how good everyone looked - wide awake, alert and happy. Nobody looked like they had just stayed up all night through several different storms and hours of endless prayer and singing. Afraid of how I looked, I tried not to think about it, wrapped in a dirty blanket, mud all over what used to be my eyes, kneeling directly on the damp earth. But I felt alive, I felt great, better than I could remember.

The snow was subsiding, and the mocking birds and blue jays were starting to greet the new day. Johnny went back out to get more wood, and as the door opened, everyone peeked outside, gasping at the raw beauty of white snow everywhere. A big flock of wild turkeys scattered as he popped out, gobbling and screaming while they half flew, half ran up the slope toward the road.

"Nephew, thank you again for thinking of this way for your healing. This is a beautiful way. It is very special to everyone here, and to many others, and we appreciate you putting your faith in God and in this medicine to get better. That alcohol, it's no good for anyone, but this medicine, it's good for everyone. Some people don't understand it, some people think they can use it for other things, but you can't, because it is for getting better, that's all. It's not for those who don't understand it, and that's okay, because they might have their own way. But for us, it has always worked. It opens up your faith, it allows you to accept God's healing.

"Even if you don't know it yet, but I think you do, you are healed. I saw that medicine work on you last night. I saw it in the stars, in the coals, and in that medicine. I know what it has done. And you kept it all down. We were all waiting for you to get sick, but you did good. This medicine works differently with each person. Usually people throw up that much medicine, they clean out. That's good too. It's not shameful to get sick. We call it getting well, not sick. But that medicine had to go deep inside you to do its work. You had some deep problems it had to fix. And it did its job. You are going to be okay. Next time your family is going to sit up with you in your new home, this tipi. Everything is going to be okay."

Sonny passed the smoke to Duane, the Cedarman next to me. He smoked quietly, then spoke briefly, greeting his friends, his relatives, eventually everyone in a general way, then he also thanked me for sponsoring the meeting. He laughed, "I think we were all waiting for you to throw up last night." Several people laughed out loud, especially Franco. *Don't get him going,* I thought to myself. "I was ready to move over and out of your way if you did, but you surprised us all. It never happened. Nobody got sick. This was good. It was rough, but it was good. I had my doubts in the beginning, but when you finally let go, it got smooth, real smooth. I am happy to be here, happy to have been able to help. And you helped me and my family more than you will ever know. So, thank you, like that. In this way, I say thank you. Aho."

He walked the smoke to the Drummer, who took four puffs, blew the smoke on the drum and drum stick, then Duane tossed a handful of cedar into the coals and put the end of the smoke among the crackling, smoking evergreen and sat down. By now, Johnny had the fire rebuilt and stacked, radiating heat once again. He began spreading the new batch of hot embers from the fire out again, erasing the heart, filling the entire space between the fire and the moon altar, a giant half circle of pulsating red hot coals that warmed us so much that blankets, jackets, and other layers began coming off. Everybody started shifting around and stretching, reawakening for a new beginning.

After the coals were all spread out perfectly, Duane stood up again with the cedar bag and threw in another big handful of evergreen incense and announced this was for all of us, to bless ourselves in this new morning. All of us reached for the big cloud of smoke and pulled in four big double handfuls of it, blessing every part of our tired yet alert bodies, smiling and laughing silently. Then he put in a little more, and said, "This is for you, Auntie, and for the water."

I took note of that relation, suddenly interested how I fit in with everyone. If he was her nephew, logic told me we were brothers. When he sat down, I leaned over and said, "So we're brothers, now. Good morning, Brother."

He looked at me and said, "No, I think of you as my nephew, after babysitting you all night, so, actually I'm your uncle." Now I was confused, and he saw it in my look. "Each person is related to the other according to who adopts who, it isn't like blood. We cannot choose our blood family, but in here, we can choose our relatives. It is determined more or less by the medicine. Our first ceremony together and I was your helpful uncle all night, so I am adopting you as my nephew. You will see how it works with time. Some have children older than them, and others have parents younger than them. It is a spiritual family, so the rules are different. It doesn't matter much, just that we recognize that we are all relatives. These are all of my relations. You will no longer call Lilly-Ann by her name. It is Auntie from now on. And it sounds like Sonny has also taken you as a nephew, so you will always refer to him as Uncle, same as me. He is my uncle, also, so don't try to put your typical thinking into all of this. Just remember who is who. Sometimes it's actually easier, because names are hard to remember, but relatives stick in your mind forever. Good morning, Nephew."

"Good morning, Uncle," I responded.

Franco only heard that, and blurted out, "Dude, Duane is your uncle? Last night you told me you didn't know anybody in here. What's up with that? Who else are you related to in here, man?"

"Everyone, including you," I replied. He looked over at me like I was crazy, again. "Yeah, right, whatever, anyway, man...I mean...Brother."

Lilly-Ann, or, I should say, Auntie, reached into the swirling cloud of sweet smoke and pulled it over the water bucket four times, blessing it. She then flipped the handle toward the fire, symbolically opening up the bucket for drinking, and tipped the bucket toward herself slightly, spilling out a tiny amount onto the ground, offering Mother Earth the first drink. She then stood up, picked up the heavy bucket and placed it in front of the Doorman on the south side of the door, faced the bird to the fire, put the handle on the fire side of the bucket, and handed him the cup. Then she knelt back down in front of the fire on her folded blanket.

The Doorman took only one cupful, gulped it down, and passed the bucket to the man on his left, handing him the cup. Sonny said a few words, then offered the floor to anybody wanting to express themselves, what might be on their mind.

Several spoke up, very short and concise affirmations pertaining to the ceremony, healing, and all so thankful they were here. One young Indian, mid-thirties, told his story, short, powerful, and to the point. His name was Irving Tso from Window Rock, Arizona. He had been living out here for a few years, drinking and working. He was at the campground right next door, my old stomping grounds, one year ago yesterday exactly. He got real drunk with some of the locals, then blacked out. He woke up in his car 50 miles away, up in the mountains, his car wrapped around a signpost. The engine was cool, so it had happened hours before he woke up. The cops arrested him, and while he sobered up in jail, he came to the realization that his drinking was out of control. He quit that day, one year ago. This morning was his one year birthday of sobriety. He heard there was a sobriety meeting up here, so he wanted to be a part of it.

Irving addressed me pointedly, "I want to thank you for this meeting. I didn't know you last night, but I feel as if I know you now. You're like all of the rest of us, only you did what we all need to do, and that is to confess ourselves before God and man, and submit to the healing of the Creator. Your story is my story, it's everyone's story, but you wanted a better ending to your story. You weren't satisfied with giving in to this horrible enemy we all face. You asked for help, in a good way. I watched my grandpa fix up that medicine for you last night, and I saw something happen to you. I felt something happen inside you, and it happened to me and probably many others here tonight, and very possibly some that weren't here but who we prayed for."

There was a noticeable round of vocal affirmation, groaning, grunting, and "Ahos" from all present. In helping myself, I had inadvertently helped countless others with the same problem. The miracle was shared by many here, and I was to find out, even some relatives that were prayed about that night quit drinking right then, and like myself, 10 years later, never started up again.

"Your pouring out of your very soul, your honest and sincere cry for help, was answered last night by God, and the miracle will continue. You must share what you have learned in here with others that have the same problem. You need to carry this message to a hurting world. People can be helped, and they don't even need the medicine. They just need to pray, to cry out, to repent, to return to God and get among His Creation, and take that thirteenth step, that final commitment, to never say 'no' again, as my brother Red Hawk told you last night. The secret is to stop, to submit, and to empower yourself through the Creator, and never give up that power again, Never take that first drink again. That power to be free is available to all who ask for it if they are sincere, and really mean it. Taking that Thirteenth Step, in the fresh snow, never looking back, a new beginning, it is possible, and you proved it to the biggest skeptic in here: yourself. Thank you again, Brother, and good morning to you and to everyone from the doorway in to the doorway out. Aho."

Once again, when the water reached the Roadman, all talking stopped. Sonny threw cedar into the fire, picked up the eagle bone, and whistled four times, announcing the sunrise. Then he took his eagle feather, dipped it into the bucket, crossed the top of the water, then splashed the water to the four directions around him. It was just like Midnight Water. He blessed us all with the water-dipped feather, fanning half the tipi, reloading, and finishing off the other side, as we sat with outstretched hands, happily accepting the early morning baptism.

Expecting to get that drenched feeling I got during Midnight Water's baptism, I was not let down. As soon as I looked up at him flicking the big black and white feather in my direction, the rain came pouring down. I was dumbfounded, because at midnight it was very dark outside, and the fire had gotten low as Johnny sat there unable to attend to the wood. At that time, I couldn't see the feather real well,

297

only feel the large amount of water pouring on me. Now, in the pre-dawn light, which was getting brighter by the second, with a fully loaded fire going, I saw the feather, and also the water pouring down on me. I was unable to comprehend how this feather, big as it was, could hold all of that water. Even Franco felt it, commenting as discreetly as he was able, "Dude, now I'm soaking wet, man, can you believe it?"

I bowed my head and quietly thanked God again for this miracle that I knew was taking place. Thanked Him for this water blessing. Thanked Him for my life, something unthinkable only 12 hours ago.

Then I looked up, watching Sonny splashing everybody. When I rubbed my hands on my soaking arms, they were bone dry, exactly as they were at midnight. I looked over at Franco, who was in the process of discovering this contradiction of reality, and knew he was about to blast the news to everybody, so I shook my head as if to say "No!", then nodded as if to agree with the insanity of the situation. He caught on, shook his head back and forth, and rubbed his dry arms vigorously, saying nothing. Another miracle, Franco restrained himself.

When the water got to me, again I was suddenly parched. I guzzled four full cups, savoring every drop, wanting more. One or two more people expressed themselves as the water made its way to the door. Every time someone addressed me as brave, or strong, or other undeserved adjectives, I lowered my head and stared at the ground, embarrassed. If I had any pride left when I came in, it was completely gone now. And all of this attention and recognition only served to humble me more, rather than fill me up. As I emphasized many times before, nothing I said or did brought me here last night wanting to repent and be saved. I was fighting it all the way to the tipi door, and for a long time after it had rolled shut. No matter how big the capacity of my ego might have been, it was completely deflated now, fully aware that even against my strongest protestations, God had landed me right here, and I was humbled and thankful that He did. But there was no way that I could take any credit, not the tiniest amount, for what had happened. There wasn't enough of my pickled brain left to prepare and organize something as powerful and miraculous as this. Not to mention the fact that I didn't even know such an opportunity existed. So I thanked each person for their praise, and protested quietly that I deserved less than none of it.

When Johnny took his last sip of water at the door, he picked up the bucket, set it in front of Auntie once more, and she drank four full cups, thirsty from kneeling so close to the fire for so long. She then stood up slowly, pulled her shawl around herself, and carried the nearly empty bucket clockwise around the tipi back to the door, then took it outside. She came back in and, starting with the Doorman at the south side of the door, went person to person, shaking each hand or hugging them, greeting each one with a warm and sincere "Good Morning! Yah'ah'teh' ah'bin'eh!" Some, like her elderly traveling companions and husband, she would hug tightly and cry, bringing emotions to my heart that I was sure I had drowned forever. When she came to me, I stood up and hugged her firmly, as she exclaimed "Yah'ah'teh' nephew, I welcome you to a blessed and all-new beautiful day!" We stood embracing and crying for several moments, as everyone affirmed the bond.

Naturally, Franco jumped up and hugged her also, and kept repeating how sorry he was. Finally, Auntie put an end to it once and for all. "What are you sorry for? You have absolutely nothing to be sorry for. Thank you for bringing my nephew in here, Brother."

Franco beamed at the adoption, and smiled back. "Thank you, Sister, thank you. Yeah, thank you, Sister." Once Lilly-Ann got to the door, Sonny was gathering up the staff, gourd, sage, and feather fan, while Orlando pulled the drum to his mouth and blew air into the skin, pumping it up for action. Sonny announced it was time for the sacred meal. Some of the women would go out and bring in the four foods of the morning meal. Once the bowls were in place, Sonny would sing the final four songs, and the ceremony was finished. It sounded like we were moments away from leaving the tipi, but that was only a fantasy. Very similar to the timer on a football game, who announces only 12 minutes left to play, and one hour later they finally walk off of the field.

I had to admit, I heard somebody mention coffee, and it sounded real good to me. Sonny sensed the anxiousness, and said that the medicine was available for anyone who needed it. That was a signal that there was plenty of morning left in here, and if you were tired, now was the time to refuel, or forever hold your peace. Coffee sounded good, and the taste was predictable, but it wasn't going to happen anytime soon. Indian coffee was definitely on the agenda. For me, if I took the time to think about it, with the amount I had consumed hours ago, sleep was far from my mind, even being tired. The coffee thing was just about old habits and rituals that sounded good, yet were totally unnecessary. Orlando stood up, picked up the medicine bucket and bowl of dried peyote powder, and brought it over to me, the sponsor, as was protocol, and, with a wide smile, asked me if I was ready for more.

Not about to rock the boat at this juncture, I nodded in agreement. I took a tiny spoonful of the dried powder, and pushed it into my mouth. Then I immediately followed it with four fast cups of cold, bitter tea, now condensed at the bottom of the bucket. It was thick and hard to swallow. I downed them rapidly, again trying to have my throat beat my mind in the race for rejection and expulsion. The upheavals came, the muted gag reflexes pushed hard, but there was no way I was going to throw up now, after going through the whole night intact. But my body totally disagreed with my resolve, and protested all the way down. I passed the bucket, cup, and bowl fast, hoping to put the attention on Franco, so I could fight the urge to vomit without an audience. After a few miserable minutes, the waves of nausea subsided enough for me to relax so I could once again watch the morning unfold.

Franco took my mind off of the intense nausea when he started licking his lips and whispered to me about how much he loved the taste of almonds, or some other nut, fully assured by now that he also came from the nut family. One thing was for sure, to me this medicine had absolutely no taste resembling any kind of nut. It was definitely an acquired taste, one that took me several ceremonies to acquire, but I did take notice how for the old timers in here, their reaction certainly did not betray any negative response to consuming this sacred medicine, in any form. Those who have been consuming this medicine since early childhood generally enjoyed the flavor, having no mental prejudices against it, while newcomers usually aren't exactly enthralled with the taste. Duane mentioned to me earlier on how God purposely made the medicine very bitter so it could never become popular; you had to want to be in this ceremony to partake of it.

301

Soon the gag reflexes ended, and the medicine settled in, giving me energy and alertness, along with that clarity that brought total understanding to all that was being said, in any language.

CHAPTER 20

THE THIRTEENTH STEP

As the women got together the morning food, we could hear them slipping and sliding in the snow and ice, and freezing in the cold morning air. One of the men commented about the snow, and told a short story about being buried in a blizzard in a tipi ceremony in South Dakota. When the women returned they carried three bowls and the refilled water bucket. The bucket sat next to the lighter stick in front of the fire. The three bowls in a row matched the bucket, beautiful glazed surface with intricate airbrush designs that were coordinated, definitely a complete set.

Now I understood many of the items in the local "Indian Store" that specialized in all things Native, including art, beads, music, and trinkets, mostly actual Indian-made, not Chinese imitations. There was an area that had fancy, short brooms, obviously for the Fireman, along with long, ornate staffs, gorgeous fans, single feathers, many gourd rattles, brass and cast iron kettles for the drum, and various Water Bird jewelry. There was a shelf with ornately decorated bowl sets and buckets, and small cups and tiny spoons. All at outrageous prices, and I could never figure out who would buy only three matching bowls, what the buckets were for, and why anybody would want a decorated half broom. Suddenly, it all made sense as I stared at the matching bucket and bowls sitting on the ground by the fire. I looked around and recognized all sorts of paraphernalia being used and worn. But the fact that an entire ceremonial society existed right in front of me and I never had a clue really didn't surprise me, considering I had been in my own selfish world of destruction for so long, nothing would have caused me to see this. And a big community it is, spread all over the United States, in every nook and cranny, quiet, devout, strong, and spiritual relatives, with various secret tipi sites where the ceremonies are held and disappear as fast as a weekend flies by. Even on the Hawaiian Islands, and some parts of mainland Mexico, this way of life has managed to survive and flourish, changing and saving lives as it has for centuries.

The first bowl after the water bucket had corn kernels cut off the cob cooked on the outside fire yesterday by my Aunt's mom, Grandma, to me, I suppose. The next bowl was filled with canned fruit I recognized from my stocked motor home. I felt good knowing I had accidentally provided at least something proper for the ceremony. Following that was meat, but from where I was sitting, I couldn't tell what kind or where it came from. The tradition for this aspect of the ceremony, as with all else, was identical every time. Always, the sacred water of life. Then corn, unsalted and unseasoned, the basis for many Native foods, the gift from the Creator. Then came the fruit, sometimes fresh, often canned or frozen, simple yet full of energy-producing natural sugar. Finally, the meat, always unsalted and unseasoned, but always meat. This was definitely not a meal for vegetarians. Regardless of someone's attitude on nutrition and diet, this will never change to adjust to the latest food fads. What worked in the beginning is still working now, and is not about to be altered for a group of people with new ideas.

The food really didn't spark any hunger pangs for me right now, but I also knew when it came around I would probably readily eat it. Suddenly Sonny was singing the last four songs, and everybody sat up or got on their knees, right back into the moment. The singing was loud, strong, powerful. We were all singing. Some had brought out their own gourds and fans, and were joining in with the instrumentals. By the second song, the intensity was indescribable. Sonny was on his knees, but just barely. He had the staff, sage, feather, and white eagle fan in his left hand but it was up in the air, not planted into the ground as usual. He was shaking the gourd as fast as possible with his right hand, and Orlando kept up perfect beat, pounding away on the drum and singing loudly. Everybody was giving their all, a united song of praise and gratitude, of thanksgiving for the miracle.

Both Franco and I were singing along, nearly shouting, word for word to a song in a different language we had never heard before. The words just flowed out of our mouths, as if we had practiced this song for years. Not bothering to figure it out, we sang our hearts out. This was a true catharsis, and it was exhilarating. It was bright, the fire was hot, and the music was deafening. I looked around at each person, quickly making eye contact with everyone and feeling their joy. My heart raced, tears poured down my cheeks. Finally, after all of these years, tears of complete happiness.

The second song blended right into the third, without skipping a beat. We sang this one harder and louder than the last. Sonny was nearly on his feet. The only thing missing was us getting up and dancing. Fortunately, that isn't part of the ceremony.

There was a slight break from the third song to the last, the quitting song. Everybody was staring at the door, so I looked, too, not having a clue what they were looking at, or even if they really were looking at anything. It was almost like a made-up scene in a low budget movie, only it was real, and I was witnessing it. It started at the top corners of the roll down door, then worked its way down to the floor. The rising sun had just peaked over the trees, and shot bright rays of light directly into the center of the tipi. Sonny had positioned the door directly east. The light split into two giant beams that came through equally on both sides of the door, flooding the open cracks with light, then flooding the center of the tipi in orange and white. Just as the bright beams hit Sonny directly in his face and illuminated him like he was on fire, he started shaking the gourd vigorously, and Orlando jumped in with the drum. Sonny began belting out the words to the final closing song, *Gayatina.* He was lit up from head to toe, singing and shaking the gourd, looking everything like a rising spirit, a good spirit. The feeling, the singing, the visual light show, was almost too much to take in at once. The emotions were so strong, the song was nearly cried out, with not one dry eye in the tipi. I was hyperventilating, enjoying every breath of fresh crisp morning air as it filled my soul to overflowing. The light show was the perfect grand finale, couldn't have been planned any better by Disney himself. It's impossible to outdo the Creator of the universe.

I really felt like a new person, inside and out, free from my sickness once and for all. And time would prove it to be an accurate feeling.

At the last chorus, Sonny lowered the staff to the ground, then slowly raised it and the gourd in his other hand as high as they could reach, and as we all sang out the last word, everyone raised both of their hands up in unison, a final act of praise and submission.

That was followed with exhilarating groaning, moaning, "Ahos", and yelps like a pack of happy coyotes. In the distance, we heard the real coyotes respond with howls and barking, which brought laughter to everyone. The other sounds of nature resumed with the morning cries of hawks, crows, mocking birds, blue jays, wild turkeys, and dozens of different small songbirds beginning their day. The river was roaring, releasing the extra water from last night's downpour. I heard somebody talking by the river, probably a relative of someone inside who had slept in their car or truck. I felt like I recognized one of the voices, but that thought vanished as fast as it came. The road above us was beginning to get its sparse traffic, with the occasional big rig overdoing the jake brake, and the early-rising Harley riders roaring past.

It felt like we had been inside this tipi for days. Time had expanded so everything could be accomplished, a concept about time taught to me in a later ceremony that explains all kinds of inconsistencies in life that seemingly don't add up. I thought of millions of people just waking up to repeat yesterday's mistakes again, unable to stop the cycle of insanity on their own. I thought of myself, knowing my cycle of destruction was over, and could not contain my joy. Never before had I felt so sure about anything, and I knew it was real. Yet, if I tried to explain it to anybody, there was no way to convey the whole concept. I would soon find this out with my family; words had lost their power long ago with them. It would take action to prove the truth, a slow, yet successful endeavor. Thinking of my wife and kids brought tears to my already wet eyes. I wanted to go home this minute and beg for forgiveness. And I thought of my parents, all that I had put them through over the years. I wanted to hug them and tell them how sorry I was, also.

As if he had read my mind, and most likely he had, Sonny addressed me again, breaking the silence of this phenomenal moment. "Nephew, now you must make amends. But don't rush it, take your time, and don't think you can do it with words alone. How you act in the coming weeks will determine how much forgiveness, if any, you will receive from anyone. You have caused a lot of damage, over a long period of time. Don't think you can simply erase it overnight as easily as you just erased your own problem. It will come, if you are careful and wise, and use your life as an example, not your words. Very few people are going to take you seriously for a long time. But if you stay on this road," he pointed to the moon altar, sweeping his hand in an arc, following the curve of the moon, "eventually, other people are going to want to climb up and follow you on this road, because they will want what you have."

He paused long enough for his words to sink in, then continued. "But do not get proud. Keep the humility I saw you come to last night, and stay focused. You have been given a gift. For whatever reason, the Creator has chosen to bring you to this place, so do not forget where you have been. Too easily, we think somehow we are responsible for our rebirth, that our own, great power brought us back from the brink, and that we are invincible now. It is pride, vanity, and arrogance that got you in trouble, and humility and submission to God that has saved you. Do not forget it. You cannot be defeated, but you can defeat yourself, simply by thinking you can do this all alone, without God, and without your relations. We are all together in this journey. None of us can make it alone, so do not try, or this night will fade away like a distant memory, never to return. Start and end every day in prayer. Ask God for direction in all you do, and help others come to this same reality, and the road will lay itself out before you and direct your path. You will reach the end of this moon, and even beyond. Stay on this path that has been opened for you."

Duane got up and put a big amount of cedar in the coals, and told me to bless myself, to cement those words deep into my soul. I reached into the cloud of smoke and pulled it to me four times, washing it over my body, and tapping it into my chest, into my heart, breathing deeply as I went. Then Duane tossed in another handful, and told everybody to do the same, to bless themselves with this morning's sweet scented evergreen billowing up and swirling around the tipi. Everyone reached in and sanctified the words of wisdom.

As Duane stood there, he talked about the morning. "I was taught that the morning belonged to the woman, that this is the time of new life, of birth, of nurturing and growth. They also taught me that it was the time for the women to bless us, and bless the morning meal. So I am going to hand this cedar to my sister, Cheyenne, who I have great respect for, who I have known since I was little, and who just recently lost her little brother to this alcohol. I want her to share her wisdom with us and to bless the morning meal, the sacred food prepared for us." He stopped and wiped the tears from his eyes, trying to regain his composure, after thinking of Cheyenne's brother. Obviously most, if not all here, knew her, and also knew her brother, and were all quietly crying, the tissues were coming out again. I didn't know either of them, but I felt like I did, and couldn't hold back my tears either. When I closed my eyes, I saw a young, round-faced Indian boy, laughing. The picture was crystal clear, and when she showed me his photo later that day, I recognized him from my short vision.

Duane walked clockwise around to her. At the door he had to turn the lighter stick to the side, opening the gate, and passed through in front of the water bucket and behind the fire. When he came to her, he finished talking. "Good morning, Sister, thank you for being here, and thank you for your prayers. I love you, and it was good to sit up with you again after all of these years. Thank you for supporting all of us during this hard time for you and your family, Aho." He held out his hand and helped her up.

She struggled to rise up, then rewrapped her shawl around her, stretching her tired and cramped legs. She took the cedar bag and stepped closer to the fire. Duane also handed her the big eagle feather Sonny had used throughout the ceremony.

She wiped her eyes, then smiled. She introduced herself, and when she spoke, I recognized her voice. It was her who had talked to me outside the tipi just before Midnight Water and disappeared into the dark.

She started as all others had, by introduction. "My name is Cheyenne Sam. I am Din'e, from the Turtle Clan, and I grew up in Keyenta, on the Navajo Reservation. I am related to many of you in here, including my uncle, Sonny Hogan. Good morning, Uncle." Sonny answered in Navajo, and she responded in Navajo, then talked in that language for several minutes, and as she broke into tears, so did all of the Din'e speakers around me. The sobbing went on, and I just held my head low, staring at the ground through my damp eyes.

Then she resumed her English, "I am sorry, and I apologize to the sponsor, Robert Hayward, for speaking in my Native language and excluding you from my conversation. I just wanted to say a few things to my relations in here that can't be expressed completely in the English language, because some words in Din'e don't come out the same in English, and English is not my first language, so please forgive me." I looked up at her and nodded, barely letting out a quiet "Aho", feeling very self-conscious, not even considering her possibly offending me in any way during her sorrow.

"I will tell you as best as I can, but first I want to thank you for sponsoring this meeting, from the bottom of my heart. I really needed this, and got what I came for. I heard about this meeting, and drove 12 hours right after I got off work to attend this prayer service, and today I will drive 12 hours back home, only with great joy in my heart, not the sadness and the anger that I brought with me. So thank you, Brother, for putting up this meeting, even though I think you really didn't know what to expect. I know what has happened, and many things happened to me last night and this morning, and I really needed that. As I said to you outside the tipi at midnight, you have a lot of power, I can see it, and I saw it last night when my uncle gave you that special medicine from the stars, just like my father used to do when he was alive." She paused for a second, then went on. "And like my uncle said, that power is not yours, it comes from the Creator, but it is real, and you need to learn how to use it in a good way, now that you are a part of these ways." As she spoke, she pointed to the moon and the fire.

"This alcohol, this evil curse to my people, to all people, it doesn't care who it kills. In fact, it only wants to kill, that is its whole purpose. Don't let those Super Bowl commercials fool you, it doesn't make you big, and strong, and happy, and get all of the girls. That is the lie, and you know that now. It wants to kill you, and destroy your family, and all families. It tried to destroy mine, and I almost let it."

She stopped again, and wiped her eyes with a tissue. "Last week, we were having a little gathering at my mother's house in memory of my dad, who walked on to be with the ancestors one year ago. He had diabetes, and even though he was a Roadman, and healed hundreds of people in ceremonies just like this, he couldn't heal himself, and he accepted that, and my mom accepted that, but none of us kids ever accepted it. We have been angry with the Creator about it ever since, at least until last night. But on that day last week, one of the teenagers in our little neighborhood, if you could call it that, was drinking with his friends, like they do every day. Only on this day, he decided to take his brother's car while he was sleeping off a hangover, and race up and down the dirt road by our house. He drove past our house maybe 100 miles an hour, everybody inside yelling and laughing, thinking they were having a good time on that alcohol. We all came out to the road, and he spun around and came racing back. Before we could react, he hit a big ditch in the road, lost control, and headed full speed for our front yard. He couldn't see where he was going in all of the dust, and we all ran to the house, all of us but my 11-year-old little brother." She stopped talking, and began sobbing, along with almost everybody else.

After a while, she attempted to finish. "He was a beautiful, innocent boy, so smart, so happy. He just wanted to watch the fast car, that was all. He really thought that mailbox would protect him." She cried louder and bowed down in pain.

"We buried him three days ago, and it was the hardest funeral I have been to, harder than my dad's last year, harder than my best friend's two years ago, harder than my niece's only a few months ago. And I have been to so many other funerals in my short life, and my dad's was the only one that wasn't because of alcohol, one way or another.

"So I have been angry. Angry about alcohol, angry that people use it, angry that we don't do something about it, angry that God lets it ruin lives. But last night, the medicine showed me something, and I learned a lot looking into the fire. And I watched as that medicine did a miracle on a hopeless drunk, and I got filled with compassion and understanding. I saw my brother with my dad last night, and they are happy together. My brother had the hardest time losing Dad, they were so close. He would sit next to him in the ceremonies since he was one-year-old, and could mimic everything Dad did. They are together again, and they are happy. It doesn't bring him back to me, to Mom, but I can give my mom some good news."

She stopped and cried again, then resumed. "And, I saw something else. I saw that teenager in jail crying. I could feel his shame, his remorse, his pain, and I know it was real. That boy hasn't known anything good about family in his home, they are all alcoholics, and that is all he knows. But he has to live with this for the rest of his life. And he will be in jail or prison for a long time. And in there, he will only learn how to get worse, and come out of there worse than he went in. Well, I'm not going to let that happen. The medicine showed me last night another option, and it is called forgiveness, something I would not have come up with on my own, but something my dad would have tried to teach me about this situation. I'm going to help that boy, either in jail or out. I'm not going to let alcohol turn one meaningless death into another.

"It is time we start fighting back. We have been complacent for too long. We have allowed this to rule us for too long, and now we have to get stronger than it, because we are stronger, we just have forgotten. And watching the demon of alcohol leave the sponsor last night was a sign for all of us. It can only win if we give it permission. We have to stop allowing it to take our lives. We have to stop giving it our permission to kill us."

The affirmations were loud and plentiful, Red Hawk being the most vocal with his signature Kiowa war cries. Sonny blew on the eagle bone whistle four times. A line had just been drawn in the sand, and the warriors were preparing for battle, a war that was long overdue.

Cheyenne addressed me again. "And to the sponsor, Robert, don't forget what my grandma told you early on, because she knows what she is talking about, and we can all learn from the Elders things that we might never learn on our own. The next time you come in here, your home, you have to have your family with you, because your success depends on being all together as one. You can't be unequally yoked. And they will come in here, no matter how impossible it sounds right now. I have seen bigger miracles than that in here. I saw a bigger miracle in here with you just last night. That was hard. If they see that you are really better, not by your words, but by your actions, they will follow you to the ends of the earth. Blood is that way. And you will also find many other people come out of the darkness willing to follow you into the light. So you have to be good, be sober, stay right with the Creator, because you can't give away what you don't have. You can't lead people unless there is a reason to be followed."

I heard her words, and they sunk in. When Mom had told me that I had to bring my family in here only hours ago, there was no way it was going to happen, in my mind. Right now, that felt more like days ago, a lifetime away. So much had happened, it seemed impossible that it was only last night, or maybe even early this morning. And as Cheyenne repeated those words, I knew she was right. Not only did I have to bring my family into this way of life with me, at that very moment, I also knew for a fact that they would be in here the next time this tipi would be set up. I knew it just as surely as I knew that I would never crave alcohol again, or need to fulfill that craving. And time would prove these feelings to be true; they would come in the next ceremony, and I would never drink again. My life would never be the same again. I had turned the corner.

Cheyenne again thanked me, then went around thanking each person, adding a personal touch to everyone she knew, and wished all of us a good morning. Then she prayed in Navajo for at least 20 minutes, then again in English, crying out loud every time she mentioned her brother. Then she dropped a huge, overflowing handful of cedar into the coals, walked clockwise to the front of the fire, and used the eagle feather to bring the smoke to the bucket and the three bowls. Then she opened the door slightly and used the feather to bring the morning sun in and blessed the food and water with that. I was blinded momentarily with the sunlight reflecting off of the white snow just outside the door.

She threw in another large handful of the cedar, and told all of us to bless ourselves, and wish each other a beautiful morning. Then she returned to her blanket and sat back down. Duane walked around and picked up the cedar bag she had set in front of herself, shook her hand with the one-up, and one-down Peyote handshake, and returned to his seat, handing Sonny the cedar bag on his way.

Sonny went forward and threw cedar in the hot coals, then he ceremoniously picked up the big, dried Peyote Chief off of the altar, waved it four times in the sweet smoke billowing up, then, starting to his left, held it up high and showed it off slowly to each person, circling the entire tipi. As the Chief faced each person, they lifted up both hands to receive a blessing as it went around, creating a wave just like at the ballpark, only just with their arms, not getting completely out of their sitting position. By the time I figured out what was happening, it was too late, so my hands and Franco's missed out on the wave. He put the Chief into its own container and back into his oversized cedar box along with his feathers and fans, the gourd, and other paraphernalia.

Orlando untied his drum, rolled up the skin and squeezed out the excess water, wrapped it with the drum rope, and put it into a leather bag, then put his drumstick into his cedar box. He got up and poured the water inside the drum onto the ground at both ends of the moon, then added the coals in the drum to the coals in the fire in four different locations and put the drum in that same leather bag. He picked up all of Sonny's boxes, his own box and drum bag, tossed some cedar into the coals, waved the whole collection over the sweet smoke four times, and walked out of the tipi to put it all into their truck. When he returned, he picked up the lighter stick, made sure it was out, then picked up the four tiny sage leaves that the Chief sat on, and the sage bundle that had traveled around with the staff all night, and brought it to me. He handed them all to me, thanked me, and said to keep these in a good place, in remembrance of the night. I thanked him and shook his hand one time, and Duane put them in his cedar box until I could put them into my truck. He said, traditionally, many people write on the lighter stick the date of the ceremony, the Roadman, the sponsor, and the reason for the meeting. Then they often keep the firestick and sage over their front door for protection, something I would come to notice at many different people's homes.

Once the Chief was put away, it got fairly casual, and the laughter began in earnest. Lots of jokes and comments relating this to past ceremonies, and a lot about the weather throughout the night, and of course, Franco quickly became the source of all kinds of mirth, with or without him adding to it. Just as Johnny added some fresh sticks to the fire, it got unmistakably dark again, as if someone had turned off the sun. A cold breeze snuck under the canvas, and the opening of the tipi completely clouded over. Johnny picked up the water bucket and cup and passed both to the man on the south side of the door, who drank two cups of water and passed it to his left. Johnny started passing the bowls of sacred food to follow the water. The man at the door took a big spoonful of corn, and passed the first bowl. He did the same with the fruit, then a handful of what looked to be shredded beef, and it all got slowly passed around. When I looked up through the top of the tipi, I saw a newly familiar scene of thick snowflakes drifting in. As the food went around, the jokes and laughter began, followed by people telling stories about being snowed in and staying hours longer because of the weather. I was dumbfounded, being only one of two people present that knew snow was extremely rare here, especially this time of year. My aunt cleared up the confusion for me, as she nearly shouted above the chatter to me. "The Creator had to erase all of our tracks we just made to get the sacred food. Remember, you are going to make fresh tracks in new snow."

Both Franco and I laughed, then stopped suddenly, realizing we were the only ones laughing. She wasn't making a joke, she was stating fact. Apparently the show wasn't totally over just yet. I started wondering what could possibly happen to top it all off. I certainly didn't need any more convincing. When the food came, as expected, hunger pangs started dancing around in my stomach. I took a spoonful of corn, at first shyly, not used to sharing utensils since my commune days decades ago. Once I realized it had to be safe, peyote being a strong germicide, I enjoyed several spoonfuls of corn and fruit, then a good handful of the unsalted shredded meat. Once I bit into it, I recognized it to be the buffalo I had put in the motor home, far tastier than mere beef.

Franco was anything but timid as he stuffed the food into his mouth with the entire audience appreciating his primitive antics. I finally nudged him, reminding him there were still many left who hadn't eaten. By the time the food made it to the door, the sun had peeked out through the clouds, and the snow had recoated the ground with fresh powder. Within minutes, the sun was out, the sky was blue, and the animals were back at their noisy best, competing with the noise of melting ice and snow dripping on and from the tipi. People began putting on jackets and sweaters, standing and stretching, shaking out their blankets and preparing to exit, once again talking about coffee and muffins.

Sonny stood and announced one last time, "Good morning to everybody, and remember, God...Loves...You," he said, slowly and firmly.

Johnny stepped out and rolled up the tipi door backwards so it couldn't unroll, and mentioned to the next in line on my side for each person to grab a bowl on the way out. I stood up next to Franco and almost fell back down, waiting for my leg muscles to catch up with my mind. I stretched and rubbed my cramped legs, slowly bringing the blood back into circulation. The line in front of us moved out.

I took a step, then remembered. I counted each step, walking completely normal, with a regular, if slow, stride, to the door. My left foot was at the base of the door on number twelve. I ducked out, under the low opening, sticking my head outside, into the bright sunlight reflecting off of the blinding white snow. Everybody had turned right, walking around the tipi clockwise, touching each pole through the canvas. I looked down to the fresh powder piled against where the door had been, and noticed everybody before me had purposely not stepped there, leaving it completely smooth and untouched. I brought my right foot outside and took my Thirteenth Step into the white snow. I stopped, and took in a deep breath of cold, brisk, mountain air, savoring the moment.

I walked out, and stepped quietly through the new snow, tears pouring down my cheeks. I was making new tracks, on a new day, in the new fallen snow. All of my old tracks were buried, gone. I kept walking, breathing deeply, and crying. "Thank you, Creator God. Thank you, Jesus. Thank you, Holy and Great Spirit. Thank You."

I walked away from the tipi and a little ways up the snow-covered road and looked around, taking it all in. The air was scrubbed clean, the animals were scurrying about and flying around. I looked up the side of the mountain, and noticed the trees above us were all green, with no trace of snow on them. As I looked around the mountain, I could see a definite line where the snow ended and the trees began. From this vantage point, it was apparent that it had snowed locally. Very locally.

Like only right here, around my tipi, in this tiny little section of the river valley.

I watched as the last people filed out of the tipi, some circling it to touch each pole, others walking to the motor home for coffee, some heading straight for the restrooms. I started to walk back, when I noticed an older man and what looked to be a teenager getting up from my favorite boulder on the riverbed and starting to walk down the river. They definitely weren't in the tipi last night, and were undoubtedly who I had heard talking outside at sunrise while we were still inside. I focused on them, and could faintly hear the man talking. I did know that voice, but from where? As I watched them walk away, the older man with a long, braided, gray ponytail turned back and looked directly into my eyes. I knew those eyes, how could I ever forget them? He smiled and waved, then kept on walking. I froze in my tracks, my mind racing to put the words and thoughts together. For a few seconds I was completely unable to speak as they disappeared down the river into the trees, engrossed in their conversation.

Finally, I yelled out loud, "CHINO...CHINO!" Everybody looked up at me, then down where I was directing my call. By now, Chino and the young Indian were out of sight and beyond hearing distance, drowned out by the sound of the roaring river.

Franco came running up to me, shouting all the way. "Right on, Brother, right on. I'll bet ol' Chino can hear you, wherever he ended up after all of these years, man. I remember that crazy Indian, too. Who would have ever thought his predictions would turn out right about everything? Someday, Brother, maybe we will see him again, who knows? Now, let's go get some coffee, man.... what a night.... Are you okay, Brother?"

I stood looking down the river for a few seconds, then smiled broadly, feeling happier than I had felt in longer than I cared to remember. "Yeah, Brother, I am definitely okay. Let's go get some of that coffee."

AHO.

EPILOG

AFTER THE CEREMONY

When Franco and I returned home later that Sunday afternoon after the ceremony, my wife and children were nervous, at best. Franco ranted on and on about how I was cured and my drinking days were over. Naturally, everyone was very skeptical. I knew deep down inside he was right, but I did not speak about it, because they had heard and seen this all before, far too many times.

However, over time, they saw the change, and my actions spoke louder than any words could have. My wife, Sandra, began to chip away at the wall she had built, and slowly, cautiously, wanted to believe it to be true. When Sonny and Lilly-Ann returned a few weeks later to run a ceremony in the desert nearby, I invited Sandra to the ceremony, not totally sure she would accept. She did, and that ceremony marked a new beginning for her and for the whole family.

Later, I sponsored a ceremony for our marriage, and then one for my family. They all attended each, and the emotional outpouring in those ceremonies was empowering and also draining, yet so necessary, as it brought us all back together, better than we ever were before. I learned that my healing was not complete if they also did not get to deal with all of those years of abuse. Events that took place in both ceremonies were even more powerful than my first healing ceremony. Everyone knew what they were talking about that fateful night when they insisted I bring my family along with me for the miracles that were to follow.

As of this writing, twelve years later, I have not had a drink, nor the desire to drink. My life hasn't been perfect. In fact, the adventures really only just began that night, and God had, and still has, many lessons for me—some easy, many hard—but all of these lessons are intended to bring me closer to our Creator, and share the love that He has for every one of us. This new way of life came to full fruition once I had made my amends with my family, and all of those I had hurt over the years.

The Native American Church, and the Ceremony of this church, is not just a passing whim, it is a way of living. And as you read more of my stories, you will see how it gets better and better if you stay on that Red Road, and how God challenges us to grow in awareness and truth and quit hiding from ourselves, from each other, and from Him. The message here is simple, and does not require that everyone try to find a ceremony of the Native American Church to participate in. Just the opposite. Everyone needs to find their path to the Creator, based on the traditions and teachings found in their personal heritage and culture. This ceremony is my heritage, from the Native American culture, and is not for everyone. But The Truth found in this ceremony that set me free is the same for all cultures and it is revealed to us through His creation. You will hear it in that still, small voice in the quiet and solitude of nature, and that Truth will set you free. Follow Him, and he will lead you to greener pastures, and you shall not want. Take that Thirteenth step of faith, and live again. God bless.

APPENDIX

The following is a detailed explanation of the Sacred Sacrament, Peyote, and how and why it has become so demonized and maligned, and the truth behind the myth.

Forget marijuana, opium poppies, the coca plant, and blue agave. If you can. They have all had their detractors, and they also have all caused so many problems. Overuse and abuse go hand in hand with each one of these plants. Communities, societies, and civilizations have suffered from the excessive use of these botanical wonders. Their medicinal possibilities are defensible, but casual and recreational use consistently turns into abuse, creating casualties all around them.

But show me documentation of consistent, harmful abuse leading to negative consequences of the tiny cactus that botanist know as *Lophophora williamsii*, and I will show you government propaganda in the same insane context as *Reefer Madness!* I was able to get much more information on the sacrament of the ceremony than the ceremony itself, before there was the internet to turn to. Since I had eaten it so innocently when I was 14-years-old, and periodically over the years after that, I was already familiar with its effects, and was able to wade through all of the nonsense filling the reports about "scientific data" pertaining to its properties. Although I spent many years in the underground drug trade, and fully aware of all legalities associated with those drugs I peddled, I had no idea the United States government was so disproportionately obsessed with the use of this little succulent cactus, especially since its only consistent use was for religious purposes. For a brief period of time, during the late 1960s and early 1970s, the Hippie movement did its best to pervert its sacred use and tried to turn it into a recreational drug, as they did with anything and everything that could even remotely alter their debased mindset. They chewed Morning Glory seeds and smoked banana peels, licked frogs bellies, and ate fungus right off of fresh cow manure.. So their habits were hardly anything on which to base federal drug policy.

Other than that undeserved blemish in its million year history, there is no instance that peyote has ever caused any societal problems, except for the irrational response authorities have had to it over the ages. Quite the opposite. Those who use it as the medicine that it is, have endless stories, legends, and documentation of its healing properties. Miraculous healings that include incurable disease, cancer, diabetes - the list is long. And in recent centuries, those who regularly employ it in their ceremonies have used it to stop alcohol and drug dependence...completely. The adherents to the beliefs of the Native American Church use it to get off of alcohol and drugs, and stay off, saving friendships, marriages, and lives.

You never hear of peyote addicts breaking into cars late at night to steal a stereo to trade for some peyote before they go into withdrawal. There are no underground cartels trafficking in peyote smuggling and sales, making millions of dollars supplying a desperate crowd with their cactus. Nobody has been jailed for driving under the influence of peyote, arrested for domestic abuse while raging out of control on peyote, or sentenced for murder while delirious on cactus. Well, maybe. The United States government probably has accused Indians of all of those crimes and more for using peyote, but those charges are frivolous, at best.

Anyone who has ever ingested peyote will attest to the fact that it just doesn't work that way. And as far as damage to health, study upon study actually show beneficial results from its use. An in-depth, long term study of two identical neighboring Huichol Indian tribes in northern Mexico, compared genetic mutations, birth defects, and generational health between the two, one tribe consuming large amounts of peyote regularly as part of their religious culture, while the other tribe never consumed peyote, all other factors being comparable. The surprising results showed the peyote users were of better overall health, lived longer, happier lives with less problems, and had absolutely no chromosomal damage in their progeny.

So why would the federal government be so absorbed with proclaiming this benign cactus in the desert, used by a tiny segment of the population only for religious purposes, a dangerous, addictive narcotic, on legal par with crack cocaine and heroin? In a country always claiming to have been founded on the principals of freedom of religion, freedom of expression, and freedom of speech, what possessed the authorities, all the way to the Supreme Court, to outlaw the oldest, most peaceful religion on the continent, to raid church services, destroying ancient, sacred religious artifacts, jailing old men, women, and children, and burning family tipis to the ground? Old news, you must be thinking. Actually, this was happening right up until Congress amended the American Indian Religious Freedom Act, originally passed on August 11, 1978 (42 U.S.C. 1996), in 1994. The original act in 1978 did not allow for the ceremonial use of peyote specifically, so that loophole enabled the over-zealous Drug Enforcement Agency, under orders from some obsessed, racist FBI leaders, to continue raiding the ceremonies under the guise of stopping the "rampant abuse of Peyote" among Native people.

Later, the Supreme Court even furthered abuses by law enforcement authorities against Indian ceremonies in the Employment Division v. Smith, 494 U.S. 872 (1990), where they ruled against the sacramental use of peyote again and allowed the termination of employment of a Native American (Smith) who admitted to going to a Peyote Ceremony on his Saturday off, even though his work was above reproach and, unlike his employers, he did not drink alcohol. Finally, Congress recognized the hypocrisy of denying freedom of worship to the original inhabitants of this country and overruled the Supreme Court and amended the 1978 act, calling it the American Indian Religious Freedom Act Amendments of 1994 (Public Law 103-344 [H.R. 4230]- Oct. 6, 1994), including Section Two, the "Traditional Indian Religious Use of the Peyote Sacrament". Yet, some states still occasionally use scarce and valuable resources to search, harass and temporarily jail leaders and members of the Church to this day. They, interrupt sacred ceremonies and abuse elderly attendees, destroying ancient, sacred, family heirlooms, forcing the longest operating church in the nation to continue to keep ceremonial grounds secret, and worship in fear of harassment in what is supposed to be the United States of America. You have to go way back in history to find the cause of this glaring hypocrisy.

When the government had succeeded in cornering, starving, and rounding up the surviving tribes scattered across the country and relocated them onto Reservations, promising in Official Treaties with Sovereign Nations that they would leave them alone and take no more of their traditional hunting grounds, they had hopes of these uncivil peoples starving to death and dying off from diseases, some introduced intentionally to speed up the process. Never really expecting the Indian problem to last much longer, they thought it was more or less going to just fade away.

But as more and more settlers, miners, ranchers, and farmers spread out across the country, land was at a premium. Treaty after treaty was voided, and the government seized more Reservation land to satisfy the demands of a growing population. Feeding the Indians surplus white flour, sugar, bad meat, and lots of alcohol turned them into a dependent people, unhealthy, but alive nonetheless. Boarding schools, covert blood dilution programs, isolation and oppression tried to destroy cultures, heritage, family ties, and behavior, but they kept hanging on. Afraid of uprisings, escapes and revolt, all activities involving any kind of gathering of people were banned. Any Native religious ceremony, dance, pow-wow, or other cultural meeting was aggressively stopped. The Ghost Dance, a movement of hope practiced by a prophet of peace, spread rapidly across the West, from California to The Dakotas, and caused major panic among military generals in charge of Indian welfare. These tensions led to tragic massacres of splinter groups of tribes. The military decimated unarmed men, women, and children with automatic guns and cannons.

Afraid of more imagined uprisings, the Calvary clamped down on all social life on the Reservations, any and all ceremonies were forbidden. The Peyote Church, one of the few respites of hope and spiritual awakening during that dark period, was under attack. Setting up their tipis late at night, out in the wilderness, running the ceremony through the night, ending it at sunrise, taking down the tipi, cleaning up the area, and moving on before the security team came searching, kept the movement alive, albeit scared and intimidated.

Using paid infiltrators from traditionally competing tribes to keep the tribal security forces informed, authorities realized the Peyote Church was helping the hurting, and keeping attitudes positive and upbeat. The last thing the Calvary wanted were Indians that didn't act defeated, so they found out what the whole resurgence was based on. Using committed missionaries intent on saving the heathen savage souls, and overzealous Bureau of Indian Affairs flunkies, they began a heavy handed attack on peyote, petitioning the government to declare this cactus dangerous. So zealous and obsessive were the early accusers against peyote, that in the rules and regulations hastily drawn up to clamp down on the church the name of this "horrendous, deadly" cactus was misspelled. Many of the first laws banned the mescal bean, a totally unrelated tiny, red legume used as beads for necklaces and other decorations. Public declarations enumerating the imagined dangers associated with peyote, peotl, mescal, mescal beans, and peeyotee, plus other pathetic identifications, not only stirred the white population into a frenzy, they also did a stand up job scaring many tribal leaders and Reservation Indians not yet familiar with the Peyote Religion. They ignored evidence that showed the groups and tribes involved in the Native American Church were the people who stayed away from alcohol, had families intact, were productive and tried to survive as peacefully as possible.

The campaign to hide the truth about peyote, and demonize its users as "crazy and dangerous" was carried out with the ardent support of the government, the military, the BIA, and the Reservation missionaries, and it succeeded. Federal and state laws were passed banning its possession and use. To make these laws have teeth, the BIA convinced the new Drug Enforcement Agency to declare Peyote a narcotic, without the usual testing and evidence of "danger to society".

The cactus has over 24 competing alkaloids. One of them, if reduced and refined, could produce mescaline. This was all that was needed to put the cactus in the same category as cocaine and heroin. They failed to report about the stronger alkaloids that produced vomiting if consumed in great quantities. Also, the taste of the cactus is perhaps the most bitter, least attractive taste found in any type of food or herb. The involuntary reactions of rejection caused when it is put into the mouth have prevented any attempts to consume enough to get the effects from the mescaline worth the suffering required. The fortitude needed to consume this cactus and sit up all night on the ground, praying and singing, hardly makes this an attractive drug experience. There are easier, more fun ways to get high. This does not even enter the realm of getting high. Other than keeping church members awake, similar to coffee, and able to withstand hours of sitting in one place, concentrating on prayer and healing, there is no wild, hallucinatory LSD-like reactions; all of that is fairy tale and propaganda. Because it does have the ability to clear the mind of much of its clutter, things can be seen for what they really are. Visions of reality have been turned into hallucinations by carefully crafted anti-Indian rhetoric. Very much the same as the early proclamations of violent, murderous black men coming from the ghettos to "rape and kill white women" while stoned out on the "evil marijuana", as in *Reefer Madness*.

As mentioned earlier, we were never taught the correct way to use marijuana, so it shouldn't be used by us. That doesn't mean whoever does know how to use marijuana shouldn't use it, if there is anyone left who does. It is *their* medicine, not ours. We were taught the correct way to use this medicine, peyote, and that is the only context in which it can be used. The problems associated with alcohol, marijuana, cocaine, opium go back to it not being used as a medicine, as taught by Elders and passed on generation to generation. We are fortunate to have retained the knowledge on how to use our medicine, and we benefit greatly because of it, in spite of a new government of strangers attempting to regulate it and dictate to us how it is to be used. The irony is the harmlessness of the Peyote, the benefits it brings, and the effort to demonize it is completely irrational, all based on a long ago prejudice that warped into a never-ending persecution of a people, a sacrament, and a church. Most people today have been conditioned to roll their eyes and cringe when even the word peyote is mentioned. It means "crazy" to almost everyone. It shows how successful the government was in distorting the reality of peyote to further their agenda. Never mind the current media and public craze over "energy drinks", containing dangerous and questionable ingredients, all just fine if they have no connection to an Indian ceremony. It is almost entertaining to those of us who know the truth about peyote to see the reaction most people have to it, yet those same people have no problem taking daily doses of anti-depressants known to actually cause depression and suicide, and potent painkillers that result in addiction and overdose every single day of the year.

When you consider the Holy Sacrament of the Catholic Church is wine, and the abuse of alcohol causes more problems worldwide, broken homes, families, relationships, accidents, and death, than any other substance, yet there is no attempt to eliminate its ceremonial use. Prisons and jails are filled with people who did unthinkable crimes while using alcohol. There is a whole industry built around trying to help people stop abusing it, but it would be blasphemous to suggest the Catholic Church stop having wine with its communion. Yet this tiny, spineless cactus that sports a beautiful flower each spring, with literally no history or documentation of abuse, or any negative effects on health, no addiction, no disrupted families, relationships, no overdoses or death, is maligned, attacked, prohibited, and persecuted. It is the only substance known to have a consistent record of helping large populations of Native alcoholics quit drinking, and stay sober, made illegal because it is used as a sacrament in a Native American Ceremony.

Perhaps the saddest result of this intense government crusade is the new attitude among many Native people unaware of the facts, who reject peyote and its miraculous healing properties, passing up opportunities to get well from what is killing them, and slowly dying from new, westernized medicines that really are deadly and dangerous. Many of the Elders cannot understand this paradox.

The American Indian Religious Freedom Act Amendments of 1994, Section Two, passed by Congress and signed into law by President Clinton, was to override an incredible Supreme Court ruling, where the Justices agreed unanimously it was a bona-fide religious ceremony, yet the DEA designation of peyote as a narcotic precluded freedom of religion to apply to the Native Americans and ruled it illegal for them to practice their religion. After the Act became law, it allowed American Indians, with a minimum of ¼ blood quantum of a federally registered tribe, to participate in the ceremony, and possess the peyote. This stipulation was demanded by the DEA so that as time goes on, and as Indians marry out of their tribe, as blood quantum becomes diluted, eventually the ceremony will be obsolete, once again illegal for all; careful, government planned obsolescence.

The irony of the DEA dictating religious policy is astounding, as their agents drive past entire communities destroyed by alcohol, heroin and methamphetamine, on their way to raid a tipi in the desert with a handful of peaceful people singing and praying to God in the oldest religious ceremony in these United States.

These are the facts about Peyote, and I write them to enlighten the reader so that you don't finish this book and still have a lingering doubt as to whether peyote is a Sacred, yet harmless cactus, or that wild and crazy drug you have been conditioned to believe it to be. The general attitude towards peyote is completely negative, but as I have explained, there is a reason for this, and it has nothing to do with the actual plant, but everything to do with how the DEA has successfully confused the truth, for reasons that do not belong in a country that claims to be tolerant of other religions, especially one that predates this country's founding.

John Halpern, M.D. Assistant professor of psychiatry at Harvard Medical School, also the director of the laboratory for integrative psychiatry for the alcohol and drug abuse division and research center, is the only recognized scientific expert of the Native American Church of The United States, and has completed the largest government funded study into the neurocognitive and psychological consequences of peyote use within the Native American Church, and found no evidence at all of any problems. Doctor Halpern had the following to say about this book relative to his extensive scientific knowledge and personal connection to peyote and the ceremony of the Native American Church; "A brave and beautiful vision, a healing that is very personal and direct is within these pages. It is not an accident that Robert Hayward has been saved from the ravages of alcohol, and the reader will understand why Robert's "miracle" is available and accessible to all who come to pray that right way around that fireplace. There is no "hallucinogen" within Peyote the Holy Sacrament: there is only profound love and healing and an unlocking of one's humility to begin at the beginning for that right recovery, no shortcuts. The Thirteenth Step dispels all sorts of negative assumptions [made] by those that don't know. Every Native American struggling in addiction needs to find a copy of this book: it will give you strength to put one foot onto your right path for the good life you can have and were meant to have. There are no current medical treatments offering a more reliable or profound healing than through this Peyote Way. May The Thirteenth Step be your next".

A Brief History of Indian Removal

There is the history about Native America that we all learned in school, and then there is what really happened, which brought Indians to the Reservations and ripped their true culture right out from under them. Many rewriters of history claim the indigenous people were violent and bloodthirsty and were in the process of killing each other off when the Europeans arrived. Just reading Christopher Columbus's journals that he wrote during and after initial contact with the Natives relate a story of a gentle and welcoming people, far from the dangerous savages that sent fear and hatred that supposedly inhabited the "New World".

The problem, according to Columbus, and subsequent missionaries, was the fact that these kind and friendly savages weren't baptized, and therefore were doomed. The only hope for them was conversion into a religion that required the understanding of a big book, so until they gave up their pagan lifestyle and learned to read and write, they were all headed for damnation. This is where cultural ignorance cost the lives of literally millions of people. Had the conquerors stood back and observed, they might have realized the host people of the new land lived a more "Christian" life than most, if not all, of the missionaries trying to change them. And once it was learned that this new continent had that precious yellow metal in its mountains, rivers and valleys in abundance, the only thing the Natives represented was a roadblock to riches. Had the Natives of this northern continent been killing each other anywhere near as plentifully as the invaders started killing them off, this would have been an uninhabited land with dried skeletons everywhere long before they arrived.

When the Europeans started their organized push westward in the unending quest for land, wealth, and resources, that is when the tribes started fighting each other, as they were forced into neighboring hunting grounds just to survive. The ripple effect went all the way across the country. Tribes were moving or being moved into territories far from their traditional areas, and into other tribe's hunting and farming grounds, creating tensions and fighting that ruined any hope of unified resistance. Following right on their heels were settlers, prospectors, ranchers, farmers, and the relentless mounted Seventh Calvary. Soon the government had to start relegating tribes to small, controlled plots of land, so the new stewards could have unfettered access to all usable space, civilizing the untamed wilderness.

Prior to this rapid devastation of all Native life, the people lived their religion. They knew the only way to be connected to their Creator was to be intimately connected to the Creation. They were in touch with all things natural, not because it was cool, but because it was necessary for survival. They needed to know and understand the seasons, the cycles, and all of the intricate details that kept life functioning, so they could function. And a constant contact with God gave them the inner strength needed for everyday living. They had no hospitals. Nature provided the remedy for pretty much everything that could ail them.

Mass disease and epidemics were not a part of their existence until it was introduced from a foreign land and people. Alcoholism, drug addiction, sexual and domestic abuse literally did not exist until it was taught to them in the boarding schools and orphanages. The average lifespan was over 100 years before Reservation commodity foods, sugar, and alcohol became a new way of life, cutting life expectancy in half within one century.

Now, alcoholism, drug addiction, diabetes, heart disease, and suicide are higher among Native Americans than any other group or race, all unknown before the invasion. It is for these reasons that life on the Reservations is what it is. People are always commenting on the fact that these Reservations are dirty, filthy messes, and full of drunks, and why should we care. Because this is not who we are, and how God meant us to live. But there is hope. The resurrection of our original culture and ceremonial life, without harassment from the federal government, is what will restore us to our true selves. If we are allowed to pray as we always have, and we all do, without alcohol or drugs holding us down anymore, our spirit will return, and the circle will no longer be broken.

Thank you for your understanding.

Aho.

About the Author

Robert Hayward was born August 23, 1959, the ninth out of ten children, to very loving and devoted parents. His parents were animators who met while working for Walt Disney. They were part of the original crew that developed Mickey Mouse, Pinocchio, The Three Little Pigs, and many more.

In the late 1970's Robert studied at Laguna College of Art and Design, in Laguna Beach, CA. In August of 2000, he was commissioned to design and build a roadside monument to honor a fallen Native American firefighter, who lost his life while protecting the La Jolla Indian Reservation in San Diego County. Robert will graduate from Palomar Community College in San Diego, CA, in 2011 earning a Certification as a Licensed Drug and Alcohol Counselor (CAADAC).

Robert has been studying and writing about Native American history and religion for over 30 years. Linked to the Native American community by blood, he has been mentored by traditional Medicine Men and Roadmen since his youth.

Robert Hayward maintains a blog at:

http://roberthayward.nativesonpublishers.com

Lightning Source UK Ltd.
Milton Keynes UK
UKOW03f1135100517

300894UK00001B/42/P